LEARNING

TO

CARE

*Pastoral Work
in the Local Church*

DAVID CLARKSON & STEPHEN MCQUOID

Partnership
Churches networking for mission

glo

PAL
OVERSEAS PUBLISHING AND LITERATURE

First published 2023 by Partnership (UK) Ltd, GLO Europe, and OPAL Trust

Abbey Court, Cove, Tiverton EX16 7RT, UK

27 26 25 24 23 / 5 4 3 2 1

British Library Cataloguing in Publication Data
A catalogue record for this book is available from the British Library

ISBN 978-1-9160130-8-7

Typeset and cover design by projectluz.com
Printed and bound in Great Britain
for Partnership (UK) Ltd, GLO Europe, and OPAL Trust
by Bell & Bain, Glasgow

Series Preface

This book is a further title in a series being published jointly by OPAL Trust,[1] Partnership,[2] and GLO Europe[3] (including Tilsley College[4]). Previous titles in the series are:

> David Clarkson and Stephen McQuoid, *Learning to Lead: Next Generation*, OPAL Trust, 2013
>
> Stephen McQuoid, *Learning to Share the Good News: Evangelism and the Local Church*, OPAL Trust & Partnership, 2019
>
> Jeremy McQuoid & Stephen McQuoid, *Learning to Preach*, OPAL Trust & Partnership, 2020.

The titles are an example of collaboration between bodies which serve a significant group of independent local churches which are found in the UK and in 155 or more countries across the world.

The purpose of the series is to provide material of help to church leaders, and others who are active in church life and work, in local churches which are committed to team leadership and every-member ministry, and therefore

---

1. **OPAL [Overseas Publishing and Literature] Trust** provides literature for the Majority World. It provides affordable Bibles and other good Christian literature to missionaries and national workers alike, in many countries worldwide, and has permanent book depots in Zambia and the USA, as well as in the UK.

2. **Partnership** and its predecessor body existed for six decades specifically to encourage, strengthen, and support local independent evangelical churches which are committed to the biblical gospel and to team leadership and every-member ministry. One way in which it did this was through publications aimed particularly to help church leaders and other volunteer workers in such churches. As a result of discussions between a number of bodies and church leaders in recent years, it has been decided that Partnership should cease operations from 1 January 2023 and allow other bodies to continue its ministry as and if they wish to do so.

3. **GLO Europe** is a Christian mission organization dedicated to bringing the good news of Jesus to a world that is lost. Its vision is to establish church planting teams throughout Europe and to support them and local churches through short-term mission trips. It is also committed to training and equipping Christians for mission and ministry so that they can share God and their faith effectively.

4. **Tilsley College** is the training arm of GLO Europe and is based at Motherwell in Scotland. It offers a range of one-, two-, and three-year accredited residential courses at very economical fee-rates (all including siginificant, on-the-job placement experience), part-time study through open access to the College's regular teaching, evening class study in local areas (Joshua Training), and online study.

have many unpaid church leaders and other volunteers who are vital to the life of their churches. These church workers generally have little time and opportunity for formal training for their responsibilities. They are keen students of Scripture, have active devotional lives, and often much experience in the Christian service which they undertake. But, for the most part, as has been said of the armies of the American Civil War, they have learned 'to march by marching and to shoot by shooting'—that is, they learn by doing. Such leaders and workers are essential to the life and work of the church, and it is evidently impossible, and in principle gravely limiting, for Christian ministry to be carried out exclusively by trained, paid workers. But, very often, volunteer workers are only too conscious that they could do better if they had some 'continuous professional development' (CPD) for their tasks. It is the purpose of this series to provide relevant and helpful material which can be used in this way. For some topics in the series, the material is simply print. [For *Learning to Lead* there is, however, a related training course which is accessible online (see [URL reference] for more details).]

While the aim of this series is to help voluntary Christian workers, we have no doubt that those who have had the privilege of formal training for Christian work can profit from the books in this series, if only by way of 'brush-up' and CPD for themselves!

The books in this series are not produced for profit by commercial entities, nor do writers, editors and sub-editors receive remuneration for their work. Any surpluses on sales will be used to finance further such publications and to subsidize the distribution of books in the Majority World, so that church leaders and others can benefit from them when otherwise they would not be able to do so.

Contents

MAKING THE CHANGES
FOCUS ON THE PROCESS OF CHANGE

Introduction

Who this book is for

We have been involved for many years in training young people for leadership in Christian ministry. It has been obvious in the course of this work that most of these young people go on to take up leadership positions with little practical knowledge of how to do pastoral care effectively. In this context, we thought that it might be helpful to write a book offering guidance to young or new leaders who want to understand how they can better support the people for whom they are responsible. Having embarked on this project, we discovered there was also considerable interest from existing leaders who felt they had received little training in pastoral care, and from church members who were actively engaged in caring but wanted help to do it better. We have sought to present the material in a way which will be helpful to people in these three categories, but we also wanted to help every Christian understand what pastoral care is about and that they have a part to play in doing it well.

The approach we have taken is to outline some basic principles so that they can be easily understood and applied by anyone who seeks to offer Christian care to someone in need. We believe that every Christian can offer pastoral care to another, sometimes at a very basic level, and sometimes with considerable spiritual insight. We also appreciate the specialist help provided by professional counsellors who have received formal training in the use of psychological principles and related therapies. However, this level of Christian counselling is beyond the scope of this book. Our focus is on encouraging ordinary church members to show love and care to others.

Many Christians think they should not get involved in pastoral care because they do not have appropriate training or qualifications. We recognise the value of training, but we also recognise the huge contribution to be made by someone who has a love for people and a desire to see them grow in their faith. It is remarkable what a listening ear, compassion, and patience can accomplish. One aim of this book is to encourage readers to understand, that no matter how inadequate they may feel about themselves, they can make a difference.

1. Who we are

Neither of us are specialists in the field of pastoral care, but we have both been involved in different aspects of Christian ministry for many years. Whether it be teaching in Bible college, leading Christian organisations, or as elders in local churches, we have inevitably been involved in seeking to help to fellow Christians in difficult circumstances. We have each handled a range of complex and difficult pastoral situations and know what it means to drop everything to deal with a crisis. Consequently, we are writing as people who have learned 'on the job' and we are still learning. We do not claim to know all the answers, but we do bring life and ministry experience which comes from real engagement with real people.

Both of us have also been called upon to advise church leaders who have found themselves in, for them, uncharted territory. This has allowed us to see close-up how pastoral care operates in a wide variety of contexts. We believe that by drawing on our own experiences and from our observations of others, we might be able to help a new generation of carers to provide high-quality care and point them away from repeating the mistakes of the past.

2. How we wrote

As the joint authors of this book, we have collaborated on every chapter, but we each took responsibility for assembling the content and format for particular chapters before bringing our thoughts together on each chapter. We have used the first person singular 'I' on many occasions without identifying which of us was writing.

Throughout the book we have provided examples of real-life situations to illustrate particular points. In all such cases we have changed the names and omitted details so that the person used in the example cannot be identified. On these occasions we have used the plural 'we' and 'us' and sometimes these references relate to occasions where we worked together on a particular project. We have also provided generic case studies where we brought together several 'typical' problems which do not relate to any particular person. In many of these cases, for simplicity, we have given the individual a fictitious name, sometimes male and sometimes female.

In this book we have also made frequent reference to 'church members'. We recognise that not every church has a formal membership and indeed some choose not to for a variety of reasons. Our use of the term 'member' is not to suggest that structure as a recommendation; rather we use the term to describe someone who is a regular attender in a church.

3. How to use this book

This book can be used in a variety of ways, depending on the needs of the reader.

- It can be read as a conventional book for those interested in pastoral care. As you will see from the table of contents, we have tried to arrange the book in a logical order. Many readers will want to start at the beginning and work through to the end.
- Some readers may want to use it as a reference work and so to dip into it when seeking information on a particular subject. Each chapter has a numbering system to enable readers to find their required section more easily and quickly.
- It can serve as a training manual for any church or organisation wishing to train members in pastoral care. In this context, the numbering system will be particularly useful. We have also included study questions and/ or case studies at the end of each chapter.
- Some may find it useful in a small group or house group setting, as interested Christians reflect on, and discuss, the importance and practicalities of pastoral care.

- It can be a resource book. At several locations in the book, and particularly in Appendix 3, we have highlighted some websites and other resources we have found to be helpful.

However you choose to use it, we hope you will find this book helpful and a blessing.

Acknowledgements

In writing this book we are indebted to a range of other writers and people who helped us bring it together. Our bibliography gives details of specific books that we have found helpful and we particularly reference the work of Gary Collins and his masterful book, *Christian Counselling*. All of these works have advanced our thinking and understanding of how pastoral care functions. We would also acknowledge the significant help of Allison Hill and Margaret Clarkson who were heavily involved with us in the project. Special thanks should also be given to Neil Summerton and Jo Jowett for their help in editing the book.

LAYING THE FOUNDATION

General introduction and biblical basis

CHAPTER 1

Restoring pastoral care

Finding Cinderella

When I remarked to a friend that I was involved in writing a book on pastoral care, his immediate comment was that pastoral care was the Cinderella of church activities. When I asked what he meant by that, he replied, 'Unimportant people do pastoral care. The important people—the leaders and decision-makers—give their time and energy to the tasks they think matter, and this does not include pastoral care. People with power don't rate pastoral care highly.'

I disagreed with such a negative assessment but, as often with such criticisms, it contains a kernel of truth. In many churches we have relegated pastoral care to a place of secondary importance. Many Christians see such activities as evangelism, preaching, and visionary leadership as essential to church life, whereas they regard pastoral care as more peripheral. It is seen as something desirable, but not essential.

It is ironic that, at the same time as pastoral care has diminished in importance in the church, non-religious groups such as schools, universities, and even football clubs, have taken up the concept. Their concern is for the holistic development and wellbeing of those under their care. Also, over the last thirty years, humanists have made significant progress in developing a network of people to provide pastoral care for non-religious people. The organisation, Humanists UK, provides celebrants for marriages, officials for funerals, and seeks to provide a counselling service in hospitals, prisons, and universities for those who are not religious.

1. Why has pastoral care lost so much ground in the church?

Pastoral care has changed as a result of the advance of secularism and, in some cases, secular therapies have replaced pastoral support. Religious leaders are no longer held in the same esteem as in the past and are often viewed with suspicion following the many allegations of child abuse and clergy malpractice. People reject the idea that someone else, far less a religious person, should be a source of guidance for their lives. They are committed to the view that everyone has their own truth and should be allowed to live their lives by that truth.

The experience of many Christians is that pastoral care in church has been much neglected and poorly delivered. One of the most common complaints and criticisms of the church from members is that, when difficulties arise in their lives, no elder visits them or expresses concern. This is the reason most often cited by people when deciding that they no longer wish to continue in church membership. There may be some truth in this but, in our experience, it is more often the case that elders do not have the time or expertise to do the job as well as they would like to.

Elders are very busy people. In many churches they are bi-vocational and have difficulty balancing the increasing demands of secular employment, responsibility to their families, and the significant time requirements of running the church. The demands are often impossible to meet and expectations are so high. In some evangelical church traditions, the pastor in a church often has to act in the role of counsellor, marriage guidance specialist, CEO, business manager, event organiser, caretaker of the building, and much more. This may well explain why it is increasingly difficult to find people willing to undertake the task of pastoral care.

It is also the case that pastoral issues are becoming more complex. Matters such as lack of spiritual progress or marriage breakup have always been around, but the contemporary challenges of domestic abuse, deterioration in mental health, addiction, and sexuality have become much more prominent.

A further reason for this marginalisation is that many people have a flawed concept of pastoral care. The popular perception is that the pastor or elder must deliver all pastoral care when members of the church find themselves in crisis or difficulty, usually relating to times of illness. It is flawed at a biblical level because the teaching of the Bible is that, while pastoral care is a crucial task of eldership, God has also given pastoral gifts to a broader range of people. It is flawed at a developmental level because it perpetuates the notion that pastoral care is something the elders give and the members receive; the implication is that members have no role in providing care, which creates a culture of dependence. The concept of one man providing all the pastoral care is also flawed at a practical level because it is impossible to deliver and, in fact, inhibits the growth and development of the church.

It is our conviction that, if we do not return pastoral care to centre stage, the effectiveness of the church will be significantly diminished. For these reasons and many more, we feel a book focussing on the practical issues around pastoral care could be very helpful. Our prayer is that this 'Cinderella' activity can be turned once again into a princess admired by all.

However, we need to emphasise that the pastoral care described in this book is overtly Christian, meaning that it is based on Christian values and the belief that the power of God is available to change the subject's life. Historically, pastoral care was described as the 'cure of souls', which focused on the spiritual needs and development of Christians. We feel it is essential to maintain this dimension and commend the book to you in the hope you will find it not only useful but life-changing.

2. What is pastoral care?

Since this book is about pastoral care, we must now clarify what we mean by this term. If we're building a house, we need to have the plans in front of us to know what it will look like when it is completed. Similarly, we need to understand what God, the divine architect, has in mind for the individual Christian and the church.

The Bible has given us a clear blueprint. In Colossians 1: 28, Paul says that the focus of his ministry is to 'present every Christian mature in Christ'. Similarly, regarding the church, Paul says that God has given apostles, prophets, evangelists and pastor-teachers 'to equip the saints . . . so we can all come to maturity in Christ.' (Eph. 4: 13) God does not want us to remain spiritual infants. He is looking for growth in knowledge, love, and holiness, which are marks of maturity in Christ.

In the same way, God is looking for growth and development in every local church. He wants to see love expressed, faith developed, and holiness demonstrated in deep loving relationships with himself and with each other. God is looking for every church to show how redeemed people live under the Lordship of Christ.

So, when we consider God's intention for the Christian and the church, it is immediately apparent that moving on to maturity involves growth and development. Paul expresses great frustration that some in Corinth had failed to progress in the things of God. They were still infants needing milk instead of solid food (1 Cor. 3: 1, 2). In a similar vein, the writer to the Hebrews expresses surprise that so many needed to be taught primary-school lessons when, in fact, they should be teaching others (Heb. 5: 12).

Both writers emphasise that staying in the same spiritual condition for long periods is not what God wants, either for the individual Christian or the church. God's purpose is to see us becoming more and more like Jesus, and pastoral care has a major part to play in this process.

If the Christian life is a journey from new birth to spiritual maturity, we can see some parallels in physical journeys. Imagine driving along a winding road at night through hostile territory. It is almost inevitable that at some point we will take a wrong turn or become exhausted. Some unexpected crisis or adversity will cause us to get stuck somewhere along the way. Enemies are also trying to prevent us from arriving at our destination. They will try to impede progress, send us in the wrong direction, and sometimes even leave us wounded by the wayside. The journey of faith has many hazards, so we will need to keep our eyes firmly fixed on the goal if we are to arrive safely.

Of course, it will be much easier for us if we do not travel this road alone. What if there were people willing to help and provide us with food and shelter when we need it, give us clear directions, and provide support when enemies attack? We need people to help us navigate the twists and turns of the journey and, when we get knocked off the road, help us find the way back. This often simply means speaking a word of encouragement when spirits flag or providing a cup of cold water when we are thirsty. On other occasions, the help needed will be much more demanding. Because of some sin or crisis, we may find ourselves languishing in a ditch, not knowing how to get out. We need someone prepared to get down into the ditch with us and lift us back on to the road.

Helpers along the way

Ephesians 4: 12 says that God has given gifted and experienced leaders to equip his people, prepare them for service, and bring them to maturity in Christ. We know this is a key role of pastors and elders, but maybe we are not so aware that the Bible equally teaches that all God's people have a role in this process. Let's take a simple example. In Leviticus 19: 18 Moses says we are to 'love our neighbour as ourselves'. The details spelt out in the chapter depict how the people of God are to live together in community. We are told not to defraud or cheat our neighbour but to treat him fairly (11, 13) and we are not to slander him or gossip about him (16).

The New Testament is no less explicit regarding life in community: 'The greatest commandment is to love God with all our heart and our neighbour as ourselves' (Mt. 22: 36–40). We are to do good to our neighbour and love him or her in the same way that Christ loved us and laid down his life for us. If we are to become like Christ, we must reach out to our neighbours. The parable of the Good Samaritan illustrates that if our neighbour is in need, our task is to help them. The instruction to care does not depend on the colour, creed, or social standing of the person in need, nor does it depend on whether or not we like the person.

So far, we have seen: (a) that the elders have overall responsibility for pastoral care, and (b) every member has a part to play in this. But when we examine the New Testament teaching more closely, there seems to be an intermediate group of workers, loosely categorised as deacons. We can think of Timothy and Titus, Priscilla and Aquila, Phoebe, and Dorcas. These people are examples of individuals who used their gifts and calling for the benefit of their communities. Paul and Peter established teams to help in a range of ministries. Many churches today see examples like these as pointing to a group of pastoral carers often designated 'the pastoral care team'. These comprise people from the congregation who show an aptitude for this work, are set apart by the church, and are directly accountable to the elders.

When we pull all these ideas together, the picture that emerges can be summarised in the diagram below:

The pastoral spectrum

Church member	Team member	Elder
'All'	'Some'	'Few'
Level 1	Level 2	Level 3

We see the pastoral spectrum as a continuum but, for simplicity, comprising three broad groups. At one end we have every Christian showing basic Christian love and care (we call this Level 1); at the other end, the pastor and elders providing support at a deeper level (Level 3); a pastoral care team in the middle (Level 2). Our conviction is that the people in the local church provide a reservoir of skills and care to meet most of the problems likely to be encountered in church.

We now need to tease out something of what is involved at each level.

3. Level 1: every member care—'all'

Jesus says we are to love one another (Jn. 13: 34); then Paul says we are to do good to all men (Gal. 6: 10) and pray for all men (1 Tim. 2: 1). Regarding relationships in the church, Paul says, 'Be kind and compassionate to one another, forgiving each other, just as in Christ God forgave you.' (Eph. 4: 32). Verses like these (and many more) describe the bottom line of Christian living. They also form the bottom line of pastoral care.

Pastoral care starts with living as a Christian, paying attention to the little things, and generally looking out for each other. We can show a caring spirit through small acts of kindness, such as delivering food parcels or tidying an old person's garden. We can see it in a willingness to help even when it is not convenient for us, putting the other person before ourselves and being ready to listen and encourage. It calls for a rejection of the 'me' culture, so that when we notice someone has been missing for a time, we try to make contact with them. When we see someone looking worried or distracted, we draw alongside to enquire about their well-being. We can never know the impact we make just by sitting with someone over a cup of coffee and listening to their story. This simple act of kindness could be life-changing.

When we look at pastoral care in this light, we realise immediately that the qualities required are well within our capabilities. The requirement is not for in-depth counselling skills or extensive training, but for engaging with people, sometimes at a very practical level in everyday life, using the basic human skills of being good neighbours to those around us. It is called 'every person' caring, because every Christian can do it.

Maybe you had never thought that just living a Christian life brought you into the category of pastoral carer. We hope you will see things differently now and take on board some of what we have been suggesting. We have described caring at level one in very basic terms, but this in no way implies that what we do is ordinary or inconsequential. On the contrary, 'level 1' care is the bedrock on which all other care is built.

I remember speaking to a lady who wanted to become a member of our church. She was from a non-church background but had been coming for some time and had recently made a commitment to follow Christ. I asked her why she had come to the church and why she wanted to be a member. I have to confess that I hoped she might say that it was the quality of the teaching and preaching which had so impressed her, but she didn't say that. She said that some years earlier, she had gone through a very difficult time and had been greatly helped by a Christian neighbour. The neighbour didn't preach at her but showed her much Christian love over several months, such that when her circumstances improved, she asked if she could accompany her neighbour to church. And the rest, as they say, is history.

This is a salutary lesson for us all, and particularly for preachers. The biggest influence on people coming to Christ is not how good the preaching is—it's how much Christians care. As someone powerfully said, 'People don't care how much you know till they know how much you care.' It has always been a source of great encouragement to me that, even in churches with no formal care structures, when a crisis such as bereavement or serious illness arises, people respond spontaneously and generously. They do it without being asked. These kinds of action are expressions of primary Christian caring.

Paul Tripp says, 'I am hit with the utter simplicity of biblical personal ministry (pastoral care). It is not a secret technology for the elite, but a simple call to every one of God's children to be part of what God is doing in the lives of others. It is basically just a call to biblical friendship!'[1]

Two things need to be said to conclude this section. First, pastoral care, as acts of kindness, begins at the level 1 side of our spectrum. We cannot properly do pastoral care at the second and third levels if we have forgotten how to care at the first level. Secondly, level 1 care is not only about acts of kindness: there is also a spiritual dimension.

The Bible tells us that God is love and our acts of kindness to other people are expressions of the love we have experienced from God. But the Bible also says that God is light, indicating that he is true and holy. We are also to express that aspect of God's character in caring for other people. The New Testament clearly instructs us in this regard when it says we are to build up one another (Rom. 14: 19; 1 Thess. 5: 11), admonish one another (Rom. 15: 14), teach one another (Col. 3: 16), encourage one another (Heb. 3: 13), and care for one another (1 Cor. 12: 25).

The historian, John McNeill, says that from passages like the above, it is evident that Paul was trying to establish an atmosphere in the early churches in which spiritual help, mutual edification and correction were a normal feature of Christian behaviour.[2] Obviously, Paul sought to build 'mutual edification and correction' into the church culture. He encouraged every Christian to correct others who might be embracing wrong doctrines and rebuke people whose behaviour or attitude fell short of the demands of Christ. He did not see admonishing as a put-down but as a stepping stone to maturity, which it is when motivated by a spirit of brotherly kindness. The members were in this together and each wanted the best for everyone else.

We have moved far from this ideal community experience, and it could be argued that twenty-first century culture, with its focus on individualism, is a far cry from the community togetherness of the first century. But, just maybe, we need to learn to overcome our inhibitions and develop these community practices which help us to progress towards maturity in Christ.

---

1. Paul David Tripp, *Instruments in the Redeemer's Hands*, Kindle Edition, p.27.
2. John T McNeill, *A History of the Cure of Souls*, Torchbooks 1965, p. 85

This spiritual dimension of care begins at level 1, but takes much more of a centre-stage position in levels 2 and 3. Those involved in caring at these levels need to develop the skills required to bring about change in people's lives.

4. Level 2: team member care—'some'

Some members of the congregation discover that they are gifted in pastoral care and feel a burden to serve God by using this gift to bless others. They have seen considerable growth and development in their own lives, having gained a knowledge of the Bible and how to use it in helping others. Their relationship with God has deepened over the years, which has enabled them to make a difference as they reached out to care for others. This spiritual progress can be recognised by others who see that these carers are serious about serving God. And because they can relate well to people who are in trouble or losing their way, those in difficulty often seek out their help.

Lots of pastoral work at this level is undertaken by those who have no 'official' pastoral position. Ministry team leaders come into this category. They are highly focused on the task of the team, but they also recognise that part of their ministry includes the spiritual development of team members. Being a member of a church team is an excellent opportunity to give and receive encouragement. Praise and recognition can be offered when someone does well, or encouragement given when they feel under pressure—and they may do the same for us. Our strong recommendation would be for every carer to get involved in team ministry. All of this illustrates that pastoral care is often best delivered through the close relationships formed within the church's natural networks. It also highlights that pastoral care is a two-way process. We are not always givers *or* receivers; we need to learn to be both.

In most churches, there will be people who offer pastoral care at this level. They often do it informally, but some churches have found it helpful to establish a formal pastoral care team. The people on this team will be, for the most part, taken from the group we have just been describing. We will discuss the formation of a pastoral care team in chapter three.

5. Level 3: elder care—'few'

The elders have overall responsibility for pastoral care in the church and members refer matters to them which are too sensitive or too difficult. We have described pastoral care at Level 3 as 'elder care', but not every elder will have the skills necessary to offer care at this level. There may also be people in the church who are not elders but have particular gifting and experience to offer care at Level 3. Leaders will want to recognise such people and ensure their gifts are used. Level 3 carers will display the characteristics indicated by Paul in 1 Timothy 3 and Titus 1. They will also have an extensive knowledge of the Bible and know how to use it in pastoral care situations.

This review of the pastoral spectrum shows that care is required over a range of issues and at many levels. At its most basic, it can be a simple conversation on a topic of concern lasting for just a few minutes as an enquirer seeks advice and clarification; it can also be lengthy and complex, requiring elders coming alongside a troubled individual over a period of months.

As we said at the beginning of this section, pastoral care is a continuum and all of us will fit somewhere into that spectrum.

6. Towards a definition

We have said a lot about the people who offer pastoral care without attempting to define it. Someone has said, 'pastoral care is very difficult to define, but we know it when we see it', or as a cynic might say, 'we know it when we don't see it.' Pastoral care is multifaceted, so it will be difficult to incorporate every element into one concise statement. John Piper, for example, defines biblical counselling as a conversation which 'is God-centred, Bible-saturated, emotionally-in-touch use of language to help people become God-besotted, Christ-exalting, joyfully self-forgetting lovers of people.'[3].

Piper's statement is full and helpful, but often we need something a little more straightforward. So, we might say that pastoral care is the ability to get alongside others, identify with them in their circumstances, and encourage them to grow in grace even when life is complicated. Alastair Campbell writes, 'pastoral care is, in essence, surprisingly simple. It has one fundamental aim: to

---

3. John Piper, https://www.desiringgod.org/articles/gods-glory-is-the-goal-of-biblical-counseling

help people to know love both as something to be received and as something to give.'[4]

We find a biblical definition in Colossians 1: 28, where Paul admonishes and teaches everyone 'so that we may present everyone fully mature in Christ.' In this book, we seek to provide practical advice, so at several points we have taken this verse as our baseline. However, we recognise that behind what seems like a simple, straightforward statement lies a wealth of elements, some of which we have identified above, and others will be developed more fully in the chapters that follow.

7. What pastoral care is not

Pastoral care does not mean we have to say or do something, but our task is not to solve every problem brought to us. When people ask for help, our first instinct is to start looking for a solution. But often, what's needed is just for someone to come alongside individuals and listen to their stories. It means seeking to understand what they're feeling and sharing how the Bible offers hope and strength in their time of need. There is much wisdom in the saying, 'Sometimes the best thing is to do nothing.' We can do much harm by rushing in too quickly with our perceived solutions. In any case, we place a heavy burden on ourselves if we imagine that we can solve every problem or remove every difficulty.

Equally, pastoral care does not mean we have to say or do nothing. Those who hold to this view think that caring means simply asking questions, listening, and providing support to the individual. They believe that the individual already knows the answer to his or her problems and that if we build a supportive enough relationship, they will be able to work out solutions for themselves without our telling them what to do. This is a mistaken and unbiblical view. The verses we have quoted earlier in this chapter indicate that we are to instruct, encourage, and admonish, which implies an ability to guide the person to a biblical perspective on their situation. Also, when the carer offers biblical advice or challenges unwise attitudes, it enlarges the individual's self-understanding and expands the range of solutions open to them. Stephen

---

4. Alastair Campbell, *Paid to Care?*, SPCK, 1985, p. 1.

Pattison says, 'The trouble with empathetic listening which remains non-directive is that eventually it can leave the person seeking care, trapped within the boundaries of their own horizons. People need the challenge, guidance, and perspectives of others if they are to grow and change.'[5]

This takes us on to our third point which is, don't just be 'nice'. Churches are good at being 'nice', for example, by providing a warm welcome at services or sending a card to someone who is ill. Sometimes as Christians, we think it is enough that people speak well of us. But the problem is that being 'nice' can also imply being bland, inoffensive, and irrelevant. Many people's unspoken thought is that the church may be 'nice' but is not for them.

Making ourselves available to our neighbours to offer help is important, but it often requires more than practical support or acts of kindness. Pastoral care often involves hard work and tough love, sometimes requiring difficult decisions. It may well involve the messy business of getting down into the ditch to get someone back on the road. It is costly to put someone else's needs before our own.

Fourth, pastoral care is not about me. Some people see pastoral care as an excuse to speak about themselves, perhaps to enhance their own reputation or relive their own emotional experience. If you feel you need to do that, maybe you shouldn't get involved. Nor should there be any suggestion of superiority/inferiority in the relationship. The caring relationship is not one of teacher and pupil where one has all the answers which the other should gratefully receive. It is rather much more about two people relating to each other on an equal footing, together seeking to find God's purpose and direction for the way forward.

Finally, pastoral care is not professional counselling and the two must not be confused. Professional counsellors have much to offer in their own areas and there will be occasions when the needs of an individual are such that the person will be best served by referring him or her to a counsellor and preferably to one who is a Christian. We must know our limitations and not presume we can handle problems requiring specialised treatment.

---

5. Stephen Pattison, *A Critique of Pastoral Care*, SCM Press, 2000, chapter 3.

8. The God dimension

It is important to remember that we are co-workers with God (1 Cor. 3: 9). The development of individual believers to become Christ-like is God's business and whatever changes may take place in the life of the individual will be because God brings about these changes. God is the primary change-agent and our role is secondary. We must be careful not to impose our ideas or agenda, but help the person to find God's purpose for his or her life.

It is essential to bring Jesus into the conversation. This does not mean that it is necessary to quote Scripture, pray, or push religion at every opportunity, but it is to highlight that the answers are to be found in God and not in us. We are only the channel through whom God may choose to bring blessing to the individual.

Of course, if we want to see God transform the lives of others, we must be equally passionate about seeing God transform our own lives. Paul says, 'keep watch over yourselves and all the flock' (Acts 20: 28). This is very challenging. Only when we are in a deep relationship with Christ, and are experiencing his love and transforming power, can we communicate the same to others.

The critical factor in pastoral care is not so much what we say or do, but who we are. This has both daunting and encouraging aspects. It is daunting in the sense that we are conscious of our own failures and unworthiness. We are often at a loss to know what to say and fear we will get it wrong. But it is also encouraging in the sense that, ultimately, it is not about us—our performance or ability. It is God, and he alone, who can bring about lasting change.

9. Some concluding observations

Some of the information discussed above may sound a lot to take on board, but for your encouragement, the example below shows the impact pastoral care can have on individuals' lives.

The ability to offer support, even in the most tragic circumstances, is seen in the following excerpt taken from the book *Let's Roll!* by Lisa Beamer. Her husband, Todd, had been a passenger on Flight 93 which was hijacked on September 11, 2001. He, with others, had attempted unsuccessfully to keep control of the flight. Lisa had been wakened early in the morning by friends who knew that Todd was travelling on that plane, but no one knew what had happened to it for some hours.

For Lisa and her family, it was a very anxious and stressful time. Many people came to help and comfort. Some offered counsel and prayer, while others brought food or took care of the children. But she highlights one lady whose input was very significant. The lady's name was Jan Pittas. Lisa writes:

> At one point, in the middle of the day, during a lull in the activity in my room, I was staring blankly into space. I looked across Todd's and my bed, and there was Jan Pittas, one of our more quiet-natured friends, just sitting on the opposite corner of the bed, quietly praying for me, not talking aloud. Not talking at all. I didn't want to talk; I wasn't able to talk, and with her sweet, gentle spirit, Jan knew better than to try to talk to me. But her presence in the room was comforting. "Thank you, God, for sending Jan", I prayed.[6]

At that point, Lisa did not need explanations or theology. She just needed someone to be with her. Any of us can do that but it takes much wisdom and empathy to know when to speak and when just to be there.

For further reflection

1. If pastoral care is about presenting everyone mature in Christ (Col.1: 28), what are the signs of growing maturity?
2. What are some of the things that impede spiritual growth and what role has the pastoral carer in helping overcome these?
3. In this chapter, we looked at three different levels of pastoral care. Level 1 involves all church members, level 2, the pastoral care team, and level 3, the elders or church leaders. What kind of pastoral care do you think will take place at each level?
4. In what sense do we work alongside God as we do pastoral care?

---

6. Beamer (with Ken Abraham), *Let's Roll!: Ordinary People, Extraordinary Courage*, Wheaton IL: Tyndale House, 2003, p. 170.

CHAPTER 2

The biblical basis

Pastoral care is woven into the fabric of Scripture, as seen in its grand narrative and its detailed instructions and exhortations. The question is asked at the beginning of the Bible, 'Am I my brother's keeper?' and an affirmative answer is everywhere assumed. Responsibility for each other is based on God's character and his covenant. God takes an active interest in human affairs, expressing grace and kindness, yet demanding obedience to his word. Central to the covenant that God made with Israel is the expression, 'I will be your God and you will be my people', highlighting that they were to be one people under God, caring for each other as God cared for them. The relationship was much more communal and corporate than individual, although the latter was never absent because one person's sin could have consequences for the entire community.

In the New Testament, pastoral care is grounded in the life and ministry of Jesus, who provides both a pattern and a standard recognised and implemented by the early Church and more fully explained in the epistles.

Having given a brief overview, we shall look in more detail at the biblical evidence under two headings—underlying theological principles and some specific instructions.

1. Underlying theological principles

The character of God—Hesed

The word 'Hesed' is often translated as 'mercy' or 'steadfast love' and describes God's covenant relationship with his people. It speaks of God's compassion, faithfulness, and reliability (Ps. 36: 5). It is unchanging towards us and will endure forever (Ps. 118: 1). The writer of Lamentations could affirm, at probably the darkest moment in Israel's history, that 'The steadfast love [*hesed*] of the LORD never ceases; his mercies never come to an end; they are new every morning; great is thy faithfulness' (Lam. 3: 22–23 (RSV)).

'Hesed' describes who God is and speaks of his desire, not only for our salvation but for our wholeness and wellbeing. Those who have received God's 'Hesed' are called to reach out to others with the same love and care that God has lavished on us. We see this in Zechariah 7: 9–10, 'Administer true justice;, show mercy and compassion (Hesed) to one another. Do not oppress the widow, or the fatherless, the foreigner, or the poor. Do not plot evil against each another.'

The self-sacrifice of Christ

The movement of Christ from heaven to earth, from unimaginable splendour to squalor and shame, is truly breathtaking. The coming of Christ into this world to give himself for us on the cross is the fullest expression we have of how much God loves us. Jesus came among us and shared in our distress and pain, reaching out to the most vulnerable, giving himself totally for our benefit and calling on every Christian to follow his example.

The calling of the Church is to love as Jesus loved. Our problem is that we like to do ministry in our churches with people most like ourselves, but Jesus seems to have different priorities. He does not attach the same importance to our committees or our efficiently organised programmes. In a sense, Jesus does not spend much time in church; he is to be found more often in the company of hurting people. The compassion and kindness of the Good Samaritan did not take place in a church but on a dangerous road frequented by robbers. This principle is highlighted in Jesus' statement about how our lives will be assessed: 'for I was hungry and you gave me something to eat, I was thirsty and you gave me something to drink, I was a stranger and you invited me in, I needed clothes and you clothed me, I was ill and you looked after me, I was in prison and you came to visit me' (Mt. 25: 35–36).

Our task is to go where Jesus goes and do what he does, wherever people are in need. This is the essence of pastoral care.

The priesthood of believers

In the Old Testament, the function of the priest was to offer sacrifices for people so that they could come into a right relationship with God. Priests were also required to teach the people about God from his word. We could say the task of the priest is twofold—to bring people to God and to bring God to the people.

The priesthood of all believers means that all Christians are priests because of their union with Christ, so that there is no need for a special class of people required to bring the ordinary Christian into the presence of God. We find the doctrine in such passages as 1 Peter 2: 9, 10 and Revelation 5: 9, 10, which teach that the whole Church constitutes a holy and a royal priesthood before God. This means that every Christian can offer prayers for himself and others.

There is a close link between this doctrine and the idea of every-member ministry. Every Christian is a priest and functions in a community of priests. The Bible teaches that God has given spiritual gifts to every Christian and expects them to use these gifts for the benefit the local church and the community. We each express our identity as a member of this 'kingdom of priests' by serving God with whatever talents and abilities he has given us.

If, as stated above, it is the function of the priest to bring people to God and bring God to the people, then we can see how this ideally describes the ministry of pastoral care. If every believer is a priest, then our task is to help people reach out to God in whom alone they can find answers. The Latin word for priest is 'pontifex', which means a 'bridge builder'. We are to help our brothers and sisters in times of distress to find that bridge, which is Christ, and encourage them to cross over to the welcoming and forgiving arms of God. Pastoral care is about helping people to find God.

The doctrine of the priesthood of all believers does not receive much emphasis in the contemporary Church and we give even less prominence to the equally important principle—which we might call 'the pastorhood of all believers'. Maybe it is time to change that.

The Church as the family of God

The New Testament provides a great deal of information on the Church as a family, but for our purposes, the relationship we are to have with other church members is most clearly and strikingly seen in the 'one-anothers' of the

New Testament. The expression 'one another' occurs around sixty times, and contains both positive and negative instructions. We have not included all the references below, but have simply selected a sample to represent the range of teaching. We would encourage you to check out all the references for yourself.

POSITIVE COMMANDS
Love one another (Jn. 13: 34—This command occurs some
16 times)
Build up one another (Rom. 14: 19; 1 Thess. 5: 11)
Admonish one another (Rom. 15: 14; Col. 3: 16)
Serve one another (Gal. 5: 13)
Bear one another's burdens (Gal. 6: 2)
Forgive one another (Eph. 4: 2, 32; Col. 3: 13)
Encourage one another (1 Thess. 5: 11)

NEGATIVE COMMANDS (how not to treat one another)
Do not lie to one another (Col. 3: 9)
Stop passing judgment on one another (Rom. 14: 13)
If you keep on biting and devouring each other . . . you'll be
destroyed by each other (Gal. 5: 15)
Do not slander one another (Jas. 4: 11)

These instructions are crystal clear and easily understood. The challenge is not in understanding; it's in putting them into practice. We would encourage you to commit today to change whatever attitudes or behaviours hinder you from carrying out the explicit command of the Lord Jesus Christ and begin to care as Jesus cared. Andy Stanley said of the early Church, 'The primary activity of the Church was one-anothering one another.'

The picture of a shepherd
The Old Testament often likens the relationship of God and Israel with that of the shepherd and his sheep. Ezekiel 34 is one very vivid passage. The prophet first highlights the failures of the nation's leaders in verse 4, 'You have not strengthened the weak or healed the sick or bound up the injured. You have

not brought back the strays or searched for the lost'. This is a grave indictment against the spiritual leaders of that day.

Having made the charge against the shepherds of Israel, Ezekiel declares in verses 11–16 how God will care for his people. It is easy to read these verses quickly and not immediately appreciate how powerful they are. In order to catch their full impact, instead of writing them in narrative form, we have listed the various elements below.

> I will search for my sheep . . . from all the places where they
> have been scattered
> I will rescue them . . . from every enemy
> I will make them lie down . . . in green pastures
> I will bring back the strayed . . . those who have lost their way
> I will bind up the injured . . . those who have been broken
> by sin
> I will strengthen the weak . . . those who had lost hope
> of returning

God makes this commitment to those who are lost and broken—'I myself will be the shepherd of my sheep' (vv. 11, 12). He does not stand idly by and do nothing for people in distress, and Ezekiel's message is that we must not either.

The shepherding metaphor is further emphasised personally by David in Psalm 23 where he says, 'The Lord is my shepherd'. The idea is carried over into the New Testament where Jesus declares himself to be the 'good shepherd' and instructs Peter to feed God's sheep (Jn. 21: 15–17; 1 Pet. 5: 1–6). In his farewell address to the elders of the church at Ephesus, Paul gives this instruction: 'be sure that you feed and shepherd God's flock' (Acts 20: 28 (TLB)).

The biblical references highlight two things:

1. Shepherding is about the unstinting care of the sheep, not cruelly controlling the sheep nor the glorification of the shepherd.
2. Shepherding is an incredibly demanding occupation; it requires constant vigilance to protect the sheep from danger, hard physical exertion carrying wounded or sick sheep to safety, and knowledge of the best places to find food and rest for the sheep.

The picture of a servant

The idea of a servant runs throughout the Bible with Jesus himself being the supreme example of servanthood. The Old Testament understanding of the Messiah reaches a high point when the prophet Isaiah describes his character and mission as the Servant of Jehovah.

In the New Testament, Jesus indicates that his role in coming into the world is that of a servant. He has come to serve, not to be served (Mk. 10: 45). His radical message to the disciples is that the way to true greatness is not what the world thinks—i.e., by acquiring power—but by serving others. The way up is down; a message as radical then as it is now. We live in the so-called 'me generation' where everything centres around *our* desires, ambitions, and needs. But Jesus says that we need to turn all of that on its head and learn that we will only find true fulfilment in life in the service of others (Mt. 20: 25–28; Lk. 22: 24–26).

But what exactly is servanthood? A servant is one who obeys the instruction of another. For Christians, this means submission to God first and then to one another. It means willingly giving oneself to minister to others and to do whatever it takes to accomplish what is best for the other person.

Jesus' action in John 13 brings the meaning of servanthood into focus. The disciples were weary after a long hard day, and they were looking forward to a time of rest and recovery as they entered the room that night. It was just a standard room with a basin and jug of water at the door. One or two hesitated but thought better of it and went in with the rest. They had been discussing earlier in the day which of them was the greatest—which of them had done most for Jesus. It was a kind of power struggle, with each staking a claim for leadership.

As they sat in the room that night, anxious, embarrassing thoughts crowded in upon them. They realised they had not behaved as Jesus would have wanted. Suddenly someone got up, moved to the door, and began to pour water into the basin. It was Jesus. There was a stunned silence as it became apparent that Jesus was going to wash their feet. They knew instinctively that this was not right. Washing the feet was the job of a servant, of the person at the bottom of the heap. It was not for leaders, yet Jesus was about to do the work of a servant.

Peter refuses to let Jesus wash his feet, but Jesus dismisses his protests, saying that this is the only way in which Peter can be a true disciple of Jesus. Each one there that night knew there was a job to be done in serving the group, but each one of them said: 'let someone else do it'. Most of us, I suspect, have been there and know something of that sinking feeling that we have not done well.

Jesus clearly states the lesson for his disciples, and us, in verse 15, when he says, 'I have given you an example that you should do as I have done to you.' Jesus' action shows true pastoral care. How like the disciples and how unlike Jesus we often are when it comes to serving others. Jesus' example is a powerful visual lesson for us.

The apostle Paul in Philippians 2: 3–5 gives us an insight into Jesus' motivation when he urges us to have the same attitude as Jesus, who gave up everything for us. Paul says that we should, like Jesus, do everything out of selfless care and concern for our brothers and sisters putting their interests above our own. He continues in verses 5–11 with words of unparalleled majesty, highlighting that Jesus 'being in very nature God . . . took the very nature of a servant'.

Pastoral care, like all other Christian ministries, is about servanthood.

3. Specific instructions

Having reflected on the theological principles, we now move to specific instructions.

Most of us probably believe that the responsibility for pastoral care lies with the elders, and the New Testament does indicate that this is one of their key functions. Paul describes the required qualities in such passages as 1 Timothy 3: 1–7 and Titus 1: 5–9. Elders, and by extension those who are involved in delivering pastoral care, should be people who have grown to a measure of maturity and display something of what it means to be holy. The corollary is that no one should be appointed to a pastoral care role who is unsuited for that role or disqualified in terms of their Christian lifestyle.

In the following passages, we describe the task of eldership, so that we can see the range of pastoral requirements.

In Acts 20, Paul reminds the Ephesian elders

> of his own example (18). His life and witness were a model
> for others.
> His ministry had been with humility and tears (19, 31).
> It was not for any personal reward or financial gain (33).
> He was always available to the flock night and day (31).
> His teaching was public and private (in church and at home) (20).
> It was hard work (34, 35).

Paul thus demonstrates his total commitment to the people of God. He had given his life for their benefit and up-building, and their affection for him was unmistakable (37, 38).

In 1 Thessalonians 2, Paul describes his ministry in similar terms:

> He was not seeking the praise of men (4, 6).
> His life was a model of Christian behaviour (10).
> He was gentle and caring, like a nursing mother (7).
> He was encouraging and supportive, like a father dealing
> with his children (11).
> He did not use underhand methods (3) or flattery or deceit
> (5), but was consistent and honest.

In 1 Thessalonians 5, Paul speaks of the work of the elders (12, 13):

> They are to admonish or correct (12).
> They are to warn those who are unruly and idle, encourage
> the fainthearted, support the weak and be patient with
> everyone (14).
> They are to 'live in peace with one another' (13).

In 1 Timothy 5, the elders

> have a duty to preach and teach (17)
> to 'direct the affairs of the church well' (17)
> to do so 'without partiality or favouritism' (21).

In Hebrews 13, they are

> to use their authority well and be an example to the flock in
> their teaching, faith, and conduct (7)
> to keep watch over the members' spiritual progress, remem-
> bering they will one day give an account of their steward-
> ship (17).

In 1 Peter 5, the apostle says that they are

> to 'serve as elders with enthusiasm and submit their lives as
> examples to the flock' (1 Pet. 5: 2, 3).
> They are not to lord it over those in their care (3).

As shepherds of the sheep, they must always remember that they are under
the authority of the chief shepherd and need to carry out their duties having
regard to the instructions above. Doing so will merit 'the crown of glory that
does not fade away' (4).

Thus, the New Testament gives clear instructions about eldership and how
that task should be undertaken. It is truly a noble task and a high calling.

Everyone plays a part

Lest we imagine that these exhortations are only to elders, we need to be reminded of what the New Testament also says to us. The character requirements
outlined above are not for elders only; they provide a statement of what we
should all be aiming for in terms of our Christian growth and development.
They are the marks of maturity to which every Christian should aspire.

We should also note that many of the instructions given to elders are also
explicitly given to members of the congregation. For example:

> Elders are to teach (Eph. 4: 11), encourage (Tit. 2: 15), keep
> watch (Acts 20: 28), and admonish (1 Thess. 5: 12).

> Members are to teach and admonish (Col. 3: 16), encourage
> (Heb. 10: 24–25) and keep watch (Gal. 6: 1–2). This latter
> exhortation is in line with the wisdom of Psalms and Proverbs

showing that rebuke is an aspect of genuine friendship and
fellowship (e.g., Ps. 141: 5; Prov. 17: 17; 27: 6).

Summary

The inescapable thrust of these passages in terms of general theology and
specific exhortations is that every Christian, young and old, experienced and
inexperienced, has a duty to care for other people. All of us need to be involved.
None of us is excused.

The goal is a fully functioning body where every member loves and helps
every other member towards maturity.

For further reflection

1. What can we learn about pastoral care from the parable of the Good
   Samaritan (Lk. 10: 25–37) and Paul's address to the Ephesian elders
   in Acts 20: 17–38?
2. How does the doctrine of the priesthood of all believers, and the New
   Testament picture of the family of God, influence our understanding
   of pastoral care?
3. Paul describes his approach to pastoral care in 1 Thessalonians 2. How
   many elements of pastoral care can you see in this chapter and how do
   you think they might apply today?

WORKING TOGETHER

Focus on the nature of pastoral care

CHAPTER 3

Building a pastoral care team

Where to park an ambulance

A missionary doctor, writing of pastoral care, said, 'If people are constantly falling off a cliff, you could place ambulances under the cliff or build a fence and put up warning signs on the top. We are placing far too many ambulances under the cliff.'[1] This is a pretty accurate description of how many churches today do pastoral care. Instead of providing resources to prevent people from getting to a point where their lives are in crisis (falling over the cliff), we wait until the damage has been done before rushing to help, by which point it is often too late.

Creating a pastoral care team is one way of caring for people before they get into the danger zone. If we can help people to see the warning signs and guide them away from the cliff edge, we will be providing the support when they can most benefit from it. It is not always easy, however, to see the danger signs. Physical needs in most churches are like the visible 10% of an iceberg, while 90%, which includes most of the emotional, spiritual, and relational pain, is below the surface.

A pastoral team provides additional personnel and a formal arrangement designed to provide care in a more structured way. Having a team of people who possess, or are taught the basic skills of listening, praying with people, using the Bible, and visitation, will be a big step towards helping people before they get too near the cliff edge.

This chapter is about how to establish a pastoral care team in a local church context.

---

1. Andy Peck, *Pastoral Care Essentials*, CWR: Kindle Edition, location 695.

1. Thinking about models

No one model of pastoral care will meet the needs of all churches. Every church must decide for itself how to make the best use of resources. Some churches will create a formal structure, whereas others will go for something more informal and spontaneous. The final arrangement will depend on such factors as the size of the church, the policy agreed for providing pastoral care, and the availability of personnel.

We have no preference for any particular model, nor are we advocating that every church must have a pastoral team, though there are many benefits from having a team. And creating a designated pastoral care team may, sometimes, do more harm than good. Here are some lf the matters to be thought about:

- The congregation may not be ready for it because they feel it is a step too far. They still hold to the view that pastoral care is the job of the elders.
- Some may feel resentful of the team being given prominence and may opt out of their present involvement.
- The requirement of confidentiality can create the impression the team is some kind of elite group keeping secrets from the church.
- The fact that a team is being formed raises expectations which the church might not be able to deliver.
- If not adequately supervised, the team can do its own thing, sometimes with drastic consequences.

The dangers highlighted above should not be a reason for not having a pastoral team: we have simply attempted to create awareness of potential difficulties that might arise. Each of them can be overcome if handled sensitively.

Benefits

Having considered some difficulties associated with pastoral care teams, we must now look at some potential benefits.

Often churches form pastoral teams because the elders don't have time to do everything. The apostles in Acts 6 appointed deacons to support widows in need in order to leave the apostles free for teaching and prayer. There are benefits for a pastor (if there is one) in reducing his workload, and there are also benefits for pastoral care team members who will have opportunity to use their gifts.

One particular advantage of having a designated care team is that it provides a larger number of people to do the work. Because they are already members, the congregation will know them as people who can be trusted and, more importantly, the team will know their fellow church members, so are in a better position to see the signs of potential problems. A further advantage of having a care team is that people are already in place when pastoral issues arise. When the care provision is unstructured, churches often scramble around to find someone to deal with problems. The danger is that someone can be ignored or passed to a carer who is willing to help but is already overloaded. Andy Peck says, 'we need a care process that doesn't just depend on the free time of a few brave souls.'[2]

One objection from church members may be that pastoral care team members lack the experience of the church leaders, but it should be remembered that not every elder has pastoral gifts, and many others in the fellowship may have a pastoral heart as well as the time to spend with those who need support. Also, the benefits of utilising 'lay' people have been documented in academic circles. Durlak and others[3] have examined the literature comparing the progress of patients suffering from crisis or illness who had been referred to professional counsellors and those given help by lay 'people helpers' such as family and friends. The outcome of these studies showed that the groups who had only the help of friends and family often did better than those who received specialised counselling. It would seem that it is not so much the specialism that counts, important as that may be; what produces the greatest effect is the love and personal presence of caring people around us. Professional counsellors see

---

2. Andy Peck, *Pastoral Care Essentials*, CWR: Kindle Edition, location 171.

3. A summary of this research can be found at Robert W. Kellemen, *Gospel Conversations*, Zondervan, p. 82.

The following references are to the original research: J. A. Durlak, 'Comparative effectiveness of para-professional and professional helpers', *Psychological Bulletin* (1979), pp. 86, 80–92; J. A. Hattie and C. F. Sharpley, https://citeseerx.ist.psu.edu/viewdoc/download?doi=10.1.1.909.6659&rep=rep1&type=pdf; & Berman and Norton, 'Does_Professional_Training_Make_a_Therapist_More_Effective', at https://www.researchgate.net/publication/19261008_.

'clients' for an hour a week, whereas having the sustained company of a loving group of friends can often be much more beneficial.

This point is not to belittle professional counselling, but to encourage church members to see how much we can achieve by drawing close to people in their moment of crisis. We can make a difference!

From the observations above and the biblical teaching of chapter 2, the evidence is overwhelming that involving church members in addition to leaders is the way to proceed. So, let's suppose the church has considered all the factors and has decided to create a formal pastoral care team. What factors need to be taken into consideration to put the team in place?

Prior considerations

In the eyes of many, the proposed changes will seem like a significant departure from the church's long-standing position. We need to set minds and hearts at ease, so it is vital that leaders consult as early as possible with the congregation to ensure that everyone understands the reasons for change, how the change process will impact the church and what will be the eventual benefits. It is most important that proposals for change are not suddenly sprung on the congregation. A slower pace and fuller explanations are always better.

Members should know that the elders fully support the changes because they believe the result will mean a much better level of care. More people will have the opportunity to use their gifts so fewer people will be overlooked. In addition, there will be benefits in terms of the discipleship programme, evangelism, and social care in the church and the community.

It is also helpful to acknowledge that not everything that happened in the past was bad. Attempting to improve the provision does not imply that what went on before was ineffective. The leaders should acknowledge that much of the pastoral care, even though it was informal, was beneficial and they would wish to see this continue. They recognise the value of the many supportive conversations in the church's shared activities, for example, in the choir, the youth work, and other networks.

Church leaders should also recognise that those previously involved in pastoral care will be apprehensive that their contribution is no longer required.

They need the assurance that creating a formal pastoral care team adds value to what is already being done; it does not replace it.

In summary, the idea behind establishing a pastoral team is to deliver care in those areas which have not received enough attention in the past. This will be particularly beneficial to the elderly who belong to few networks in the church and often feel forgotten.

2. Pastoral team remit

It may be that the pastoral team will feel it is important to extend the range of pastoral activities to complement the provision that already exists in the church. It is not a good idea for the pastoral team to take over ministries the church members are already providing perfectly well. Their focus should be on areas not already covered by the existing provision. This section offers some helpful suggestions.

Pastoring people on the way in

The team could take a lead in welcoming new families or individuals into the church. We should never underestimate how stressful it can be for people to settle and feel at home in a new church, especially for young Christians. This might involve an early contact following their first visit to the church and, in due course, helping them to settle into one of the church house groups. The team would also inform new families of the range of ministry opportunities and facilities for children.

It's wise to give people time to settle in before involving them in public ministry. They need to feel sure about making the church their spiritual home and know enough about its ethos, so that they feel comfortable about getting involved.

Discipling new Christians

This is important where the church does not have an official discipleship training programme. The problem with so much discipleship training in churches is that it is spontaneous and situational rather than intentional and structured, so a pastoral care team could play a significant role here. Small groups, short courses, and coaching groups can also be useful vehicles through which to unpack the implications of discipleship.

Helping with transitions

There are, for example, opportunities to prepare young people transitioning to further education. University can be a make-or-break experience for which there is a genuine need to prepare students. Another area of concern for many parents is that, when their children reach their late teens and become involved in activities outside the church, their interest in Christian things diminishes. It is often easier for someone outside the family circle to draw alongside that person and try to help them back into the fellowship of the church. For example, a pastoral carer could help teenagers to deal with peer pressure and social media.

Caring for those on the fringe

Fringe members are those: a) on the way into the church; b) on their way out; or c) happy not to be actively involved in the life of the church. We know that relationships speak louder than even the best worship service or preaching. If members have a few good friends in a local church, they will usually be able to weather most storms; if they don't, almost anything might drag them away. Being a friend can be crucial.

We should also remember that some prefer to remain on the fringe, sometimes because they don't want to commit.

Ultimately, our job is not to force anyone to become more involved or to stop them from leaving. Jesus invited all to come to him and turned no one away, but some excluded themselves because it did not suit their lifestyle, or they were not prepared to pay the cost of discipleship. The pastoral carer needs to encourage such believers to follow Christ in a more committed way.

Those on the way out

People decide to leave a church for many reasons. Some of these are unavoidable, such as moving home or changing job, but others are preventable.

Peck provides information from several sources on why people decide to leave church:

- Changes in belief and unbelief
- Major life changes and transitions
- Lifestyles incompatible with church membership
- Not belonging or fitting in
- Disillusionment with the church
- Problems with change in the church
- Nobody took an interest in them
- Leadership problems in the church
- Conflict in the church[4]

Most people who leave don't take the decision suddenly; they just drift away. Their involvement in church activities becomes less and they make excuses until finally they don't show up anymore. This is where the pastoral team role could be critical. We could charge carers with keeping a watchful eye on people who are not around as much as previously.

Maybe someone has taken ill, and no one has noticed, or they are looking after a sick family member, in which case they might welcome support. Perhaps the issue may be one of conflict or disillusionment with the church, or simply spiritual apathy. In such cases, it might still be possible to find a solution to the problem, but even if they insist on leaving, it is better to do so on amicable terms. It would also be important to help the person find a new church. The issue is not about church numbers or keeping members at all costs, but about the spiritual development of the individual.

Using the Sunday services

Sunday services serve many purposes. They are a vehicle for teaching the Bible, explaining the gospel, experiencing worship and fellowship, and general encouragement. They can also be a vehicle for providing pastoral care. Not everyone wants a home visit or a lengthy chat; they often just appreciate having a few minutes of someone's time to ask a question. Tea or coffee time at services provides a great opportunity to catch up, encourage, and offer support. The

---

4. You can get further information at Andy Peck, *Pastoral Care Essentials*, CWR: Kindle Edition, location 1920.

caring church will seek to ensure that everyone, but particularly elders and pastoral carers, do not congregate in their own small group of friends, but use the coffee break to reach out to people on their own, to visitors, or to people who just need a little reassurance. This is a significant pastoral moment. It should not be missed, and more than that, everyone can do it. Don't squander these opportunities.

Regular visitation programme

If the church decides to create a pastoral team, it is good to incorporate a regular visitation programme into their remit. Many members of the congregation do not find it easy to come forward and ask for help, so a home visit or meeting in a neutral place like a coffee shop, can make it easier for individuals to articulate their needs. Every elder and member of the pastoral care team should commit to undertaking an agreed number of visits, which will, of course, depend on their availability, the needs of the congregation, and the number of carers involved. Some visits will be 'one-off'; others will be ongoing.

It is important for elders to be engaged in regular visitation because in recent years the trend has been for elders to take on a more management role in the church, requiring them to focus on administration rather than people. In this context, it is easy to get out of touch and not be fully aware of the issues and problems the congregation is facing. Also, congregational members may well feel that pastoral visitation is precisely what elders should be doing, and may even feel that that they are being short-changed by a visit from another pastoral team member. We strongly urge pastors and elders to do regular visitation to meet real people in actual situations. By doing this, they can provide much more effective pastoral care. Individual elders might well take a pastoral team member with them, at least on occasion, so as to legitimize them for future visitation. Having a programme that transparently covers the whole church counteracts the tendency for individual members to believe that they are only being visited because they are considered to be badly behaved or problematic in some way.

Such regular visitation programmes have a long and proud history. Perhaps the best known was set up by Richard Baxter (1615–1691),[5] whose ministry to his church in Kidderminster in the seventeenth century saw many hundreds come to faith. Besides preaching on Sundays and midweek, he systematically visited his parishioners, explaining basic doctrine and enquiring after their spiritual life.

New ministries

The discussion above has included some general examples of pastoral ministry. The pastoral team could consider starting ministries which don't already exist in the church. These might include a prayer ministry team available after church services, a bereavement support team, or a telephone contact ministry to keep in touch with elderly members. You can find an extensive list of possibilities at the locations referenced in the footnote.[6]

Follow-up

It is easy to imagine that when we have contacted an individual or visited them in their home, we have finished our work, but this is not the case. We need to keep in touch, especially if we undertook to do something arising from our conversation, for example, to have meals delivered or help to ensure an older person can access the church's virtual programmes. If we committed to some action, we must follow up either by phone or text, to inquire how a hospital appointment had gone or how the children have settled in at school.

Often, it is only on the second or third contact that the person has sufficient trust and confidence to raise the problems that are really causing them concern. People are often hesitant to open up to someone they have met for the first time, so follow up is vital.

5. You will find more information on the pastoral significance of Baxter at:
https://www.thegospelcoalition.org/article/richard-baxter-400-years-later-still-model-pastor/
https://www.ministrymagazine.org/archive/2003/11/the-pastor-and-visitation-richard-baxters-model.html
6. Andy Peck, *Pastoral Care Essentials*, CWR: Kindle Edition, location 2172 & Alison Moore, *The Puzzle of Pastoral Care*. Kevin Mayhew, 2019, p. 11.

3. Getting the right people

Having agreed that a pastoral team would be helpful for the church, and established the remit, the next stage is to get the right people in place. We strongly recommend that someone is appointed to coordinate and lead the activities of the team. In smaller churches, the pastor often takes this role, but it is usually better to give the position to someone else. Even if there is no official pastoral team, it is still better if one person oversees the provision. Appointing the right person to this key role will be crucial and will often determine the success or failure of the enterprise. We will discuss the role more fully later in this chapter.

We now move on to consider the selection of team members[7] which can often be very tricky. Our preferred method is to issue the job description and invite expressions of interest from members of the congregation. This has the benefit of making the process transparent, and nobody can say that they did not have the opportunity to participate. Another benefit is that it can sometimes reveal individuals whose gifts we had not previously recognised. The downside is that we may receive expressions of interest from people who would not be suitable as members of the team. The leaders should indicate that asking about being a pastoral team member does not guarantee acceptance.

In addition to issuing a general invitation, the leaders should approach those members of the congregation who already show gifting in this area. Recommendation by someone who knows the person is also extremely helpful (few people put themselves forward). Often those already involved in pastoral care are the best recruiters of others because of their shared interest in this sphere of service.

A more formal process might be better in larger congregations, perhaps using a short application form followed by a brief interview by a small panel of two or three people. Whatever the method, we should base invitations to join the team on character, gifting, availability, and sense of call. Whether people are approached or express interest on their own account, it is essential to have

---

7. Alison Moore, *The Puzzle of Pastoral Care*, Kevin Mayhew: 2019, p. 29. An excellent list of issues to be addressed when seeking volunteers is provided on pages 31–34.

a preliminary discussion with them to assess their suitability and to confirm that they understand what the job entails.

If one or two people express interest in pastoral care but are clearly not suitable, the leaders need to be gentle yet honest with them, supportive, and perhaps working with them to use their gifts in other ministry areas. If the leaders think the person could develop into the role, they could suggest additional training or maybe a probationary period with someone more experienced in pastoral care. However, no one should be invited to join the team who is patently unqualified, as this could damage both the church and the individual. If the right people are not available, it may be better to delay the implementation of the project.

Already stated is the importance of those appointed to a pastoral care role having the required character and personal qualities as well as time availability. We recognise that not every church has the luxury of having a range of people to choose from. It is more often the case that the choice is limited, in which case, it might be better to delay the project until the right people become available.

Understanding the job

It is important to articulate what being a member of the pastoral team involves, for example, to clarify expectations about terms of service, behaviour, support, training, reporting, accountability, and review. New team members need to understand what they are committing themselves to.

Gifting

The team will comprise a range of individuals to cover the needs of the church, so there may be old and young, male and female, and the team will seek to maximise the range of gifts within the group. Some church members will relate better to young people, whereas others may feel more at home with older people. Members of the team will have their own strengths and interests, and we should encourage them to work to their strengths, as well as involving other gifted people outside of the team where appropriate.

Availability

Not all team members will be able to devote the same amount of time to pastoral care. One may be able to give one evening a week, whereas another could be available for several. Both the potential team members and the team leader should be comfortable with the time available and expected from the outset. The team members should consult with the leader as soon as possible should there be changes in work or family circumstances.

Calling

Pastoral care team members should have a sense of the call of God, with a conviction that God has not only gifted them for the task, but that this is how he wants to work out his purposes in their lives and where he wants them to serve.

The implication of this is that they will be in it for the long-term. Their motivation will be the glory of God and the building up of his people. They will have a 'whatever it takes' attitude to achieve this aim. The belief that they are doing God's work provides a firm foundation in tough times, for example, when things are going badly or when conflicts arise. In such situations it is easy to get discouraged and be tempted to give up, so we can remind ourselves that God called us to the work and wants us to continue in it.

4. Coordination and supervision

Sometimes pastoral care requires ongoing attention, for example, routine visits or telephone contact with an older person. But on some occasions, unexpected issues can arise, often simultaneously, followed by several months when nothing very much happens. There is no way to predict and plan for this in advance and the result can be that the care provided is haphazard or poorly managed. It requires coordination to deal with emergencies, deploy personnel, and ensure problems don't go unnoticed, and that no one gets overlooked. How often have we heard people say when someone gets into difficulty, 'I didn't know about that'. In the ideal church, someone will know and take action. Situations like these highlight the importance of the team leader's role.

The personal and spiritual qualities of the person appointed as the leader should be evident, and he or she should have the full support of the leadership and the congregation.

The job specification should indicate that the leader will:

- Act as the first point of contact for members of the congregation who may require pastoral care or wish to bring someone to the attention of the pastoral team.
- Coordinate the activities of the pastoral team to ensure everything works efficiently and effectively.
- Convene regular meetings of the group and keep records of its activities.
- Liaise with other groups inside and outside the church, such as home groups or Social Services.
- Deliver or organise training and ongoing learning for team members and others involved in pastoral care such as small group leaders.
- Identify other members of the congregation as potential future members of the pastoral team.

5. Authorisation

At the beginning of this chapter, we highlighted some benefits of creating a pastoral care team in church. What starts as a good idea can quickly become more complex. The scope of this ministry area can be large and varied, so it needs coordination, and the process of appointing people with the right personal and spiritual qualifications can be challenging. We might think we can relax a little when we have everything in place, but one last problem remains: the issue of authorisation.

The church may have paid members of staff who will have a contract spelling out their contractual commitments. The pastoral care team member, however, is essentially a volunteer in a 'semi-official' capacity. This is also true of other church members, for example, leaders of the music group or youth work. Where do they fit in regarding legal technicalities when they serve outside the scope of employment law?

Authorisation of paid employees implies that the person is in agreement with church policies and practices and is accountable to the church leadership. Employees are responsible for their actions to the church and for providing care to a standard acceptable both to the church and the community. They should report regularly and timeously to the elders indicating difficulties encountered and progress made.

A further implication is that the church deems the employee to have the skills and abilities necessary to undertake the role. This involves the provision of training and support, structured supervision, and evaluation of performance. Such provision will raise the quality of care and lower the risk of things going wrong or people getting hurt.

It is unlikely that the pastoral care team member will have a formal contract, but there should be policies in place which clearly state expectations of the team member and the church. There needs to be an open discussion between the pastoral team and the church leadership outlining the limits of responsibility, and, as a minimum, it would be helpful if there were a brief, but clear role description for pastoral team members.

Raising the issue of authorisation carries with it the danger of changing the nature of pastoral team care. What started as an informal, loving commitment by members to reach out to others in the church can become something legalistic and contractual. It can easily induce a 'tick-box' mentality which is in stark contrast to the idea of simply reaching out to people in need. Those who have been doing pastoral care for years may feel uncomfortable having to be authorised to perform a role they have been doing for a long time, not needing a title or a position.

These feelings are understandable, and we would strongly recommend that the church does not become too bureaucratic and controlling. We would want pastoral care to continue spontaneously as before and, most of the time, this will be the case. However, guidelines are needed to provide safeguards covering a variety of situations, some of which might put the carer in a potentially vulnerable position.

This issue is more fully explored in Alison Moore's book, *The Puzzle of Pastoral Care* in chapter 2.9, p.134.

There is also an excellent resource at:

> https://www.presbyterianireland.org/getmedia/f1b793fd-
> 42d4-4861-90e0-9c9987caa4e4/Pastoral-Care-Teams.pdf.
> aspx?ext=.pdf

For further reflection

1. What are the benefits and drawbacks of a formal and informal model of pastoral care and which of these would best suit your church? State why this is?

2. What obstacles might get in the way of elders involving church members in pastoral care, and how might these be overcome?

3. What is the relationship between pastoral care and discipleship?

4. Discuss the following statement and explain why you think it is true or not: 'Good worship and preaching attract people to a church, but it is good pastoral care that compels them to stay'.

5. Write a role description for a pastoral care team member. This should include both the requirements of the task and the personal qualities necessary.

CHAPTER 4

The caring church

Several years ago, we were invited to help a church with a series of consultations relating to the quality of their pastoral care. Some members of the congregation had expressed dissatisfaction with the present provision, so the elders decided that they should look more closely at the concerns. The church had about 140 members and the leaders invited all the members to take part in the review. About 40 people enrolled, so four groups, each comprising a range of old and young, male and female, traditional and progressive, were formed. The groups were asked to respond to several assignments, two of which are relevant to our present discussion.

> **Assignment 1:** Describe what you think a genuinely caring church would look like.

> The four groups identified a range of characteristics, and their findings were remarkably similar. This was very encouraging because it showed an intuitive understanding of the qualities you might find in a caring church. The discussions identified a list of some ten features central to a caring church. These formed the basis for the next assignment.

> **Assignment 2:** From a list of the key features identified in assignment (1), indicate for each element, on a scale of 1 to 10 with one being poor and ten being excellent, how you think pastoral care is being delivered in your church.

This exercise, with its various assignments, took place over a period of weeks so there was plenty of time to gather views and discuss the findings. Members who had not been directly involved in the exercise were kept informed of what had been happening and a good number contributed informally. The aim at this point was to keep the church as fully involved as possible.

Several observations should be made about this exercise:

1. It demonstrated that the members of the church were providing a great deal of pastoral support informally. This was very gratifying, and the elders thanked the members for the care they were already providing, urging them to continue in it.

2. The information arising from the exercise provided a solid base from which to build on the strengths identified, and work on areas of weakness.

3. Members were happy to be involved, but it raised a level of expectation that something would happen at the end of the consultation.

4. The consultation turned out to be a very positive, even a fun experience, but it does not always turn out like this. Consultations can sometimes be divisive.

1.   What does a caring church look like?

The example described above was of an actual consultation. For the major part of this chapter, however, we want you to imagine you are looking for a church where pastoral care is delivered to a very high standard. The various elements are combined from different sources and are intended to illustrate some essential principles.

Imagine you have moved to a new district and are looking for a church where you could put down roots and find a place to serve God. Before arriving in the neighbourhood, you check out the church's theological position and maybe listen online to some sermons preached over the last few months. You have asked friends and neighbours what they think of the church and, armed with this information, you arrive on your first Sunday morning wondering if this could be your new spiritual home.

First impressions count

First impressions can make all the difference, so you ask yourself, 'Do these people look as if they want to be here?' 'Do they look happy and feel comfortable in each other's company?' 'Do they welcome visitors?' 'How will I know where to sit and will people ask me awkward questions?' Answers to questions like these will probably determine whether you will come back.

Churches need to pay close attention to this. First impressions count. Caring churches will welcome visitors, show them where to sit, and tell them what form the service will take. They go out of their way to make visitors feel at home because they want them to come back, and they know that leaving a visitor stranded with no one to talk to is not the way to do that. Caring churches reach out from the very first contact. This care will not just be provided by an official 'welcome team', but also by church members as an expression of Christian love.

Let's suppose your first experience was a good one and you would like to know more about the church. You have picked up some literature that looks good and provides a wealth of information. The leaflets provide details of activities for children, youth, and adults. The church programme is quite extensive, so there is something for everyone. They allocate members to Home Groups, which serve as the main 'family' unit within the church.

Adding to the programme of activities are discipleship training classes, marriage preparation and enrichment classes, home and hospital visitation groups, older person care, and much more. Members arrange reading and walking groups within the church, according to demand. The literature also highlights that individuals within the church reach out more widely to minister in prisons, among the homeless community, with Street Pastors, and others in supporting projects overseas.

The material is well presented with contact names and addresses for each activity. Obviously, a great deal of thought had been given to making it as easy as possible to integrate people into the life of the church. Refreshments are provided after the service, which allows you to chat with several members, two of whom invite you for coffee later that week. All very impressive.

Everybody has been very pleasant and spoken very positively about the church. Members look out for one another, and the pastors not only telephone round the church once a month, but they also have a twice-yearly home visitation programme.

Having met with several members over the following few weeks, you notice that no one at any point spoke negatively about other members of the church. As can sometimes happen in casual conversations, members may talk about others in the church or about fallouts and tensions that have taken place. However, here, no one referred to any divisions or power struggles in the church and neither did anyone speak ill of other members or point out who the 'good people' were and who you might need to 'look out for'.

You are building a picture of the church and it all seems very positive. The range of activities and facilities is impressive, and the atmosphere is warm. This church appears to tick all the boxes for caring. The one thing you need to do now is to find out what drives this programme of caring for people. You need to know more about the underlying culture and presuppositions. To find answers to these questions, you arrange an interview with the pastor.

The pastor's name is Mark, a man who you guess is in his middle 40s. You explain that you were involved at a pastoral level in your previous church and because you have been impressed with the level of pastoral care being provided in Mark's church, you wanted to know a little more about the underlying philosophy. Mark says he doesn't very often get requests to discuss pastoral care at this level and he is delighted to give you as much information as he can. Let's listen to his story.

2. Mark's story

Mark begins: 'I came to the church about ten years ago with a desire to establish a caring community. I was convinced of the central importance of people caring for each other and the community as the key to growing the church. When people see Christians caring deeply for one another, they recognise that something different is going on and ask why.

'I had a clear vision of what I wanted to achieve. It would affect every level of the church, from the oldest leader to the newest member. The leadership team would model what a caring group should look like with everybody looking out for everyone else's interests. They would set high standards of behaviour and relationships. They would resolve conflict constructively, always seeking God honouring solutions. People don't respond to what they hear, they respond to what they see, and I wanted everyone to see a group of people leading the church with care and compassion. In the early days, from time to time I asked how the church members thought we were doing in terms of pastoral care and how they thought we might do it better. I was simply sowing a seed at that point.

'But I also wanted every member of the church to catch the vision of caring for others. So, I began that process by setting up discipleship classes for new Christians and pre-membership courses for those who wished to join the church. In each of these groups, we emphasised the importance of caring for each other, participating fully in house groups, and getting involved in other activities according to the individual's interests and availability. I just quietly set things in motion, one thing at a time.

'It was very encouraging to note, even at that early stage, that some members of the church had a genuine interest in caring for others. These people already had enthusiasm and did not need to be persuaded. I spent time with them and released them to get involved in their own house groups. They just needed to be pointed in the right direction.

'There were two other groups of people I knew I needed to get to. They would not necessarily be hostile, but might be a little reluctant because of their pre-conceived ideas about pastoral care. The first group comprised the leaders of the various ministries in the church, such as leaders of house groups, music group, and parents and toddlers. They were good people, doing an excellent job in their respective areas of service.

'I took various opportunities to speak with each of them, asking how they felt their ministry was going and how well their team was functioning. Most of the leaders thought they were doing okay, but several had not fully realised the pastoral dimension of their role in relation to team members. I encouraged them to think of the implications of this, and suggested we could chat further at a later point.

'The second group I describe as the "key influencers". This is not a distinct or easily identifiable group. They are people who, because of their personality or longstanding commitment to the church, are respected by the members and whose views carry weight. People listen to them. I've been around long enough to know that if I couldn't get these people on board, I would have no chance of success.'

Now for the hard bit

Mark continued, 'It's easy to change things in the church if you tinker a bit with the structures and processes, but if you want to make real, lasting change, you need to get under the surface. We can only sustain pastoral care in the long run if the people have a heart commitment to what they are doing. The hard bit is changing the underlying culture and presuppositions of the people.

'I believe pastoral care needs to be part of the DNA of the church; it needs to be in the bloodstream as well as on the agenda. Churches are like icebergs, where only 10% of the mass is above the surface. That one-tenth represents the church programmes; the other 90% relates to what is going on beneath the surface in people's hearts and minds and it is here that the real change needs to take place. Changing a programme is easy; changing a mindset is not. Many of our attitudes and beliefs simmer beneath the collective consciousness and contribute to the church's overall culture. These have been shaped over decades by the people and events that have gone before. This explains why attempts at change have failed over the years, because leaders have appealed to the one-tenth above the surface. The focus has usually been on organisational issues, but changing the culture requires something much deeper.

'What I want to do is get every leader and member to ask, "How can I contribute to this ministry in such a way that I can help every person I contact to make progress in their spiritual life." It's about being intentional, paying attention to detail and willing every person to grow in grace. The result is that every task, however insignificant it may seem, has the potential to make an impact for eternity. We are not just teaching children in a Sunday school class, we are bringing the love of Christ to them, and seeing them as people who will be increasingly part of God's purposes for the world.'

3. Creating a culture of care in the congregation

Mark has explained with great enthusiasm what he was trying to do and how he envisaged a genuinely caring church. He has drawn you into his vision and you find yourself wanting to take part in it. You tell him how you feel, and out of interest, you wondered how easy or difficult it had been for Mark to bring his church to where he wanted it to be.

He responds, 'When I arrived ten years earlier, the church was full of cliques endlessly opposing each other. These were driven by forceful personalities who were more concerned with pushing their own agenda and reputation than advancing the cause of Christ. The previous pastor had worked hard, but tried to do everything himself with the result that he burned himself out and had to take early retirement.

'There were a few people who longed to see a different kind of church—a more caring church. They were not interested in politics and power struggles, but they knew there would be strong bids from the clique leaders to get me onto their side. I determined to resist taking sides and gently move the church towards the New Testament ideal.

'My first task was to build up trust with the congregation, so I spent time getting to know as many people as possible, making myself available to them. For two years, I just pastored the congregation in their good times and bad. Whatever crisis or difficulty they found themselves in, I was there for them. I didn't realise then but what I was doing was modelling what pastoral care looked like. The people came to trust me and when the time came to make actual changes, they had already recognised the benefits.

'At the same time, I did two other things. I preached regularly about the need to be a caring church and also about particular pastoral issues. The second thing I did was to confront wrong attitudes and behaviours. I did not go in with all guns blazing in a confrontational manner, but spoke privately with the individuals concerned, asking them if they were aware of how much damage their actions were causing to the congregation. Some did not realise the effects of their actions and did respond to my request for everyone to pull together in pursuit of a vision for a different kind of church.

'But not everyone responded positively to this approach. When the individuals concerned realised I would not take sides and that the congregation had become tired of the constant battling, some acknowledged that their behaviour had been unacceptable and committed to change. There were, however, a few who fought back and made life difficult for a time.'

At this point, Mark realises he has been talking for well over an hour so he says, 'Let me just try to summarise for you the lessons I have learned and the advice I would give to anyone trying to implement change in a local church.'

4. Some advice

Take notice of the wake-up call

'Every significant change begins with a wake-up call. It might be complaints from membership or the recognition that if we don't do something, the church will die. The best kind of wake-up call is when someone or some group catches a vision from God of a better future for the church and really wants to see it happen. When the call comes, don't ignore it.'

Get the key people on board

'Some people will respond enthusiastically, some will be a little more reluctant, and a few may never get on board. The change will adversely affect some people and they will need to be supported through it. Choose someone to lead the change who is committed and enthusiastic. Don't just choose someone who happens to be available. Never attempt to implement change without your key influencers being on board.'

Involve the congregation

'Engage the congregation in the process and discussions about policy, because, if they have no part in it, they will never own it. Never impose change on a congregation without preparing them for it first. Leaders need to understand that change can never be successful if the stakeholders are not ready or willing to accept it. Let God guide you as to what needs to change. Your people must recognise that your proposals are for their benefit and not driven by the latest fad. People quickly come to see and resent a leadership style that simply buys into the "flavour of the month". Make sure that the individual is heard and that he or she is able to express their views without being dismissed or shouted down. The aim is to bring people on board without compromising the project.

'Decide in advance how you will assess the views of the congregation. In my case, I felt we had done enough groundwork and the congregation was ready to discuss the new direction at a public meeting. But let me give you a tip. If the issue under consideration is in any way contentious, don't call a meeting of the whole church. The more vocal people will take over and quieter members won't say anything for fear of being shouted down. On troublesome issues, it is much better, although much more demanding in terms of time, for the elders to visit each family at home. This will allow members to ask their questions and elders to answer in a more productive and less emotionally charged atmosphere. It will also enable a calm discussion of the rationale behind the proposed changes.'

Change the mindset

'Cast a compelling vision of what the change will produce and clearly articulate the benefits. People will not respond unless they understand why the change is necessary and what benefits it will bring, both personally and organisationally. Make sure the vision is your own and not a weakened version of someone else's.

'Don't just focus on programmes and activities. It is essential to reach the mind and the heart. Until people are willing to let go of the reality they are living in, they will not embrace something new. No amount of pleading or coercion will force people to do what they don't want to do.'

Communicate well . . . and often

'Don't assume that leaders can command change and it will happen. It will not happen until it is embedded in the heart and minds of the followers.

'Pay careful attention to what you communicate, by whom, and how much. Communicate with enthusiasm, calling for everyone to travel together on the journey which will take them to a better place than where they are now.

'Tell people how they can provide feedback during the change process. This indicates that the leaders have not already made up their mind and are happy to incorporate suggestions and comments from others.'

Handle the difficulties

'If an individual or group is undermining the project, deal with it head-on. The problem will not go away by itself. Provide support to those who are finding the changes difficult.'

Celebrate every milestone

'No matter how detailed the preparation, the process will not always go to plan. Some aspects will not work well, while others will be better than expected. Keep everyone informed of the progress being made and, if minor changes in direction are required, let people know of these adjustments. Thank everyone regularly for their support and contribution, especially when the change has been successfully implemented. People always respond positively to expressions of appreciation. We don't thank people enough.'

It's not over 'til it's over

'I am offering these bits of advice as a way of thinking about change. It is not a "tick-box" exercise to be followed sequentially. You don't finish one phase then move to the next; everything we have been talking about is ongoing throughout the process.'

Mark finishes with two final points. 'First, you can use this advice as a general model for continuous improvement. Let your people know that the pursuit of excellence will be a basic part of the church's business, Secondly, when you have finished one project, wait at least six months before you start another. Too many changes can be as unsettling as too few.'

Mark again apologises for speaking for so long but everything he has said has confirmed that this is the kind of church you have been looking for. You thank him very much for giving so much time and promise to be in church next Sunday.

5. Pastoral care policies

As indicated earlier, sections 2–4 in this chapter have been an exercise in imagination, but we hope one which has encapsulated many aspects of good pastoral practice, as well as a good approach to leadership in voluntary groups, which is what churches are. It would be great to belong to a church like Mark's.

We need now to return to the real world and deal with a matter that many elders and pastors find daunting and that is to put on paper how the church leadership sees pastoral care. We do encourage churches to produce a paper setting out their pastoral policy. It helps to clarify thinking and in times of difficulty can be a reminder of what we are supposed to be about. We should, however, add a word of caution.

Churches, like other organizations, can spend months producing policy papers which all too often end up at the bottom of a filing cabinet rather than being implemented. The production of the paper has become an end in itself rather than a springboard to help us achieve our goal of providing the best possible level of pastoral care.

What should be in a policy paper?

The following are offered as suggestions as to what might be included:

1. The elders' understanding of pastoral care in terms of enabling people to become more like Jesus, encouraging fellowship, growing disciples and lovingly reaching out to others in gospel witness.

2. A statement about the church's commitment to providing care of the highest standard, which will follow not only guidelines of good practice as outlined by professional bodies, but also all legal requirements and the expectations of the church's insurers. This will involve a commitment to providing support, training, and supervision.

3. A statement indicating that all carers are expected to comply with the guidelines and policies of the church (and that it will be a matter for appropriate corrective action if there is non-compliance).

4. Confirmation of the importance of home and ministry groups within the church with every member having a part to play in pastoral care.

5. Information on recognising different aspects of pastoral care:
   - **Routine pastoral care**—This reflects the traditional idea that the pastor or elders of the church will regularly visit members of the congregation. The paper should indicate how often and by whom such visits will be made.
   - **Emergency pastoral care**—this arises from situations which cannot be foreseen, for example, an accident, or a member taken into hospital. We cannot plan for these in advance, but the church should have a mechanism in place to permit action when they arise.

Information should be given describing what members should do
if pastoral care is required at very short notice.

- **Longer-term pastoral care**—the kind of situation envisaged would
  be if a member of the church were to be in hospital for a more
  extended period or to be suffering from chronic declining illness in
  the home or where, for example, an older member had no family
  and would simply require company from time to time.
- **'One another' pastoral care**—this term is used to describe the
  ongoing discipleship and development of the members of the
  church as outlined in chapter three.
- **Elder pastoral care**—this would relate to how the elders approach
  pastoral care required by more serious issues arising in the fellowship.

6. Details of how the pastoral care leader (if there is one) can be contacted
   and information on his or her role.
7. A request to members to point out any perceived deficiencies in pastoral
   care arrangements or make suggestions for improvement.

For further reflection

1. What would you expect to see in a church that describes itself as a
   caring church?
2. What obstacles might prevent a church from becoming a caring
   community, and how can these be overcome?
3. We cannot teach Christians to care for each other, they are either caring
   people or they are not. Discuss.
4. Select three New Testament examples of practical love being shown in
   a church context and discuss what we can learn from them.
5. Do you think the following statement is true and why? 'When someone
   comes to your church for the first time, you have 60 seconds to make a
   good first impression and whatever impression you give will determine
   whether or not they will return.'

Focus on pastoral care needs

CHAPTER 5

A Room with a View

You may have seen the 1985 film, 'A Room with a View', and you may even have read the E.M. Foster novel on which it was based. It tells the story of a young woman called Lucy who, on a visit to Florence, is disappointed to discover that her room does not have the view of the river Arno that she had been led to expect. The book is set at the beginning of the twentieth century and describes Lucy's relationships with the different people she meets.

Just as the characters in the novel bring their individual perspectives and attitudes to the novel, so, when it comes to pastoral care, people today also bring their unique personalities into their relationships. Some of the most significant influences that shape our outlook are the experiences we have at different stages in our lives. Viewing life as a series of stages helps us to better understand the role of pastoral care. These stages are not identical for everyone—nevertheless we have many experiences in common.

In his book, *Christian Counselling*, Gary Collins identifies five stages of life and describes the issues and difficulties many encounter as they move from childhood to old age. In this and the following chapter, we follow Collins' outline but use our own material. We will briefly describe some of the issues that are likely to arise in each stage of life, and at the end of each chapter, we will offer practical suggestions as to the kind of pastoral input that could be of help. If you require more information, we recommend you consult Collins.[1] It is an excellent resource.

We will look at these stages by using our imagination and thinking of a large house which includes five rooms for family members, with additional

---

1. G. R. Collins, *Christian Counselling*, Nelson, 2007, pp. 213–291.

communal rooms. While each room has a view to the outside world, our task
is not to look out, but to look in and observe the joys and struggles that the
occupants encounter. We shall stand in the doorway of each family room and
try to catch its atmosphere in order to understand better what is going on in
the lives of those who live there.

So, let's begin our tour of the house.

1.   The playroom

We start our tour in the playroom where we observe the youngest members
of the family. The children will be part of the life of the church because a
children's church operates, or perhaps a midweek children's club that feeds
into the Sunday programme, or just simply because their friends are there.
Whatever the reason, they add to the diversity in the church family and they
need to be cared for.

Childhood is a time when children should be protected from the cares
and worries of life and have the space to enjoy their lives in a relaxed and safe
environment. Life, however, is rarely that simple, and many children, including
those who come to church, can have a range of experiences in their young lives,
some of which are far from positive; some may even be dangerous.

Parents play a huge role in a child's life, and their actions shape how that
child develops. Christian parents also have a particular responsibility to help
their children spiritually. This will involve praying for and with their children,
and talking naturally with them about issues of faith. Besides prayer, there is
value in reading Bible stories to children and teaching them about God's love
for them. Doing this can be a profound blessing, especially when done in a
loving family where the parents are willing to spend quality-time in interacting
with their children. This kind of family environment is undoubtedly preferable
to one in which parents subject their children to stern indoctrination that puts
more emphasis on rules than supportive relationships.

Time, of course, is a precious commodity, especially when work and other
pressures crowd in. However, part of the responsibility of a Christian parent
is to prioritise and deliberately give time to family life. There is also the need
for Christian parents to live consistently and embody what they claim to
believe, so that their children can see living examples of faith. Pastoral care of

children in the church needs to recognise the special experiences of childhood and that some children who will be part of the church family will not be from Christian homes.

Looking into the playroom brings back happy memories, but when we step back from the doorway, we quickly realise that life can be very different for many children. The following are some challenges that children can face as they grow up, and an awareness of these will help us to care for them better.

A. Unstable home life

One of the critical challenges some children face is growing up in an unstable home environment. This can be true of Christian and non-Christian homes. The instability can come from many sources, including relationship problems within the parents' marriage, inconsistent or harsh parenting, or external circumstances beyond the family's control. Nine-year-old Matthew lives in just such a home. Both his parents are Christians and regular church attenders. However, his parents do not get on well together and frequently argue in front of him. His mother is extremely moody and sometimes, following a heated argument with his dad, she will ignore both her husband and Matthew. His dad also has a very busy job, and when at home he wants his own space, so he doesn't spend much time with Matthew. If mum is out, he puts Matthew in front of the TV and then retreats to his own games console. Worst of all, both parents are critical of each other in front of Matthew, which confuses him and robs him of emotional security. As a young boy he longs for attention and affection, but little is on offer from either parent.

Children are usually very attuned to the atmosphere that exists in a home, but at the same time they are often powerless to do anything about it. This increases their sense of vulnerability. Difficult home circumstances can create anxiety and guilt: anxiety because of the pervading uncertainty, and guilt because deep down, the children think they are contributing to the problems within the home. This may not be the case, but the feelings of guilt are nevertheless real.

B. When busyness takes over

Life for many families can be frantic, where time pressures are acute and quality family-time becomes almost non-existent. For some families, life is an endless round of clubs and activities, busy working lives for parents, and children who are under pressure to succeed in school. While these things are legitimate, they tend to be disruptive to the extent that families cannot spend quality-time together. I have been in homes where families seldom eat a meal together or where children are allowed to spend an unhealthy amount of time in front of a screen because the parents have other things to do. By contrast, I recently spent time with a family in Albania where both parents worked, but were committed to making time together a priority, even if it meant sometimes cutting back on work shifts. They invited me to enjoy pancakes with them. Arriving at their apartment, I found most of the family in the kitchen making the pancakes and the rest organising the evening's entertainment. The pancake supper was a relaxed event, filled with lots of conversation and laughter. The jam that we lavished on our pancakes had been a summer project when the family had gone to a fruit farm at harvest time to handpick the fruit, and had then spent an entire weekend at home making dozens of jars of jam. It was a simple activity, but done together as a natural way of strengthening bonds. It struck me how different this is to the experience of many families.

C. Psychological abuse

For many years, campaigners have been expressing their concern about the use of corporal punishment in the home. Whatever we may think on this matter, evidence suggests that psychological abuse, which is far more subtle, is at least as damaging for children as corporal punishment, and the impact can be very long-lasting.

Psychological abuse can take many forms and can manifest itself with varying degrees of severity. It can occur, for example, when parents are always critical, have unrealistic expectations of their children, or allow their own moods and attitudes to permeate family life to the detriment of everyone. Parents can also be overprotective or talk too openly about matters that are inappropriate for their children to hear. Parents can be erratic in showing affection to their children or not showing any at all. Equally, they can be inconsistent in disciplining their children and they can even humiliate them, all of which causes confusion and fear. None of this leaves physical bruises on the child, but it can scar them emotionally.

D. Poverty

Poverty also harms children. This is an outside pressure that makes life difficult for both parents and children. Given the materialism of our culture and the status that we attach to possessions, poverty can be a very real problem for families. However, we need to be careful not to suggest that poverty will automatically mean that a home will be troubled or unstable. My own home life was far from affluent, and we were able to afford few luxuries. We could never compete with the wealthier families in our church, but our parents' constant love and care more than made up for it. While many less well-off families offer children a loving and happy home life, there is an abundance of evidence showing that poverty contributes to difficult circumstances and diminished opportunities, not only in childhood but in later life.

A prime example was a family we worked with some years ago. There were five children and neither parent worked. They lived in social housing which was inadequate for their needs, in an area that was neither pleasant nor safe. There was a lack of recreational facilities, the family had a poor diet, and both parents smoked, none of which was good for the children. Going on holiday had never been part of their experience. Arguments in the overcrowded home were common, making simple things like doing homework very difficult. The result was that the children underachieved in school and had no real ambitions or dreams for their future. Their parents did what they could, but poverty marked the lives of their children. Not untypical of such situations, the children grew up with the same limited outlook on life as their parents.

E. Physical and environmental problems

Physical problems such as ill-health can also affect families, some of which have to deal with disability, depression, children with ADHD, and chronic illnesses. This means that parents need to spend so much time caring for family members with these illnesses that they have little time left for the other children. A similar situation arises for many single parents: a mother or a father, working hard but struggling to care for the family. The children in any of the above situations can be hugely disadvantaged through no fault either of themselves or their parents.

I do not find it difficult to imagine because I know situations just like these. They are sadly very common, and the children who experience them have a monumental struggle to get out of that environment in order to make a better life for themselves.

The range of circumstances described above have repercussions beyond the individuals concerned. Most parents are caring and loving, and have high hopes for their children and their future, but when these don't materialise, it is easy to lose heart and feel a sense of failure which often has a knock-on effect on the children. Likewise, when children find themselves in a difficult or stressful environment, they often play up and become very disruptive. This is understandable, given the problems in the home. Their behaviour, which may be a cry for help, makes matters worse by putting them on a collision course with parents, school, friends, and anyone else they come across. Guilt, anger, and frustration can lead to such problems as emotional volatility, attention-seeking, and temper tantrums.

How should church respond?

It is important that we understand the issues children face, but we must also be aware that, underneath the happy smiles specific children may be damaged by one or more of the problems mentioned. Churches tend to assume that none of the above could be happening to any of "their" children.

So with this possibility in mind what factors do we need to consider?

It is wise to make no assumptions. Every child is different, so any action must be based on knowing the individual child well and understanding their context. We should link this with warm acceptance of them, and where children might play up, the church should show patience and understanding.

The church should also provide a stable environment for children. An old proverb states, 'it takes an entire village to raise a child'. From a spiritual point of view, it takes a whole church to disciple a child. Adults, teenagers, and other children have an important role to play in making every child feel welcomed and cared for. They need to feel secure, be able to trust the people around them, and feel that they belong. Only then will they have the confidence to ask questions and explore their faith and the other issues affecting their lives.

Many people become Christians when they are young, precisely because of the love and acceptance that they receive in church. This is an essential part of pastoring children, helping them not just to discover faith and grow spiritually, but emotionally and socially too. Church attitudes towards children can have a very positive impact on their development and outlook on life. On the other hand, if a church is not welcoming and understanding, the children can be turned away from faith and miss out on the benefits of being in a more stable environment.

2. The den

We move on to the next room of the house—the teenagers' den. Life for young people at this stage can be both exciting and frustrating.

It is one of the fascinating phases of human development. We sometimes label it as adolescence, and it refers to that period in life when young people transition from childhood, through puberty and into adulthood, by which point they should be mature enough to look after themselves and take personal responsibility for decisions affecting their lives. During this time, young people experience physical growth together with sexual, emotional, intellectual, and social development. It can be a challenging and even confusing time of life. They are no longer children and don't want us to treat them as such, but they are not yet adults. There can be a craving for independence while, at the same time, a struggle with taking on extra responsibilities. This can make the teenage years a rollercoaster of emotions and mood swings. They can be on a high one moment and thoroughly depressed the next.

It is also worth stating that what teenagers experience today differs greatly from the experiences of previous generations. Theirs is a world filled with gadgets, mobile phones, social media, access to a whole range of entertainment, media and gaming, music, a vast array of hobbies, and sometimes drugs. When we couple this with significant study pressure, career expectations, and a culture which is increasingly post-Christian, we can see it is a lot for a young person to handle, especially at a time in life when they still lack emotional maturity.

Growth in this period is not constant and orderly, but there are three observable and overlapping phases which are usually described as early, middle, and late adolescence, and we shall use that terminology here.

Early adolescence

Early adolescence is from around age ten to age thirteen. During these years, physical change takes place. Growth spurts can cause young people to feel awkward, clumsy, and self-conscious. Body image often becomes an issue and can cause anxiety and embarrassment. This physical growth also includes sexual development, which brings its own stresses. Young people at this stage can also lack confidence, experience shyness, and be very susceptible to peer pressure. They are very much afraid of being different or left out.

All of this coincides with the transition to high school, which is a whole other world for a young person. They begin to realise the existence of the opposite sex and experience teenage crushes. Young teens also have a great capacity for 'hero worship', and at the same time they want to become a little more independent from their parents, which can put pressure on family relationships. This is a time of life when young people begin to think more deeply and question adult attitudes and behaviour.

Middle adolescence

The next stage is middle adolescence. While there may be fewer physical changes, this is a stage where they need to discover who they really are and deepen their friendships and relationships. When this need is combined with an intensification of sexual urges, particularly in boys, powerful forces are unleashed. Given the highly sexualised nature of contemporary society, together with diminishing moral values, learning how to control these urges becomes paramount.

Many young people struggle with temptation and in certain contexts they are encouraged to experiment sexually. Peer pressure continues to have an enormous influence on them and it's not always positive. Young people often encourage each other to push boundaries, boasting about and exaggerating their sexual experiences, which causes tension within the family as parents try to set limits for their teenage children. The reality is that sexual activity among teenagers is not uncommon and, indeed, is regarded as the accepted norm. This is the kind of environment in which our church young people live, and it would be naïve of us to imagine they are immune from the pressures of their peers. The danger is, of course, that sexual experimentation can go too far and result in unwanted pregnancy or sexually transmitted disease. The pastoral carer's role is to help prevent this happening, but if it does, to offer support to those concerned.

Boredom and moodiness are common and problematic in middle adolescence, putting pressure on family life, especially since there is still a heavy dependence on parents who provide money, transport, food, and much else besides. Because parents are concerned for their children and support them in so many ways, they find it very difficult when their children do not listen and reject any advice offered. Teenagers, however, have a different perspective. Contemporary culture influences their attitudes, telling them what to think, how to behave, and portraying parents as the enemy, preventing them from doing what they really want. These middle adolescents are greatly affected by the many voices around them, but, at the same time, they do recognise the love of their parents. The difficulty for them is knowing how to reciprocate it in expressing appreciation and love to their parents.

This can lead to a breakdown in communication in some families, especially if the teenagers spend many hours each week in their rooms or playing computer games, appearing only occasionally to forage for snacks. A fictitious example is William. He lives with his mum because his parents are divorced. He is 15, not particularly sociable, and going through all the lows of his mid-teens. When he comes home from school each day, he prefers to go to his room rather than talk to his mum, which she finds very frustrating because she would like his company. He spends hours on his games console and, while he joins his mum for meals, he still doesn't communicate much and resents being made to sit at the table. He shows little interest in anything, including his future, which is reflected in his modest grades at school. When his mum presses him to discuss what he wants to do when he leaves school, he reacts badly and is often abrupt and rude. This doesn't help their relationship, especially as he never seems to bring himself to say sorry. He loves his mum, but rarely shows it, and while they continue to share the same house, they have little meaningful interaction.

The internet also has an enormous effect and influence. Young people can access so much online, and the proliferation of gadgets makes this increasingly easy. Many young people get much of their information and life values from the internet, a medium which is difficult to regulate or control. This can so easily lead to an unhealthy diet of pornography, unsavoury comedy, and violence.

Late adolescence

We usually describe the third phase as late adolescence. At this point, real maturity develops, when young people become more able to think through issues and make their own decisions. During this period, they might begin an apprenticeship, get a job, or go to university, all of which can present new opportunities and challenges.

Life also becomes more serious. No longer can they afford to be complacent about the future because it is already upon them. They also know that the decisions they make have implications which need to be thought through carefully. The same is true of relationships. Teenage crushes have passed and the capacity to form deeper, long-term relationships increases. This is a time to be set priorities and make important life decisions.

As part of this questioning, there are several big issues that young people have to deal with before they enter the next phase of their lives. The first of these has to do with their identity. When they are growing up, their identity is very much bound up with the family. They fall under the shadow of their parents and that is how they see themselves. Now, however, they are about to launch out, make their own decisions, and work out who they really are. This can be a daunting task, but unless they deal with these issues and decide who they want to be, they will never leave the secure atmosphere of the home. It is, of course, possible they will want to emulate their parents or even some other family member whom they admire while still following their own path. However, sometimes young people decide, for a variety of reasons, that they do not want to be like their parents. Perhaps something about their parents' lives has disappointed or angered them and they want to make a clean break with their past. This can cause tension in the family, especially if the young person is still living at home.

Second, they need to think about what they want to do with their lives. If you were to ask a young teenager what they want to do in the future, they would probably give a half-hearted answer or just shrug their shoulders and mumble, 'dunno'! Even if they do respond, it will probably be something unrealistic like a professional footballer or a fighter pilot or some career path they are never likely to follow. At the latter phase of teenage experience, this changes and what they want to do with their lives comes sharply into focus. If they still don't know, it can become unnerving.

The extent to which young people develop ambitions depends on several factors such as their capabilities, motivation, success at school, opportunities available, family support, and their determination to make a success of their lives. Whatever the answer to these questions, they have much to work out.

A third issue concerns relationships. When they were younger, their relationships are centred around their own family life, where they live, and the school they attend. Now, in late adolescence, they are widening their social networks, and as relationships become more mature, serious questions need to be addressed. How influenced are they going to be by the pressure exerted by their peers? How will they handle conflict? What discernment will they apply when choosing friends? Also, when it comes to relationships with the opposite sex, what boundaries will they put in place? This latter point raises the issue that today's young people (including many Christians) have little or no objection to same-sex relationships. This is a pastorally complicated matter, especially given the changes in our culture. Anyone questioning the legitimacy of same-sex relationships risks being denounced as homophobic. At the same time, the Bible is clear in its condemnation of such relationships, so much wisdom and pastoral sensitivity are essential.

A final question relates to what these young people are going to believe. Again, when they were younger, they listened to and accepted the belief system of their parents. Many people become Christians when they are children or young teens. As they get older and ask questions, they often develop a scepticism regarding faith. This is particularly true if they go to university, which is why a university experience can make or break many young people. Some 70% of young Christians drop out of church in their early 20s[2].

Part of the questioning has to do with authority: 'Why should other people tell me what I should believe and how I should behave?' Of course, these questions come at a time of a developing desire for intimacy and increased awareness of their sexuality. The values that churches and parents promote are at variance with what many young people want to do and this can lead to an internal conflict.

At this stage, young people are also well aware of the mess that older generations have made of the world. They can see the economic injustices that modern free-market democracies have propagated. When very expensive cars drive past homeless people sitting on the footway, young people see not only inequality as the wealthy flaunt their affluence, but also the damage caused to the environment by those who still insist on driving petrol-guzzling SUVs. They do not always feel positive or optimistic about the world they are inheriting.

In all of this, we should not forget the influence of mass media, social media, and popular culture. Contemporary culture and the education system have encouraged young people to think for themselves, act autonomously, and believe that they are special. The provision of 'safe spaces' can make them unwilling to listen to other opinions. The influence of social media also means they develop a worldview that is often radically different from what was generally accepted a couple of generations ago. Some experts fear that young people no longer inherit a cohesive value system from their parents. Instead, they look to the mass media, peers, and other potentially unreliable and misleading sources to shape their future beliefs.

Many young people also feel their Christian parents do not fully appreciate the pressures that young people face in our modern, permissive culture. They also think their parents have unrealistic and unhealthy attitudes towards sex in particular. At the same time, they feel a pressure to conform to adult standards, even when they find it difficult to commit fully to them. They want to be real, to express their doubts and ask questions, but they fear that they will be

---

2. https://lifewayresearch.com/2019/01/15/most-teenagers-drop-out-of-church-as-young-adults/

misunderstood if they do this. They combine this with a perception that the church does not appear to care about things like economic injustice, racism, the environment, health, and social and political issues. It is no wonder that many young people lose interest in church during their teenage years. Often it is not because they think Christianity is untrue; they just think that the church's approach to spirituality is too narrow and restrictive. Moreover, when they do ask questions, they often find the responses too dogmatic and simplistic.

How do adolescents react?

Young people respond to these complex personal and societal changes in a whole variety of ways. For some, life is just a struggle. They feel lonely, alienated, and withdraw from friends. Boredom, apathy, anxiety, and depression are common, making it difficult to relate to them though they still need a listening ear.

Other adolescents may act out and behave in socially inappropriate ways. This is not always deliberate and conscious, but, in doing so, they are pressing the self-destruct button. This behaviour can include excessive drinking, drug abuse, lying, stealing, crime, and general rebellion. We could ask, what do they gain from this? Possible answers could be that they may feel empowered or simply want to challenge authority, elevating themselves in the eyes of their peers. Even if it leads to notoriety, at least they are being noticed, as there is nothing more painful to them than being ignored. When this acting out collides with overactive hormones, it can be a heady mixture. Young people can become involved sexually, not because of a deep love for each other, much less a commitment, but rather to gain acceptance, meet emotional needs, and ease their pain. These kinds of factors contribute to unexpected and often unwanted pregnancies.

A smaller number of adolescents just run away from it all. This running can be literal, with significant numbers leaving the family home each year. It can also be metaphorical. They can withdraw from the world, become reclusive, and in the most extreme situations may even attempt to take their own lives. Self-harming has also become alarmingly common, involving both physical harm such as cutting themselves and eating disorders.

Thankfully, many young people don't behave like this. They recognise that life can be complex and sometimes unfair, but they face up to it and are willing to seek the support of friends and adults. They respond well, face their difficulties with courage and, in the end, they enjoy and flourish during their teenage years.

How should churches respond?

What can a church offer as it knocks on the door of the teenagers' den? The first thing that the church needs to do is build strong spiritual foundations. This is vital and should begin with young people at a very early age. Lessons taught and values learned when children are young will inevitably be part of their spiritual fortification during their teen years. Even if they do not become Christians or engage with the church until their teens, it is important to invest in their lives so that they understand what it means to follow Jesus. They might not live consistently, but if they know what they ought to do, it will help to prepare them for the challenges of adolescence.

This input can take various forms. It includes the basics of teaching them how to read the Bible and pray, encouraging them to be consistent in doing so. In the same way that Jesus had to teach his disciples to pray, more mature church members can teach young people. But it also goes beyond this. We need to teach our young people how to handle life from a Christian perspective. Our culture is post-Christian, so the attitudes and values that young people very naturally absorb will often conflict with biblical principles and standards. The corrosive influence of living in such a culture needs to be countered by the teaching that young people experience in church. This is a huge responsibility for those in the church engaged in teaching at any level.

Whatever method of teaching is used, whether formally or through small group work or one-to-one discipleship, some analysis of culture from a Christian perspective needs to be included, together with practical Bible teaching on how to live as a Christian in a fallen world. Young people need to be taught how to communicate openly and to relate to others. They need to learn how to deal with problems and challenges in a Christlike way and how to trust God in difficult circumstances. Some young people will have come from Christian homes where they learned these things in the family. Others, however, will have come from homes where no one is a Christian and where family members may be hostile to Christianity. Mere formality or religious 'show' will not impress. Young people value authenticity and thoughtful responses to their questions. Even though they may not always accept the church's position, they want to be treated seriously.

The church also needs to provide relevant teaching about the everyday challenges that young people face in life. The school system provides some of this, but, in our increasingly secular society, it is often devoid of any moral content and lacks a Christian perspective. Young people need to understand the dangers of alcohol, drug use, unrestrained sex, and a range of other related issues. However, it is not just as simple as giving them a science lesson on the dangers of these things to their health. Rather, they need to see a bigger picture of the implications of lifestyle choices. Yes, their health is important and should be protected, but God also wants them to have 'life to the full'. There are very positive reasons for living a healthy lifestyle and finding meaning and joy in positive actions and relationships.

It is crucial to demonstrate what a healthy Christian lifestyle looks like, and to help young people to discover the art of good decision-making. Positive and robust role models in the church can make a significant impression in this regard. Prayer must also be part of the equation, and we should not underestimate what a perilous journey young people take through their teenage years.

If the church can offer the experience of community, it will be one of the best protections that young people can have amid the issues already mentioned. If they genuinely feel a sense of belonging, they will be much more hesitant to leave the church. This is much more than just laying on more meetings or church events. It is about people in the church family wanting to engage with each other and doing life together. This was something I was privileged to have once I had become a Christian. Unlike many of my peers, my father did not teach me to drive, even though he would have gladly taught me. Instead, a car mechanic in his thirties named Joe took an interest in the young people in our church and, while he was not a preacher or an up-front person, he cared for us and encouraged us to get involved in church. He offered to teach me to drive, which resulted in many long journeys during which we would talk about faith and what it means to be a consistent Christian. I did learn to drive, but more importantly, I gained a sense that I was part of a spiritual family where people would look out for each other and try to walk with God together. Role models like Joe are worth their weight in gold in the local church.

In concluding this chapter, we must remember the range of circumstances affecting our young people. Their parents may or may not be Christian, and their family life may or may not be happy or stable. Young people can find themselves caught in relationship struggles that occur in the wider family; for example, their parents may not have a good relationship or may even be going through the painful throes of divorce. For all the reasons above, and many more, churches need to give much thought to supporting their young people through hard times and to demonstrating a counter-narrative of the joy and satisfaction of living a life in the service of Christ.

We will visit several other rooms in the next chapter.

For further reflection

1. How would you pastor a single-parent family with three children, one of whom has significant behavioural difficulties?

2. How would you respond if a 15-year-old Christian girl from your youth club confides in you that she is pregnant?

3. How would you advise parents who have just been told by their teenage son that he is gay?

CHAPTER 6

More rooms, more views

1. The ensuite room—the young professionals

Our tour now brings us to the ensuite room where the young professionals live. These are the 20s and 30s who are much in demand in the workplace and in local church life. Within this group, there is a wide diversity of life experience and personal circumstances.

The twenty-somethings

First, there are the twenty-somethings. They have left their teenage years behind and are becoming a little more independent. Many will have gone off to university, but increasingly, they live at home and study locally as this is a more affordable route to take. Even after university, many continue to live with their parents because they don't yet have sufficient income to get on the property ladder. Those who have left home for good often rent or share a flat until they become more self-sufficient.

The rate at which they pull free of family ties will depend on the family dynamic. It is not surprising to find a 21-year-old who is very independently minded and rarely consults his or her parents on any issue. Likewise, there are plenty of 30-year-olds who still maintain a close relationship and dependence on parents and would hardly decide anything without consulting them. There are no right and wrongs here, just varying family set-ups and different personalities at play.

Singleness

Many twenty-somethings are single, which can cause loneliness and self-questioning, even if their singleness is a choice. Margaret is an example of this. She has a good job, lots of friends, and is heavily involved in her church. Everyone around her assumes that she is content with life and that she either has not looked very hard for Mr. Right or that she does not want to get involved in a serious exclusive relationship. None of these assumptions are true, but with a busy career and a lack of social opportunity, no relationship has developed. When she turned 30, she became very conscious of the years passing. She is now 36, continues to be busy and committed to church life, but she is apprehensive about remaining single now that most of her close friends are married and her mother seems to talk about nothing else.

Singleness can be a very positive and exciting lifestyle choice at this stage as a single person can enjoy both independence and a life full of activity. Many single people are aware of the advantages and make the most of them, developing strong social networks and deep friendships, and they can use their freedom to be a great blessing to the Kingdom of God. The mission organisation that we work with is so grateful for the outstanding contribution single people have made to the ministry.

For those who do get married, life is not necessarily straightforward. The cost of living, work pressures, housing, career choices, church and social networks all add to the stress young married people feel. Some young couples have also struggled because of interference from parents. In such situations, a theological principle stated in Genesis 2: 24 is important: that 'a man leaves his father and mother and is united to his wife, and they become one flesh'.

The thirty-somethings

By the time people enter their thirties, they are settling down into a more established pattern of life. Many will be married, have mortgages and families of their own, but for others singleness will still be an issue. This is a stage at which additional pressures can manifest themselves, such as intense competition for jobs, meaning that employers might expect more from their employees. The thirties and forties are the time when, for professional people, they are at the height of their effectiveness. They have a useful mix of qualifications and experience and are therefore a valuable part of the workforce. Often, they will carry heavy responsibility at work and will do their jobs very competently.

Ironically, some of these younger, competent people go to churches where the leadership is significantly older and sometimes much less able than they are. Ryan, for example, works for a well-known bank in the City of London, managing a team of around 150, which is over three times the size of his church. He has a six-figure salary and controls a budget in excess of tens of millions every month, but his church would not consider making him an elder because he is only 38 years old. The three elders who are in leadership are all over 70 years old. Because Ryan unsurprisingly finds church frustrating, he focusses his energies and talents on work.

Family pressures

Married couples, at this stage, find themselves taken up with family. I was 30 when my first child was born, and over the next couple of decades, she and her siblings occupied much of my time and energy. These are formative years, and parents only have one chance with each child to get it right. This creates a significant challenge. On the one hand, parents want the church to provide culturally relevant activities for their children. On the other hand, many want to be actively involved in church life and to enjoy fellowship, but their work and family pressures make this difficult. The church can meet this need, but it is more difficult if there are lots of services which are not family friendly. However, if the church offers quality fellowship, opportunity for service, and well thought-out programmes, it is possible to attract and inspire busy thirty-somethings.

Despite all the joys and benefits, people in their twenties and thirties also experience failures and frustrations. Family and work pressures can put marriages under strain and couples can find themselves becoming distant in their relationship. Even being committed Christians does not protect them from this danger. When I first met Michael and Alice, they were in their late thirties, doing well in their professional lives, committed to the church, and parents to two young children. Michael's job involved some unsocial hours and occasional trips away from home. As a couple, they remained faithful to each other and devoted to their children. Yet in the busyness of life, they spent very little quality time together. After a while they began to notice how impatient they were with each other and how often they argued. Even though they were both quick to apologise, they found it increasingly difficult to move on. When the quarrels became very loud and affected their daughters, they prayed together about the situation, but the arguments continued, as did the sense of guilt and failure. Thankfully they have now worked things out, but looking back they realise that their many obligations had put their marriage very much in the balance.

Work pressures

Frustrations and failure surface at work as well. The thirties are a time to get established in a career, but this can bring its own tensions and discouragements. I have spoken to many young professionals who felt they were bypassed for promotion. It's hard to graduate from university, join a company, and then ten years down the track find that a colleague who joined at the same time as you, is now your boss, especially if he is demanding or unpleasant.

However, lack of success may not be the only issue. People sometimes discover at this point in their career that the job they chose or the company they work for is not what they expected. Coming to that conclusion when you are single and in your early twenties is one thing. At that point, it is still relatively easy to have a total change of direction, but, if you are 35, married with children, and have a significant mortgage, such a radical change is much more difficult. Like John, an engineer friend who told me his current job was boring and the company was not very good to work for, but he feels stuck. He would like to move on, but with a young child and bills to pay, the need for job security outweighs everything else.

Loneliness can also be an issue. This might sound strange for a young couple with children who appear to have everything they could want. But career development and family are a busy mix and often young couples find that they have little time to be with friends and relax together. This is especially the case if they are both working. Of course, this will only be for a limited period of time; once the children grow up, they will have more freedom. That season, however, can last for many years. The feeling of loneliness often grows slowly. Initially, it is exciting to be in a career with potential, and deeply rewarding to begin a family. But as time goes on, couples like this, if they are not vigilant, can slowly and unintentionally drift away from their social circle. They get to the point where they realise they have very few friends and feel life is passing them by. They might even feel too tired to re-establish a social life, which accentuates the loneliness.

2. The study: the middle years

Now we come to the fourth room. It is said that life begins at 40, though in talking to many 40-year-olds, one could be tempted to think otherwise. In theory, people in their forties should be able to enjoy good health and improved financial security. So life ought to be good. Many, however, find the number 40 to be strangely threatening and upsetting. For married couples, especially couples with children, this decade can be one of increasing responsibility and worry. Many couples in their forties have teenagers, which brings a whole other world of challenge. At the end of these teenage years, parents have the experience of children getting married and leaving home.

Many see mid 40s to mid 60s as middle age and the very idea of this can cause people to worry. For the first time, they sense their mortality, sometimes with an increasing feeling that their best days are behind them. Statistically, once someone is in their late forties, they have fewer years ahead of them than behind.

Despite the pressures of this age group, the interesting thing to note is that in society at large and in church life, middle-aged adults still make most of the decisions, and earn and dispense more money than other people. They fill most leadership positions and exercise most of the power, which can give the impression that they are invulnerable. This is not the case.

Personal change

Middle age is a time of change, and not all of it is to be celebrated. The first and perhaps most obvious change is physical. We live in a society that values youth and image, and puts high currency on physical fitness. This adds pressure to those who are increasingly aware of their body image: hair going grey, baldness increasing, skin becoming coarse, and bags appearing under the eyes. Few of these changes are aesthetically pleasing. There is also a decrease in physical strength and stamina. In women, the physical changes are accompanied by the menopause, which some find very traumatic. Some researchers believe that a similar, though less noticeable, change may occur in men. All of this reminds people at this stage that time is marching on and there is no going back.

There can also be psychological change as middle-aged people become aware that they will have a limit to their working life. At 25, they think of what to do for a career and it feels like the best of life is still ahead. At 55, they are more aware that they might only have 10 or 15 years of productive life left. So each year becomes more precious. Of course, some middle-aged people are desperate to retire, especially if they don't enjoy their work.

Pressure at work

These middle years also contain a mixture of emotions. The excitement and challenge of establishing a career are long gone. Those with highly responsible jobs often feel under pressure, especially if they have ambitious subordinates working for them. They end up working all the harder, not because of a love for their jobs, but because they feel the threat and want to prove they still have a place in the workforce. The problem with this dutiful approach to work is that it can be joyless. Equally, it is not uncommon for middle-aged people to feel they have not and will not achieve their career goals, which can bring a sense of genuine sadness with questions and regrets. Paul, for example, did business studies at university and then joined a small family firm where he was happy, but moved to a much bigger company after about ten years because he wanted to climb the career ladder. He worked well, was a loyal and committed employee, and again enjoyed what he did. However, his climb up the career ladder was not as dramatic as he would have wanted. Also, one of the younger employees, whom he helped to train, got promoted over him and is now his immediate superior. He still likes the job and still works hard, but this does not detract from his sense of loss at never really making it. His boss remains a friend and is good to work for, but Paul still feels a little jealous of him and wonders why he was bypassed for the top job.

Trouble at home

Home life can be a challenge for middle-aged couples who are now busy people, juggling lots of responsibilities and with much less energy than they had 20 years ago. In addition, there can sometimes be the anxiety of transitioning their children from their teenage years into adulthood and then seeing them leave home, with all the resultant emotion. There can be regret or even guilt over past parenting failures and a feeling that they are no longer needed or useful to their children. This can become acute if their children are not good at keeping in touch or if they have moved away from the area.

Added to this, there is often the concern for ageing parents. The term 'sandwich generation' describes a situation where someone has responsibility for both children and ageing parents. Both duties need to be held in balance, which can be difficult, especially when each creates demands simultaneously. For single people, ageing parents can be a particular concern, especially if their married siblings leave them to carry most of the responsibility for their parents.

Because life can be so draining, some replace active social lives with more time spent just watching TV. This habit needs to be resisted, either with exercise or mind-stimulating activity. Some of the best things that middle-aged people can do with their spare time will be to join a gym, take up a hobby, or get into the habit of reading good books. Leading a healthier, more active lifestyle at this stage will be good preparation for the challenge of old age.

Danger signs

The constant routines of life and a growing impatience with each other, resulting from years of marriage, can create difficulties and even conflict in the relationship. Some marriages are held together by dependent children, so when they leave the danger sets in. The marriage has lost its sparkle and a sense of boredom and weariness has crept in, seen in a decline in intimacy, in similarity of interests, and in ability to communicate, all of which should serve as a warning. Tragically, sometimes the boredom or stress of their lives can lead to extramarital affairs as happened with King David (2 Sam. 11: 1–5). When David had his affair with Bathsheba, he had enjoyed a successful career as king, had a family, was a devoted worshipper of God, and was middle-aged. None of these things prevented him from falling. The danger is obvious, as are the implications. When a teenager makes a mistake and 'goes a bit too far' in experimenting sexually, the situation is usually recoverable. When a middle-aged man or woman (with children and grandchildren, church responsibility, and a wide social network) sins, the fallout is devastating.

3. The granny flat: the older years

We finally look into the granny flat, which leads us to thinking about old age. Across the western world, this segment of society is getting larger as life expectancy continues to rise. In the UK, there are now approaching 13 million people who are over 65 (that is, almost 1 in 5 of the population). People often worry that in their old age they will be financially, intellectually, and physically challenged, but the reality for many is that this is not the case. Many older people are financially secure, enjoy good health, and lead active lives, so we should be careful not to generalise. I have met people who look and sound old and frail at 50, but I have also met others in their mid-80s who are energetic, upbeat, and full of life. The rate at which people age will depend on their physical and emotional makeup, their health record, their circumstances, and their environment.

As with middle age, physical changes are taking place. Some of these are very obvious, such as greying and thinning hair, losing teeth, and sometimes weight loss. A marvellous, but somewhat depressing description of old age can be found in Ecclesiastes 12. Read it in the Living Bible and you will understand why growing old can affect a person's self-esteem, especially in a culture where physical attractiveness is so valued, and the effects of ageing are feared. This issue can be accentuated if older people pay less attention to their appearance. A decline in energy means they are not so able to look after their home.

Other bodily changes are less noticeable. Older people find that their eyesight and hearing are not what they once were. They find that energy levels and reaction times decline, as does their memory. Older people take longer to respond to situations and process information more slowly. They also take longer to understand new ideas or develop new skills which is why they often find new gadgets and technology intimidating. The decline in mental ability is most apparent where quick decisions are required, for example, when driving a car.

Again, we need to be careful not to assume that this decline is evenly spread throughout the ageing population or that it will necessarily make a difference to an older person's life. In reality, while older people do slow down, this is not usually marked enough to make a big difference to daily life. They will still be mentally sharp enough to do everything they used to do, including learning new things, and developing new skills. They have also accumulated a lifetime of experience and wisdom which can be a real asset to their own life and the lives of others.

Health issues

The general ageing of the bodies of older people can cause their bones to become more brittle, their joints stiffer and often more painful, and if they become sick, it diminishes their powers of recovery. Health is among the biggest concerns of older people and, while many will not have to cope with long-term debilitating health issues, some will, and that can be a source of frustration and anxiety. Some will suffer to varying extents from arthritis, high blood pressure, and heart disease, and many will be on long-term treatments for these, but unless they are severe, life can continue as normal. Much will depend on how they confront these issues and what resources are available to them.

Finance

Some older people worry about finance and all the issues related to this. Retirement brings not just a departure from work, but also an end to their salary. For some, pensions may be sufficient to ensure that they will be well provided for in retirement. For others, however, their pension provision is modest and will cause a significant change in lifestyle, particularly where people rely on nothing more than the state pension. If their ability to budget is limited, this can cause further financial stress. Equally, if they lack practical skills, getting simple repairs done to their home or car can become a worryingly expensive business.

Company

Older people also need company at least as much, and possibly even more than younger people. They require mental stimulus to remain sharp. Many older people have found that when they retire they miss the social connections that work provided and their declining health has limited their ability to go out and meet people. Friends and family also move away and older people are left feeling they have no one. Added to this is an increased sense of loneliness and vulnerability when their spouse, friends or relatives die.

The combination of all of this can greatly affect a person's self-esteem. Older people, particularly those who had been influential in their earlier lives, can end up feeling they have no role or significance which can be potentially devastating. They long for someone to listen to them, but often find there is no one. Worse still, sometimes well-meaning friends and family treat them like children and assume them to be incompetent, adding insult to injury. Rapid changes in society and culture can also be disorientating. Their world which once appeared so simple is now complicated and they increasingly feel they are living in a strange and frightening land.

How older people handle these changes depends to a large extent on their outlook on life. Having a positive mental attitude about getting older and choosing to make the most of life can make a decisive difference to the experience of ageing. Positive people are also easier to be with, so they more naturally attract friends.

We can see the very different experiences of old age in the example of two 80 years olds—Peter and William. Their previous lives were, of course, different, but they also shared lots of things in common. Neither was a highflyer, but they both had good jobs which paid reasonably well so they enjoyed a decent lifestyle. They also both married and have children and grandchildren. Both were heavily involved in church life and had leadership and preaching ministries. Even now, in their retirement, they share things in common. They still attend church, are married and in good health, and they both enjoy a positive relationship with their families.

Now that both men are well into their retirement, the differences in their lives are very stark. Financially, William was better prepared for retirement. He saved more diligently, paid off his mortgage quicker and put more aside, particularly towards his pension. As a result, while he has less spending money than before, he and his wife can still afford a good foreign holiday every year and take fairly regular weekend breaks, something that Peter and his wife cannot afford. William also filled his life with hobbies and activities which continue to this day. He loves books, he and his wife both enjoy painting, and he is still a member of a local hill-walking club. Despite his advanced years, he is still active and has lots of friends and a positive outlook in life. Peter, on the other hand, spends his time watching TV and pottering in his garden, but not much else, and he and his wife often feel lonely. Moreover, being too old to preach and no longer in leadership has hit him hard. He feels underutilised and goes to church more out of habit than passion. William is in the same position, but because his life is generally more fulfilling, he does not feel the loss so much. Because he is also more positive and sociable, he is not short of friends at church or visitors at home. He and his wife also host their church small group which they find very rewarding. These two similar men have very different experiences of ageing.

Old age does not need to be traumatic, and the church can play an important role in preparing people for it. There can also be risks, for example, getting involved in issues such as an individual's personal finances. Despite this, good pastoral care can nevertheless involve helping people to make wise plans about their future life and their later years.

Preparing for the retirement years

What does preparation for old age look like? It is not just about having some pension provision or savings; it is also about living carefully and managing expectations. Money can stretch much further if people are careful and good stewards of what they have, which of course is a biblical principle.

But, while financial provision is important, there is more to planning than just money. There is also the issue of keeping fit and healthy. This is an important Christian discipline; our bodies are the temple of the Holy Spirit. A fit person will not only be better able to withstand the ravages of old age, but they will also have a better quality of life. Fitness, of course, is not just about the body; mental health is equally important. Older people who have not developed interests or hobbies will often struggle with all the time that they have on their hands once they retire. It is the easiest thing in the world to spend entire days watching television, which has potentially serious physical and mental health implications.

As well as needing friendship and social interaction, older people need to feel useful. If they can be encouraged to serve others, this will help to develop relationships and provide a sense of fulfilment.

We should not forget the spiritual dimension. It is easy to assume that because someone has been following Christ faithfully for many years, that this will just continue. Often it does, but sometimes people find that dealing with the challenges of old age is the greatest spiritual battle they have faced. I have cared for older people who have experienced serious spiritual doubt and cynicism because of their declining health and loss of a life partner and lifelong friends. Good pastoral care encourages older people to keep going, walk closely with Christ, and surrender each day to God.

How can the church help?

The church is an ideal place to develop social networks and receive practical help. All it takes is a little imagination and a lot of determination. However, this must involve more than just meetings. Churches need to have programmes designed to bring older people together in a relaxing atmosphere. This does not mean that the church leaders or others within the church have to do lots of work. The best activities will be the ones that the older people organise and run for themselves. They are not there just to be served by others, but to serve each other. Churches should also include older people in other activities where they can mix with the different generations. Again, this can bring lots of mutual benefits. In one particular church, the youth fellowship meets in the homes of three pensioners in rotation and the older people not only offer that service, but love the buzz of young people in their homes. In another church, older people are asked to volunteer to babysit, do home visits, and to offer prayer for people who ask for it.

Investing in older people is actually a good growth strategy for the church, given that a significant proportion of the population are retired. A church that runs positive, age-appropriate, life-enhancing programmes will be a very attractive place for older people. Such churches not only give dignity, purpose, and self-worth to older people, but also build goodwill with wider family members. Old age can be challenging, but it need not be a crisis. With a little creative thinking and planning as well as good pastoral care, old age can become a time of rich fulfilment and blessing.

Reflecting on the ages

We have spent the last two chapters looking at the various age groups represented in our churches and also the unique challenges they present, and we have now finished the tour of the house. Good pastoral care demands a thoughtful approach that looks at people's needs, and endeavours to address them. As we have seen, each stage of life presents challenges and experiences most people will feel to varying degrees. It is therefore important, when planning pastoral care, not just to see the church as a single collection of people, but as different people at different stages in their lives.

For further reflection

Assignment 1

Write a short outline for a marriage guidance course highlighting the key issues you think should be included. Finish off by making a shortlist of factors that make for a healthy marriage.

Assignment 2

Write a short paper on the advantages and disadvantages of singleness and describe what churches can do to integrate single people into the life of the church.

Assignment 3

Select three people of different ages (one under 21, one middle aged, and one retired) and ask them what the biggest challenges are at their stage in life. Having listened to their challenges, what advice would you give each of them from a pastoral perspective.

CHAPTER 7

Life's highs and lows

In chapters five and six, we thought about the different stages in life and some of the challenges those stages present. However, we also know that, because life is unpredictable, all kinds of experiences intrude into our world, some of which will be positive, and others entirely the opposite.

We shall now look at some of these experiences and explore where pastoral support might be required. Let's begin with some of life's joyful circumstances, which may seem a little strange because many people assume that pastoral care is only necessary when life is going badly. The problem with this view is that it only highlights the negative and sad aspects of life. However, as Christians we need to learn to affirm and celebrate the joyful events in people's lives. Doing so not only enhances relationships; it also enables us to recognise God's gracious hand in our lives.

So, what are the positives we need to celebrate?

1. Causes for celebration

We are getting married!

First, and perhaps most obviously, there are big family events such as weddings. These, of course, can have their stresses, but they are beautiful occasions, remembered for the rest of our lives. Marriage is a special occasion where the church can express love and care. This care should begin long before the wedding itself. The pastoral care established in the teenage years takes on special significance when two people start to develop a relationship. We should not underestimate the value of having someone to offer guidance and help. Every relationship has its ups and downs, particularly so perhaps, if the couple are relatively young or they are new Christians. As such, there is significant benefit in having a trusted friend to guide them through whatever questions, doubts, or misunderstandings may arise.

At this stage, the advice offered will be low-key and unobtrusive, but, as the relationship becomes more serious and leads to engagement, we should offer marriage guidance either in the form of purposeful conversations or a formal course. Such a course could include building a God-honouring relationship, learning to pray and discuss spiritual matters together, decision-making, conflict resolution, and using the home for God. Many married couples have become more fully integrated into the life and service of their church because caring members walked with them during the time leading up to marriage and by being available in the early years.

When a child is born

Derek and Linda were a newly married couple who did not wait long to begin their family. They were a couple with significant potential, but their commitment to church life was fairly limited. When their first child came along, an older couple in the church took an interest in them and their growing relationship led to some earnest and helpful conversations about faith. The older couple asked Derek and Linda what kind of parents they wanted to be and what values they wanted to convey to their children. The seriousness of having a family dawned on them and, with encouragement from the older couple, they began to pray together and discuss spiritual issues in a way they had not done before. When their child was born, they asked the older couple to become godparents and to be more involved in their lives as a new family. The pastoral input at an important time of celebration in their lives proved very significant.

Graduation

Brian was a young Christian from a non-Christian background who attended his local church as a teenager because Christian friends at school invited him to the youth group. He became a Christian just before going to university to study medicine and probably grew more as a result of his involvement in the university Christian Union than he did going to church. Once qualified, he continued to attend the church, having secured a new job in one of the local hospitals. In the same church, there was a consultant cardiologist who realised that he might be able to help Brian and encourage him as a Christian. The consultant phoned him and invited him round to his home for a meal.

Over the meal, they discussed lots of things, including the challenges and benefits of a career in medicine. The consultant asked Brian what spiritual challenges he thought he would face during his career, and that led to a deeply meaningful and significant conversation. Brian was both challenged by and appreciative of the input, so when the senior physician suggested they could meet up periodically to continue the conversation, he readily agreed. Over time, these meetings led to a strong friendship in which the older man prayed faithfully for his young protégé and did all he could to support him. Today, more than a decade later, Brian is a medical missionary in a hospital in Africa, but he attributes his direction in life in no small measure to the interest and care that the older man had invested in him.

Now for the negatives.

2. When everything changes

Empty nest syndrome

We have been thinking about the joys and challenges of new beginnings, but now we must reflect on what happens when things come to an end. One such transition occurs when children decide that they are ready to leave home, perhaps for work or study or marriage. The house suddenly goes quiet, activity ceases and parents realise a new phase has begun which has been described as the 'empty nest syndrome'. On the one hand, it is a joyful time of celebration because it is a real coming of age, but parents can also experience deep loneliness with all its emotional effects. Again, this is a pastoral moment where the pastoral carer can support these individuals and help them see that this is also an opportunity to make positive changes in their lives. They suddenly have more time to invest in their marriage, and in other people. Good pastoral care can make a difference in turning the new circumstances from a potentially negative experience to something positive.

Bereavement

Few things are as painful and difficult to cope with as the death of someone we love. However, death is part of everyone's experience, and we need to support others in their times of bereavement. How we do this pastorally will depend on the circumstances. Outlined below are three very different scenarios to illustrate the significance of context.

First, there is Giles, an 82-year-old man with a loving family. He was a Christian, very involved in his church for many years and through it had built up a wide social network. For most of his life, he enjoyed good health and a comfortable lifestyle. After many years of what was a happy life, he began to decline. When he reached his eightieth birthday, he developed arthritis, his memory began to fade and, as if that were not enough, he contracted cancer. His last six months were very unpleasant and distressing for his loving family who watched him suffer. When he died, his family were devastated because they had lost a husband, father, and grandfather, but they were relieved that his suffering was over and were grateful that, as a Christian, he was now in the presence of Christ.

In a very different situation, Stephen and Rachael were expecting their first child. As Christians, they had plans to have their baby dedicated and their church shared their joy at the prospect of a new member in the church community. In the final few weeks of the pregnancy, doctors began to raise concerns about the baby's health. Once born, the baby was put on a life-support machine. Various tests confirmed that the little boy could not live without being sustained by the machine, so the painful decision was taken to switch it off and allow the precious little boy to pass away peacefully. The church pastor tried to comfort Stephen and Rachael with the thought that God had taken their little son into heaven, where they would one day meet him again. They were much comforted by this thought, but it did not remove the profound pain of losing their child.

Finally, we have the example of Raymond, who grew up in a single-parent home where his mum completely spoiled him. He was a clever boy and did well in school, but frequently found himself in trouble, exacerbated by his poor choice of company. After school, he took an apprenticeship and got a job, but he began to experiment with drugs, leading to a downward spiral.

As a result he lost his job. This made his drug habit and heavy drinking even worse, which resulted in him getting into trouble with the police. Late one night his mother received a phone call from the police to say that Raymond had been killed in a car crash. He had been drinking and had lost control of the vehicle. She was distraught because this terrible incident had compounded all the emotion of years of worry.

Clearly, in each of these situations, the families involved suffered loss, but for the family of Giles, the circumstances of his life and his Christian commitment eased their grief. In offering pastoral care, it is vital to take into account the different circumstances of each bereavement. There will be times when you want simply to remind the grieving family that the person who died lived a good life and now is in heaven. On the other hand, if the person was not a Christian, your focus will be on providing comfort and support to the family.

When bereavement does happen, some general pastoral guidelines are useful to remember. First, it is good to contact the family as soon as possible. This takes a great deal of courage because often we don't know what to say or are afraid that we might say the wrong thing. However, this is a moment of crisis for them, and they need support. This could be as simple as making a phone call, but it could also involve a personal visit.

A visit does not need to be long. It is just good to be there to express sympathy and offer whatever help might be needed. It is equally important to remember that we are not going to 'solve' anything. We cannot bring the dead person back, nor can we take away the pain of those who are grieving. At this point, we should be sparing with our words. It is often enough that we are present with our friends in their time of need.

Sometimes the offer of practical help is much appreciated. Registering a death and organising a funeral can be complicated, especially when grief is raw. A busy family might welcome the offer of babysitting or even the provision of meals so that they can make arrangements for the funeral. In all of this, it is good to remind the person that God is loving, understands their pain, and has compassion for them. The reading of Scripture is also appropriate, even if the person is not a Christian. Psalm 23: 3 & 4 are obvious verses, but the Psalms are full of comfort, as are other passages throughout the Bible.

The funeral itself is a sensitive moment, but just being there is important. In my experience, people do not forget who has attended the funeral of a loved one because it means so much to them. The presence of friends at this difficult time is important, as is contact after the event when the person or family try to get back to normality. The adjustments after the funeral often provide the greatest challenges. The house is quieter, the chair is empty, and a host of memories flood in, accentuating the grief. A phone call or spontaneous visit at this time can make such a difference.

Relationship breakdown

Before we look at pastoral care in relationship breakdown, we need to consider what makes relationships healthy. Much research has been done on what factors are characteristic of stable, long-term relationships. These include commitment to the relationship, joint decision-making, good communication, the ability to work through conflict, and developing shared interests. We can encourage all of these through the general routine of pastoral care.

Broken relationships can have a significant impact on people's lives and add to their feelings of stress. Two friends have a fallout and become embittered, a family gets strained to breaking point, and siblings stop speaking to each other. Sadly, there is also the harrowing and complicated issue of separation and divorce. Circumstances around marital breakdown and divorce can be incredibly complicated, particularly when children are involved. Their presence heightens the stress of the situation; the children also become vulnerable as their parents argue with each other. Again, there are some necessary things to think about before getting pastorally involved in conflict situations like this. Wise and sensitive input will not in itself stop the conflict and save the relationship or marriage, but it can limit the extent of the damage.

The first thing to remember is not to take sides. This can be extremely difficult as each partner will want you to agree with them. Of course, very often in these situations, one member of the couple may be at fault, for example, a husband might have had an affair and refuses to end it. There may be occasions like this where it is appropriate to condemn wrongdoing because God does. Nevertheless, your job in pastoral care requires you to stand back from the emotion of the situation so that you can offer support and help the couple seek God-honouring solutions.

When a marriage breaks down, irrespective of who is at fault, significant complications often have to be dealt with. We need to help the person being pastored to confront these issues and not just react out of hurt. Children must be regarded as a top priority, so parents need to think about how they can spare the children further pain and anxiety. They might also need to make financial decisions, including about what to do with the family home. It can all become messy and painful. Of course, the pastoral person should not make the decisions, but rather help the couple to think carefully about how they will handle their future relationship.

If the couple are part of a church, it is also very easy for other church members to get drawn into the dispute and for warring factions to form. Church members must also hold to the commitment of supportive neutrality, which means they must be careful not to add to the problem by gossip, which exaggerates everything and results in a great deal of inaccurate reporting.

Quite apart from the practical issues already discussed, the one overriding factor is, what does God think of this situation? The individuals concerned need to be asked what they think God's preferred outcome would be. It is easy for everyone, including the pastor, to think that the situation is so bad that divorce is inevitable. We need to believe and convey to the couple that God can change every individual and every circumstance. We are not suggesting that this will be easy. It will require repentance, forgiveness, trust, and reconciliation, all of which will be very humbling and very demanding.

When the couple take a final decision as to the outcome, they will need to be given care, possibly for many months or even years. During this period, some very sensitive matters, such as forgiveness and trusting God, will need to be raised. Bitterness and anger are very destructive emotions which can affect a person's relationship with God and with other people. The pastoral carer should endeavour to protect the person from succumbing to these emotions and should pray with the person that healing will take place. Divorce is painful, but where forgiveness and a measure of reconciliation can be achieved, not only are the people themselves in a better position to move on, but God also gets the glory for bringing hope where previously there was only pain.

Illness

Most people experience suffering at some point in their lives, usually through ill health. Chronic or debilitating conditions are particularly burdensome and can affect a person's emotional and spiritual wellbeing.

When seeking to provide pastoral care to those who are suffering, we very quickly realise just how limited and weak we are. Glib words are of no value, often causing more harm than good, and often there is little or nothing the carer can do to help the sufferer. Aside from divine healing, there are no solutions and no instant remedies. All we can offer is emotional support and a listening ear. Often the best way of caring is just being there for the person and doing simple things like hospital visiting, making reassuring phone calls, and offering prayer or practical help.

Suffering can sometimes bring about good things in a person's life. Some Christians have found that in their suffering they have experienced a sense of God's presence and have grown spiritually as a result. We have all known Christians who remained cheerful and thankful to God, even though their lives were marked with suffering. Of course, this is not always the case, as suffering can also have the effect of leaving people with all sorts of questions, and it can leave them feeling angry towards God, and consumed by self-pity.

Each person responds differently to health concerns. But there are some basic things to remember when pastoring people who are sick. First, never doubt the struggle that ill health issues can entail. When someone is feeling fragile and when whatever treatment (if any) they are receiving does not appear to solve the problem, they can be greatly discouraged. An old adage says that you should never judge a man unless you have walked in his shoes. That is true when dealing with people who suddenly find they are struggling with illness. Unless you have had cancer, or have struggled with your breathing, or have experienced a constant gnawing pain, or the weakness that can accompany chronic fatigue, you will never really know what it feels like. Don't underestimate the physical and emotional toll that it takes on the individual.

Second, offer hope. When someone suffers from a chronic life-threatening, or terminal illness, hope is hard to find and, while we believe that God can heal, we know from experience that often he chooses not to do so. This raises profound questions which cannot be fully answered. But we can point the sufferer to God's love and presence in our lives, sustaining us in our suffering. There is also the assurance that, even should the worst happen, there is eternal life and unspeakable glory. A verse that I never tire of quoting is Revelation 21: 4—'He shall wipe away all tears from their eyes.' This is a verse that looks forward to a time when we can enjoy the paradise that Jesus has prepared for us and in that place, there will be no suffering and sadness. This is the Christian's ultimate hope, and it changes things, enabling suffering Christians to be courageous, joyful, and to grow spiritually.

A third element is that of learning to accept God's will and continuing to live to please him. All kinds of questions are raised when someone who is seriously ill prays for healing, and God does not seem to answer. They ask, 'why would a loving God allow me to suffer?' Our deepest questions do not always get answered in this life and part of the job of pastoral care is to encourage the person to trust that God knows best, even when he does not answer our prayers in the way that we would like. When a Christian continues to serve and praise God, despite their suffering, they experience a special kind of victory that inspires others. When I first became a Christian, I was inspired by two women—a family friend, and my own mother. These two women suffered greatly in their lives and both died at a relatively young age. But the positive and joyful way they lived their lives—their smiles, their selflessness, and their constant prayers for me—challenged and changed my life in a way that no preacher had ever done.

All in the mind

We should not avoid the significant challenge of mental health, which affects Christians just as it does those with no faith. There are some mental health conditions, such as stress, which any pastoral care team will have to face. Of course, stress is a normal part of life and can often act as a stimulus to perform at a higher level. However, it can sometimes become so severe that it affects our whole being—our moods, concentration, digestion, sleep patterns, and even our memory, leaving us with the feeling of stress and exhaustion. Closely related is anxiety, which again we all experience to a certain level, but it too can become so acute that it robs us of any kind of peace. People who suffer from anxiety will often not react normally and will overreact to most situations.

Depression is another pervasive mental health condition which manifests itself in many different ways. The word 'depression' is probably overused, but the symptoms include a lack of interest in anything, poor concentration and energy levels, a loss of appetite, and an inability to relate to others. People with depression will feel that a great cloud hangs over them which will not lift, so that merely talking to them or offering positive advice has little effect.

Many mental health conditions require or benefit from professional treatment, which includes medication. It is vital in pastoral care to encourage people to get professional help when necessary. It is not a failure or a reflection of someone's spiritual life if they need medication, even requiring it for years. Even if this is not required, pastoral care needs to be sensitive and patient. Carers need to be good listeners; they need to listen not so they can respond but so they can understand. Someone suffering from a mental health condition will feel isolated, and having a friend who tries to empathise with them in their circumstances can be a great encouragement. Again, using the Psalms can be a source of much encouragement because they express the kind of internal battles that are part of mental health challenges.

It is interesting that in 1 Kings 19, Elijah suffers from what looks very much like depression. He had lost all interest in life (v. 4), was ignoring his responsibilities, his self-esteem had plummeted, and, in this darkest of moments, he wanted to end it all. God cared for him during this personal crisis, not by reprimanding Elijah for his lack of faith or calling on him to 'pull himself together', but by drawing near to him. He woke him from his sleep (vv. 5, 6) and provided him with food. Elijah went back to sleep again and when he awoke there was more food before him to help him regain his strength. Here was true pastoral care, recognising the physical and psychological needs, then offering hope and new direction.

3. Other life challenges

Pastoral care is sometimes required when people find themselves in difficult or unwanted circumstances. Singleness comes to mind here. While some choose this life and believe this is God's will for them, others remain single involuntarily and, for them, the single life can be a heavy weight to carry.

First, there is the challenge of having physical desires that cannot be fulfilled. Some will find this a greater struggle than others, but Christians who are single need to recognise that their lives will require great self-discipline. However, just as Jesus lived a fulfilled life as a single man, so single people should be encouraged to recognise that their life can still be full and productive.

A second and possibly even greater challenge is that of loneliness. Even in a church setting, it is not easy to witness your friends and contemporaries getting married and having families while you remain single. This is accentuated when you think about activities like eating out, going to the cinema, or going on holiday. Married couples can do these things relatively easily, but they are more difficult for single people to do on their own. Milestone birthdays, such as turning 40 or 50, are reminders they have no partner to share their life.

How we treat single people is very important, especially in the church. We should not see them as if they were a special case or a pastoral project, but we should recognise that, like everyone else, they need friendship, company, and someone to listen and care for them. Pastors cannot provide all of these things, but they can encourage single people to develop a supportive social circle.

Another challenge we need to consider is sexual orientation. Historically, the church has not always done well in caring for people who are same-sex attracted. The church's commitment to Scripture often means that discussion of this subject focuses on theological viewpoints rather than on the need for love and compassion. The result is that those who are same-sex attracted can feel condemned and marginalised. More recently, there has been a move among some Christians to be more accepting of stable and committed same-sex relationships between Christians, and even to reinterpret Bible passages which condemn homosexual activity so that they don't have to confront the issue. Both the unfeeling condemnation of homosexuality and the theologically errant attempts to defend it are wrong and need to be recognised.

Irrespective of the theological debates which will undoubtedly continue, there are significant pastoral concerns to reflect on, not least because Christians who are same-sex attracted often feel rejected and unwelcome and, as a result, tend to hide their sexual orientation. We should begin by treating them like everyone else and not pretend that people who are same-sex attracted are so sinful as to be beyond redemption. We all have fallen human natures, and that includes our sexuality.

Pastoring same-sex attracted Christians begins with loving acceptance, not of the practice, but of the people. We would want to emphasise that we cherish them as members of the family of God and value what they have to offer as part of the body of Christ. We also need to engage openly and honestly with the 'elephant in the room', which is their sexual orientation. Unless we can talk with them about their orientation, it is hard to see how we can offer any help and counsel. For them, following Jesus will mean that they can never give physical expression to their sexual urges. I learned this lesson years ago when, in trying to empathise with a friend who struggled with his sexual orientation, I stated that I had been single until I was 28 and therefore, I could understand something of sexual temptation. His reply demonstrated the fairly empty nature of my comment. He said, 'You may have been single for 28 years, but you did eventually get married. For me, that prospect doesn't exist.'

That sense of loss or lack of fulfilment can come to dominate a person's life. We must remind them that, while society says that sexual fulfilment is the only thing that matters in this life, satisfaction and fulfilment can be experienced in the service of Christ. There is also a need to encourage faithfulness to God and moral purity. Of course, this encouragement must go hand in hand with a genuine listening ear at times when the person may want to express their disappointment and personal pain.

But pastoral care must go beyond empathy, especially because we need to help those who struggle with their sexual orientation to feel part of the Christian community. They are not abnormal; they are ordinary people who, like the rest of us, have their struggles, but also have much to offer. Good pastoral care should have expectations of them, and we should challenge them to contribute meaningfully to the body of Christ and to throw themselves into mutually enriching relationships with other people within the church. They can be helped and encouraged to build up their friendship circle, so that life can be full and they can experience a sense of community.

Addictions

We also need to think about addiction, which affects Christians as well as people of no faith. Some Christians will have struggled with addiction before they trusted Christ, and the challenge of their addiction is carried into their new life. There are of course different kinds of addiction including alcohol, food, pornography, and self-harm, to name but a few. People who do not struggle with addictions find it difficult to understand why the person is so unable to break free, while all the talk of freedom in Christ often makes those struggling with addiction feel even more defeated.

Defining addiction is difficult because this is not just some kind of physical dependency: the mind also plays a part, as does habit formation. Interestingly, Paul's wider statement in Romans 7: 19 about the power of indwelling sin ('For I do not do the good I want to do, but the evil I do not want to do—this I keep on doing') accurately describes the struggle some Christians have with their addiction.

Addictions bring short-term pleasures such as emotional boosts and diversion from other concerns (including pain), but the costs are also high. They imprison the person, causing distress, a sense of shame, altered patterns of behaviour, and a strain on relationships. Addictions can also destroy a person's self-esteem and spiritual life.

Probably the addiction that most readily comes to mind relates to the use, or rather misuse, of drugs. This need not be an illegal habit, as many people have become addicted to painkillers which they can get from a GP or pharmacist. Alcohol addiction is often more subtle. We are all aware of people who have an obvious drink problem and can no longer function well. Often, however, alcohol problems are hidden much more effectively. Take the example of Sharon, a young professional who is also a Christian. She is single, living alone, so few people see the battles she faces. Rarely does she get drunk, though she does consume too much. Every evening meal is accompanied by a bottle of wine and sometimes even more as the evening wears on. While she argues that alcohol has not taken over her life, the fact is that it occupies far too big a role and she cannot imagine life without it.

Then there is pornography addiction. This, too, usually goes unseen, not least because of the shame that addicts feel, given the stigma associated with pornography. Many Christians struggle with it, even if their use of pornography is just occasional. They usually access it via the internet in the privacy of their homes. Nevertheless, it is very real and a concerning number of Christians—both men and women—admit to their use of it.

Gaming is a similar addiction, very common among young people. Talk to the parents of teenagers and you will discover their concerns with the large number of hours their children will spend on their Xbox or other gaming consoles. Many computer games are highly immersive, drawing the player in. They create massive emotional surges, including anger and revenge, in an unreal world where the gamer, from the comfort of his own home, can kill and destroy without consequence. Games are designed to tempt, challenge, and fire up the individual so they cannot walk away. They can be fun and harmless, but they can also be violent, warped, and addictive.

Gambling can also be seriously addictive. While it is rare for Christians to have a significant gambling habit, it is not unheard of. It can take on many forms and often begins with small amounts of money, for example, by playing the lottery. Someone can discreetly place small bets through online sites, and casual betting can take place between friends. Whatever the form, it can be potentially addictive.

How do we pastor people with addictions? The answer is far from simple, not least because addictions by their very nature are tenacious and often hidden. However, acknowledging the addiction is an important first step, though one that is very difficult to take. There is a big jump from saying, 'I drink too much' or 'I look at pornography', to admitting, 'I have an addiction'. But unless people can admit their weaknesses, they can never really deal with them. This is where pastoral care begins, but not in any condemning way. Instead, we encourage the individual to recognise and admit that they have a genuine problem.

It is essential then to help the addicted person to see and wish for a better future and walk a better path. Promoting a life of holiness and a commitment to Christ are vital ingredients here. But before a person can begin to deal with their addiction, they need to recognise how destructive it is and want to be freed from it.

Negative feelings

A final area where pastoral care will be necessary is when a person is suffering from some overwhelming feeling, such as inadequacy or guilt. These feelings can be very strong and have a profound effect on their lives. Often when such feelings exist, it is because of some life experience that has left an indelible mark on them.

Aria is a good example of this. She struggled in relationships with people of the opposite sex. She found it difficult to get close to men, felt uncomfortable in their presence, and consequently felt bad about this. The reason for her strong reaction was that, as a child, an older man who was a family friend, had sexually abused her. When it happened, she was young and vulnerable, so that there was nothing she could have done to protect herself. Nevertheless, she feels a deep sense of guilt and self-loathing, which is not uncommon in such situations.

Karina is the same. She was a relatively happy and carefree child who became a reckless teenager. Her lifestyle was far from healthy and in her late teens she became pregnant. To add insult to injury, her boyfriend walked away, leaving her solely responsible for the new life within her. She was a bright girl who did well at school and had real career prospects. With support and encouragement from her parents, she had an abortion, which she thought would bring an end to her worries. It did not. Now, years later she is still riddled with guilt and, as she never married nor raised a family, she often wonders 'what if?' At those points, guilt, confusion, sadness, and self-loathing return and her life is a real struggle.

These examples help to explain why negative feelings dominate people's thinking. Their negativity, low self-esteem and, under the surface, anger, affect not only themselves but their relationships, making it more difficult to be optimistic about the future. Again, sometimes professional psychological help is needed, but in the absence of that, there are practical pastoral routes to be explored.

At the heart of these feelings is an internal battle with self. Some struggle to love or even accept themselves. This is wrong thinking and it should not be confused with humility. A humble person still has healthy self-esteem.

Someone with a low self-esteem is obsessively self-critical and dominated by negative feelings.

Pastoral care starts with a reminder that God loves us with a love that is unconditional and unmerited. Nothing in our past can stop God from loving us. However, it is one thing to recognise that love, but another to welcome and accept it. Recognising God as a loving father who welcomes us as his children is the starting point in dealing with negative feelings.

There is also a place for confession and forgiveness. Aria did nothing wrong when she was abused as a child and Karina, while suffering the consequences of her own decisions, is no worse than anyone else. The reality is, however, that whatever our circumstances and irrespective of what hurt others have inflicted on us, we are all sinful and in need of forgiveness and cleansing. This will only come about when the person acknowledges his or her condition and turns to God to receive his pardon and power. This is an important step in the process of spiritual recovery.

The idea is to develop a new narrative for our lives. The focus needs to turn from our failure and uselessness to the incredible possibilities of letting God flood our lives with power and love. In 2 Corinthians 10: 5, Paul speaks about bringing every thought captive to Christ. The devil, the great accuser (Rev. 12: 10), wants us to have negative thoughts about ourselves and, if we believe him, he will destroy us and make us ineffective as Christians. God wants and will enable us to overcome through Christ. The question is, 'Who will we believe?' As we pastor people who struggle in these ways, we need to encourage them to take responsibility for their thoughts and feelings. This is the reality of spiritual warfare and we need to help our friends, for whom we care deeply, to experience the life-transforming victory which only God can give.

None of this is easy, but the job of a pastoral carer is to work with, pray for, and encourage those they are caring for to make steady progress towards maturing in Christ.

For further reflection

1. Have you been involved in supporting people in any of the life situations mentioned? If so, how did you deal with them and how effective do you think you were?

2. What advice would you give to couples whose children have grown up and left home and what, if anything, should churches do in respect of them?

3. What advice would you give to a Christian who is struggling spiritually because of their experience of suffering?

4. We have used some scenarios in this chapter mentioning some people by name—Stephen and Rachel, Raymond's mother, Sharon, Aria, and Karina. Select one or two of these and discuss how you would seek to help them.

CHAPTER 8

What lies beneath

On 12 June 2020, the BBC reported that there had been a significant increase in domestic violence during the coronavirus lockdown. The UN described the worldwide increase in domestic abuse as a 'shadow pandemic' alongside Covid-19.[1] It's thought that the increase was due to many people being trapped at home with their abuser. There are many forms of abuse such as physical, psychological, sexual, spiritual, and emotional, all of which can have a devastating effect on the person at the receiving end.

Many churches have been caught up in the scandal of abuse of children. The #MeToo movement has highlighted the problems of men in powerful positions who make sexual advances towards women. Several high-profile church people have been forced to resign from their positions because of inappropriate behaviour.

The title of this chapter asks, 'What lies beneath' and, sadly, we must answer that virtually anything can go on underneath the surface of churches, businesses, and families. It is often very difficult to detect when things are not as they appear. Even in church, husbands or wives can be having affairs or be involved in domestic violence towards their spouse, and individuals can be stealing money from vulnerable elderly people, all hidden under the surface.

Sometimes the problem is short-term, but as in these examples, many problems go undetected for months and even years. Child abuse is an example of this, sometimes involving extended periods of grooming, leading to periods of actual sexual abuse of young children.

---

1. https://www.un.org/en/observances/ending-violence-against-women-day

Much has been written about the different groups of people who are most susceptible to abuse. The problems include physical and sexual abuse of children, domestic abuse, and abuse of older people and vulnerable adults in the home and online. The purpose of this chapter is not to go into detail in each of these areas, but to make some general observations and offer advice on how churches should handle these difficulties when they encounter them.

Pastoral health warning

Caring for people who have been abused presents particular difficulties, in part because different kinds of abuse often need to be handled differently and also because abuse can be very difficult to detect. People keep it well hidden although sometimes it takes place 'in plain sight'. The major problem, however, is that cases of abuse have legal and regulatory ramifications and may bring pastoral care into direct contact with information about potentially criminal activities. We have entitled this chapter, 'What lies beneath', not just to warn potential victims of the danger, but to highlight that carers may also have obligations which go wider than simply the interests of the subject of their pastoral care. Indeed, caring for people in abusive situations can be a minefield.

Let me take a typical scenario to illustrate the point. Suppose a woman seeks your help in a matter that is causing her great distress. You may know her quite well or it may be someone you have not met before. It doesn't really matter, because you don't know what she wants to talk about. You know the importance of being supportive and listening sympathetically, so you arrange an initial conversation in a safe, quiet place where there will be no interruptions.

The conversation proceeds amicably as you talk about things in general but, after a time, the lady begins to articulate her problem and is obviously very emotional about her circumstances. You listen carefully and little by little the picture emerges that she, and to a lesser extent her children, are being beaten by her husband. She explains something of the physical abuse she has received, describing specific incidents, and she shows you some marks on her body to demonstrate the severity of the abuse. At this point the conversation has taken an alarming turn, not just for the victim, but for you as the recipient of this information.

You want to reach out to her and bring encouragement and hope, but at the same time you are conscious that a crime has been committed and you are under obligation to report the matter to the police. You are not at liberty to interrogate the woman or decide if a crime has taken place. Indeed, should you take that line, you may be in breach of the law by compromising any subsequent police investigation. Now that the matter has been brought to your attention, you have no choice but to contact the police, including because there are children are involved. The issue of confidentiality also impinges on this situation. The lady may have thought that pastoral care implies that everything said in conversation is confidential, and she does press for that because of fear of how her partner may react to the fact that she has shared this information with you. But a pastoral carer cannot give an absolute guarantee of this, particularly once information has been given that a criminal act may have taken place or people's lives may be in danger.

What may have started out as a relatively friendly, social conversation has taken a rather different turn, and one of the main difficulties is knowing at what point in the conversation you need to tell the lady that you must refer the matter to higher authorities. This is incredibly difficult. Had she indicated in advance what her problem was, you could have spelt out what obligations you were under, but conversations seldom develop in that way.

We have sought to highlight the difficulties that carers can find themselves in and will further develop some of these problems later in the chapter.

We would recommend that serious issues such as these should be dealt with by mature Christian leaders. If a younger or less experienced Christian discovers a case of abuse, the best thing they could do would be to seek the help of a church leader or mature pastoral carer who can take on that responsibility.

1.   Is it really that bad?

It is difficult to get accurate information relating to the extent of the problem in cases of abuse. Many people do not formally report their experiences, perhaps because they don't understand that they are being abused or perhaps because they feel ashamed, or afraid of the consequences of disclosure, or maybe even blame themselves for what is happening to them. The result is that the extent of the abuse is likely to be higher than the reported figures.

Before we look at the detail, we need to be clear on what we mean by abuse.

Definition

Abuse is defined as the misuse of power and refers to any act that is perpetrated against the will of another. Acts of abuse are used to control, manipulate, or humiliate another person.

The examples below amplify this definition:

- **Physical**—like hitting, kicking, or burning.
- **Sexual**—inappropriate touching, rape, or forcing to engage in sexual acts. It can involve children and even infants as well as adults.
- **Psychological**—verbal abuse, threats, intimidation, humiliation, criticism and name-calling, stalking.
- **Isolating**—from friends, relatives, health services, and sources of support.
- **Monitoring or controlling**—tracking the victim, monitoring social media accounts, detaining at home.
- **Degrading or punishing**—not allowing the victim to eat or rewarding them for only 'good' behaviour.
- **Financial**—not allowing the victim to have their own bank account, the victim's benefits paid to the abuser, withholding money, pressurising in connection with wills, property, or financial transactions.
- **Spiritual abuse**—using Scripture and teaching or pastoral processes to manipulate and control, making unreasonable demands under the guise of spirituality, or threatening spiritual punishment.

People who are being abused often do not recognise their mistreatment as abuse, as they regard their circumstances as normal. They may be in love with their abuser and, as a result, shut out of their mind the darker side of the relationship. It often takes a long time for the person to recognise that they are being abused, and it takes even longer to conclude that they need to take some action to prevent it from continuing.

The following information, taken from government or charity sources, gives us some indication of the extent of the problem.

Domestic abuse

This category relates to adults who live together in the same household and includes people of all ages and all family structures. The statistics paint an alarming picture. The Office for National Statistics reports that the police recorded a total of 1,459,663 domestic abuse-related incidents and crimes in England and Wales in the year ending March 2021. The UK charity LWA (Living without abuse) reports that domestic abuse affects 1 in 4 women and 1 in 6 men in their lifetime, with, on average, two women being murdered each week and 30 men per year.

Internationally, the World Health Organisation in June 2022 highlighted that around 1 in 6 people of 60 years and older had experienced some form of abuse in community settings during the previous year. Rates of abuse of older people had increased during the Covid-19 pandemic. In a similar vein, the UN reported that gender-based violence, already a global crisis before the pandemic, has intensified since the outbreak of Covid-19.

These figures are truly shocking, not only because of the trauma and fear caused at the time of the abuse, but also because the effects often continue throughout the victim's life. Anyone from any culture, religion, age, or class can be a victim of domestic abuse, and while most abuse is directed against women, it can also affect men.

Sometimes, the abuse is short-lived, but it is usually long-term and often gets worse over time even to the extent that it can become life-threatening.

Child abuse

The Crime Survey for England and Wales (CSEW) estimated that in 2018–19 one in five adults aged 18 to 74 years had experienced or witnessed at least one form of child abuse before they reached the age of 16 (8.5 million people). Around half of adults (52%) who had experienced abuse before the age of 16 also experienced domestic abuse later in life, while this was true of only 13% of those who had not experienced abuse before the age of 16.

In 2019, Childline delivered 19,847 counselling sessions to children in the UK. Sexual abuse was raised in nearly half (45%) of these sessions. It has become the most common type of abuse in respect of which counselling has been given by Childline in recent years. At 31 March 2019, 49,570 children in

England and 4,810 in Wales were looked after by their local authority because
of experiencing abuse or neglect.

Cyberbullying

Cyberbullying is a more recent phenomenon in which abuse takes place online,
or on a social media platform. While not physical, it can be just as real and
damaging as forms of physical abuse. More detailed information can be found
at: https://www.bullying.co.uk/cyberbullying/what-is-cyberbullying/

No one can doubt that advances in technology have produced some stun-
ning benefits over the last few decades. But accompanying these developments,
a dark side has also emerged. Young people are very addicted to the use of the
internet and other technological devices, spending much time texting and
gaming. But there has been a corresponding rise in the number of adults using
these means to groom and abuse children. The internet allows such predators
to hide behind masks of anonymity or deception.

A Pew Research study in 2018 found that a majority of teens (59%)
experienced some form of cyberbullying.

The most common types of cyberbullying that teens experienced included:

- Offensive name-calling
- Threatening or abusive text messages
- Creating and sharing embarrassing or explicit images or videos
- Spreading false rumours about individuals to third parties
- Setting up hate sites or groups about a particular individual
- Encouraging young people to self-harm
- Being pressurised into sending sexual images or engaging in sexu-
  al conversations.

No doubt, cyberbullying has a profound effect on many teenagers and results
in considerable distress and mental anguish. Some researchers think that
cyberbullying is a contributing factor to the increase in youth suicides.

2. Could it happen in church?

The church, of course, should not be regarded as exempt from the kinds of
abuse described above. Sadly, it has fallen far short of being the place of safety,

justice, and transformation that God has called it to be, and has too often been remiss in protecting and serving those who have been victims of violence.

Abuse happens in Christian families as well as in Christian churches. It shouldn't, but it does. We know of cases where even well-known teachers have abused their wives and families over many years, both physically and psychologically, and the children have been affected by it well into adult life.

Most Christians recognise that abuse in its various forms is a real problem in society, but think it is not an issue in the church. There is a prevailing view that 'it could never happen in our church', so we don't expect to find it. We assume that everyone is honest, and no one would engage in such behaviour. The church teaching programme occasionally includes the subject in a sermon series, and we produce detailed policy papers on God's design for marriage and healthy relationships. We think we have covered all the bases so 'it couldn't happen here'.

But maybe we are not as blameless as we think. In recent years, there has been much evidence to suggest that abuse is widespread in many Christian denominations, but we, perhaps too readily, take the view that abuse could not possibly happen in our 'Independent Evangelical Churches'. This is very dangerous, and while we thank God that there have been relatively few cases, we must not close our eyes to the fact that such churches are as vulnerable as any other.

Churches provide a very fertile environment for people who might want to abuse others. They are usually close-knit communities where people chat freely with one another, often exchanging intimate details about their lives. The members work together in close, trusting relationships. There is enormous respect and trust for those in leadership, so someone in a position of authority does not arouse surprise if he or she is often in the company of one person or a small group of people engaging in legitimate church business.

Youth workers take young people on outings or to summer camps where there are many opportunities to take advantage of their position. We assume they are good people, genuinely looking after the interests of the teenagers in their care and we value their contribution to the church. They can pray or preach well and are excellent Bible study leaders. We see them as friends and co-workers. Usually, all this is true, but we need, indeed in the UK are required, to have safeguards in place for the benefit of both the children and the worker.

We are too often naïve about how the dynamics of abuse play out in church communities. So, if a child makes an allegation of some wrongdoing, we can be inclined to dismiss it, assuming the child was mistaken, or it was a harmless and misunderstood action. The truthfulness of the allegation would run contrary to everything we know and respect about the alleged perpetrator. We find it almost impossible to believe, so we fail to give the child a fair hearing with the result that victims may feel they have nowhere to turn.

Rejecting the concerns of a child in this way can have both short- and long-term implications. In the short-term, the child quickly learns that it is better to say nothing because no one will believe them, and the predator will continue his or her sordid activities with a statement to the child that this is 'our little secret'. In the long-term, the action of the predator causes significant mental and emotional problems so that, even years later, the person abused continues with the hurt of all that took place. Failing to take the problem seriously can make victims and survivors feel even more isolated and rejected.

Another important factor is that if the predator is ever caught, there will be those, sometimes even the parents of the victim who don't want to 'rock the boat'. The predator will almost certainly ask for forgiveness, and this will often be given on the basis that we are all sinners and we all need to learn from our mistakes. Some in the leadership will be concerned about the church's reputation and would like to handle the misconduct quietly and privately, hoping that things will settle down. But this option is not open to us because changes in the law require us to report all cases of suspected abuse. Society recognises the extent of abuse and has rightly labelled it a criminal activity. We can no longer regard it as a private matter to be kept within the family or the believing community.

3. So we have a problem—how do we deal with it?

Having looked at the extent of the problem, we must now consider how to respond. We begin by offering advice to individuals who may be at the receiving end of abuse, then move on to make some suggestions to pastoral carers on how best they can help. Finally, we look at the obligations placed upon churches to ensure care is offered timeously, effectively, and meets all legal obligations. (The order does not suggest that the last category is less important than the first two.)

Advice for victims

Many victims may not define the way that they have been treated as abuse. The following checklist, relating mostly to domestic abuse, may help determine if abuse is taking place. The information is taken from the Refuge website,[2] a charity supporting women and children against domestic violence (hence the use of the pronoun "he" to describe abusers, though women can also be abusers).

- Is your partner jealous and possessive?
- Is he charming one minute and abusive the next?
- Does he tell you what to wear, where to go, who to see?
- Does he constantly put you down?
- Does he play mind games and make you doubt your judgment?
- Does he control your money?
- Does he pressure you to have sex when you don't want to?
- Are you walking on eggshells to avoid making him angry?
- Does he monitor or track your movements or messages?
- Does he use anger and intimidation to frighten and control you?

Those individuals who conclude that they are being abused need to decide what to do next. They may think that it's best to confide in a friend or another family member or a member of the church pastoral team. In the latter case, it is important to remember that the person being abused must take the decision to confide without pressure from the pastoral team member. They may also decide to report the abuse to the police. They are entitled to do so and the pastoral carer should support them throughout the process. (Once the abused has confided in the pastoral carer, the latter must report the matter to the church's safeguarding officer and there is likely to be a duty for him or her to report the matter to the police and the social services department, and in England and Wales to report the matter to the Charity Commission as a serious incident.)

---

2. Quoted from the Refuge website: https://www.nationaldahelpline.org.uk/en/What-is-abuse

The pastoral carer's response

Abusive behaviour can be very difficult to detect. Perpetrators are very soph-isticated at keeping their activities secret, and victims are very reluctant to bring the problem into the open. It is not the function of pastoral carers to pry into people's private lives to find out if abuse is going on. It is, however, important that carers should be alert to the possibility of abuse taking place and can recognise the warning signs.

A word of caution is appropriate here. Sometimes what we may regard as abuse is not seen in that light by the people concerned. Some people in a church thought Jane was being exploited to an unreasonable extent by her husband. The husband regularly found excuses for not working, such as illness or lack of opportunity, but he always seemed to find time for sport and other leisure pursuits. He would ask friends or relatives to look after their small child because he had something else to do. Jane was the breadwinner for the family, sometimes having to work long hours in a quite stressful job, then coming home to make the evening meal for the family before putting the baby to bed. Jane's friends saw a deterioration in her health and were very concerned about her mental welfare.

The friends tried to raise the issue with Jane who acknowledged that her situation was difficult. However, because she had married this man, she felt a responsibility to the relationship. One of the church leaders had also spoken to Jane's husband and asked him to pull his weight in the home and not be such a burden on Jane. This made little difference to his behaviour and Jane was not prepared to confront her husband on the issue. Her friends and the church pastoral team recognised they could do nothing for Jane until she was ready to explore other options. If there is no reason to suspect that there has been any unlawful behaviour, it would be inappropriate for the pastoral care team to intervene, even though they were concerned about her situation.

It's hard to know how to help someone who is experiencing domestic abuse. Our first instinct is to protect, but we need to be careful not to rush in. Getting involved may seem straightforward, but can be fraught with all kinds of difficulties. To begin with, we do not know the extent of the problem. We may think it will be relatively easy to help the victim find a solution, but that is not always the case and there is the very real possibility we could make the situation worse. However, we should never underestimate what might be going on in any given situation so we should be highly vigilant and ready to respond if the circumstances allow for that.

If we are asked to help, it is important to offer a supportive, listening ear so that the victim knows that she is being heard and taken seriously. The first thing is to make sure you understand what the abused person is saying. It is so important to let him or her speak. Don't try to prise out details or ask leading questions, but do explain that if anyone is at risk of harm, you will need to tell someone else. It is also important to know your limits and only proceed on your own if you are comfortable doing so. As you discuss the issue, explore possible solutions and help the person to find a way forward. Offer comfort and assurance and if you think further meetings are required, agree time and place, and ask if you have permission to contact the person at home. Your task at this stage is to keep in contact on a friendship basis and with a watching brief.

Your relationship with that individual over the next days and weeks may be difficult to define but remember that you are there on a pastoral care basis only, to provide moral support. Churches should be careful not to get involved with criminal matters or take the place of social services.

4. Church response
There are several aspects to this:

How should the church respond to knowledge of domestic abuse (whether obtained through its pastoral processes or otherwise)?
Mark Conner, Senior Minister, CityLife Church in Melbourne, outlines some failings of religious bodies[3]:

1. We have not done a good job of helping to prevent domestic violence, of confronting it when it occurs, nor of helping those involved—both the perpetrator and victim.

---

3. https://www.commongrace.org.au/church_repentence_for_domestic_family_violence

2. There has been too much ignorance about the prevalence of domestic violence. Many church leaders have failed to believe that it can happen, even in Christian homes.

3. There has been much erroneous teaching about 'submission', 'authority', and 'obedience' in the home. This has led to a culture of silence and acceptance.

4. Preachers have not taught on this subject nor referred to it enough in their messages.

5. We have not equipped pastors and church leaders to address this matter, nor have they equipped their congregation members with proper responses should domestic violence occur.

6. Pastors have often emphasised forgiveness and repentance at the expense of a victim's welfare and safety.

Most churches are likely to have both abusers and victims attending, and given this, plans need to be in place to handle abuse allegations in the best possible way.

How should the church respond to allegations of abuse?

We now look at the situation where a member brings an allegation of abuse to the attention of the church leadership. The accused may or may not be a member. The important point to emphasise here is that the leadership must take the allegation seriously. If an individual has arrived at the point of making their abuse public, they at least regard it as serious. Many people have been badly let down when their complaints are not handled well or where promises of help have not materialised.

We need to be careful not to minimise the problem. An abusive relationship is not just a situation where people fallout and then make up. It is very different and often involves a continuous pattern of behaviour. The church must ensure that it gives the safety and wellbeing of the victim and any children the highest priority, and if there has been physical or sexual violence, the leaders of the church have no option but to refer the matter to the relevant authorities, and make sure that their pastoral care activities will not be judged as having got in the way of the action of those authorities.

If it involves a married couple, the church may offer marriage guidance which provides an opportunity for the couple to receive counselling to rebuild the marriage. However, while this is a laudable aim, great care must be taken because further evidence might come to light which requires reporting to the authorities. Also, the attempt to provide care can backfire and actually lead to more violence. Many victims are encouraged to seek 'reconciliation' and offer 'forgiveness' based on the belief that the perpetrator is sincerely repentant. However sometimes perpetrators pretend to be repentant and that becomes part of their method to lure the victim back into the abusive situation.

We should also consider what responsibility the church has towards the perpetrator. Pastorally, he or she still deserves spiritual support and counsel. Church leaders should challenge the person to repent and assure them of God's forgiveness if the repentance is genuine, but they should neither excuse nor minimise the behaviour. This is a difficult balance to maintain, requiring wisdom and prayer. We also need to ensure that we are complying with our legal and safeguarding responsibilities and doing any necessary reporting to relevant authorities. It may be that it should be arranged that Christian pastoral support should be given to the perpetrator from outside the congregation, though that person or organization would have the same reporting obligations if relevant matters come to their attention in the process.

We can understand the church wanting to support the abused person and this support will likely be needed for quite a long time. The aim of pastoral care in the church is to walk with the victim through these dark times and help them come into the light at the other end. Pastoral carers will want to pray with the victim, assuring him or her of God's love and presence. At some point, the issue of forgiveness will need to be raised, but that can only be done when the person is emotionally ready to consider this.

In serious situations such as this, we must ensure that key people such as trustees and church leaders are kept fully informed, as legal responsibility for the activities of the congregation clearly rests with them. It is good practice to keep written records of the date and nature of the allegation together with a note of subsequent developments and these must be retained securely, including but not only to maintain complete confidentiality.

Often these situations can be protracted, and the church needs to be prepared for the long haul. If the victim feels it is in his or her best interests to leave their partner, then the church will need to liaise with the authorities to resolve issues of accommodation and ensure that the victim and children will not be in any further danger. All of this is very traumatic for the victim as well as their family and friends, but we need to remember that leaving a violent partner is a process, not a single act. Research shows it takes, on average, seven attempts before a woman is able to leave for good.

How should the church respond to allegations of abuse involving a member of staff or volunteers conducting church activities?

Remunerated church workers are human like everyone else and can behave in ways that, while not illegal, fall short of the standards expected of a person with pastoral responsibility. These behaviours range from serious misconduct to simply being unwise in relating to others.

Again, the advice in the previous section holds good. Cases must be handled with the same impartiality and integrity towards a member of staff as they would towards a volunteer member of the congregation (and the position of a member of staff may be clearer, with more safeguards, than that of a volunteer).

The problem here is not just one of pastoral care but, with respect to a paid employee, the church also has employer responsibilities and liabilities, which adds another layer of complexity. (If the church worker is a self-employed office-holder, the terms of the contract would be relevant in the same way.) If the allegation is made against an employee and is of unlawful behaviour, the church must immediately refer the matter to the police or other appropriate authority. Because the church is itself potentially culpable, church leaders should not attempt to investigate the rightness or wrongness of the allegation.

If the police become involved, then the church will have many questions to answer: Does it have an explicit policy statement about abuse? Was there adequate supervision of the employee and was training given in this area of the staff member's remit? If the accused person is the pastor, then the issue arises as to whom the pastor is accountable. These and other issues will be very important in the enquiry.

The legal defence of the employee/alleged perpetrator will be a matter that the employee has to deal with. Clearly, the church will be concerned about the person's spiritual and emotional wellbeing, but in the context of any accusation and subsequent investigation, the church must remain neutral. The investigation involves the police and the accused only; church leaders and members need to ensure that they cooperate fully and do not obstruct, influence, or prejudice the investigation.

The church has been put in an incredibly difficult situation. It cannot continue to support the employee as if nothing has happened, yet neither can it cut off all contact with someone who is a brother or sister in Christ as if it has no further interest in the person. One possible solution might be to find a third party, either from within the church, or outside, to maintain contact with the accused and provide whatever pastoral help is needed. This third party must be clear that the task is to support the individual, emotionally and spiritually, without assuming guilt or innocence. That will be discovered through the investigation. If the accused is found to be guilty, the pastoral care may continue, but the church also needs to respect the verdict and not make excuses for the behaviour of the individual. If found to be innocent, pastoral care will still be needed, both to help the individual and to enable reintegration back into church life again. In all of this the church also needs to be sensitive to the feelings and wellbeing of the victim.

An important issue to think about is the attitude of church members towards the accused. It is important to remind the church that under law, people are innocent until proved guilty. Ask them to pray, but not make any assumptions of guilt. If the person is ultimately found to be not guilty and wishes to return to church life, members of the congregation need to be encouraged to welcome and embrace the person. If the accused is found guilty, it may be too impracticable to bring him or her back into fellowship after serving any consequences resulting from his or her actions. Real wisdom and sensitivity need to be demonstrated here and genuine repentance should always be the starting point. The church must also learn lessons from this unfortunate incident and put safeguards in place to ensure it does not happen again.

In the case of a volunteer member of the pastoral team, or a volunteer assisting with any other church activity in respect of which an allegation has been made, the immediate action of the church would be to ask him or her to step down temporarily from all service to the church. Since the volunteer is acting on behalf of the church, then a similar range of questions to the above will probably be raised. Was the individual given a detailed statement of his or her remit within the pastoral team? Were the church's expectations with respect to personal conduct made clear? Was he or she given appropriate training for the task and was there adequate supervision?

If the allegation results in a court case, then representatives of the church may well be called to respond to the kind of questions outlined above. The church should cooperate fully with the authorities, and should not attempt to cover up or justify any potential abuse.

5. Safeguarding

What safeguards does a church need to minimise the possibility of abuse taking place?

Churches have a duty to ensure that members and others using church facilities or otherwise taking part in church activities can do so without fear of abuse or neglect, and more widely we would wish that they should thereby come to no harm at all if it is reasonably in our power to prevent it

On safeguarding properly so called, there is an abundance of information, but here we will simply summarise some key points and provide useful contact details.

It is essential for churches to have a safeguarding policy and that members are aware that the church is committed to upholding the highest standards of care. Church members should also have the name and contact telephone number of the safeguarding coordinator, who will be the person to contact in the event of an emergency or an allegation of abuse.

The trustees should ensure the policy is reviewed annually, that training is given regularly to employees, self-employed office-holders, and volunteers; and that necessary checks and related administrative action are carried out timeously, efficiently, and completely. It is also important to ensure that there is appropriate insurance cover for all the activities of the church, and that the trustees and elders are seen to take these matters seriously in order to set the right example.

The policy should include such elements as:

- A general statement of the church's attitude towards abuse and its commitment to minimising it.
- Some details of how the policy will be implemented and where the policy can be accessed.
- Information relating to the appointment of individuals to paid or voluntary positions within the church.
- How people can bring allegations of abuse to the attention of the church leaders.
- A detailed description of the actions the church will take in the event of such allegations and how it will care for those affected.

Every person, whether paid or volunteer, should be given a copy of the policy and asked to sign a statement saying they agree with it and will follow its terms.

One further danger still lurks under the surface and that is the effect any of this might have on the church itself. Where trustees and elders are called upon to deal with some of these difficult cases, they need all the support they can get from the congregation. Too often congregations criticise the decisions of the elders saying they have been too harsh or too lenient, when in fact what is needed is the prayerful support of the people of God. If we are not careful, a pastoral situation like those described above will be a no-win situation for the trustees and elders as the people of God take sides in support of either victim or perpetrator. These situations call for great wisdom by the leadership and great trust on the part of the membership.

Further reading and information

As indicated earlier, there is a vast amount of information on the internet on this subject that we could not reference here. There is a number of helpful websites and we give the links to them below.

From: Durham Church of England—general plus much helpful material for local use
https://durhamdiocese.org/safeguarding-abuse-concerns/
See also https://www.churchofengland.org/safeguarding/promoting-safer-church-safeguarding

From: SCIE—Social Care Institute for Excellence
https://www.scie.org.uk/safeguarding/faith-groups/communities#case-studies

From: FIEC—general advice plus helpful video webinar on online safeguarding
https://fiec.org.uk/resources/staying-safe-when-church-is-online

From: Knighton Free Church—example of local church policy
https://www.knighton.org.uk/wp-content/uploads/2015/03/Safeguarding-policy-final.pdf

Other: Assistance with church safeguarding responsibilities:
Thirtyone:eight Creating safer places Together: https://thirtyoneeight.org/
Christian Safeguarding Services: https://thecss.co.uk/

For further study

1. Abuse is clearly a significant matter in contemporary life. What can the church do to be more vigilant about the threat, and also to care for people who suffer abuse?
2. What safeguards can churches put in place to guard against abuse taking place, both within the congregation and the wider community?
3. Describe in your own words what constitutes 'controlling behaviour' and discuss how churches can guard against this behavior among their members.
4. Bullying tends to be an acceptable social behaviour on the grounds that everyone does it, it toughens people up for life, and it is necessary in

order to get things done. How common is it in church life, and does it matter? How is it best approached in pastoral care?

5. Read the following case study and discuss what actions should be taken and what principles should govern those actions.

> **Case study:** Jodi is a married woman in her mid-thirties with two young children. She comes to church intermittently, accompanied by her husband. Their children attend kids' clubs but do not integrate very well with other children. When Jodie and her husband attend, they keep to themselves and, if they do get involved in conversation, he does almost all the talking. Ladies in the church have invited Jodi out for coffee, but she always declines. One day when she was wearing a short-sleeved blouse, church members noticed some bruising. When asked about this, she replied that she had fallen in the garden and quickly changed the subject. One of the elders offered to visit the home, but Jodi's husband stated they were too busy for a visit.

CHAPTER 9

The ticking time bomb

Having thought about some of the dark things that can exist beneath the surface in church, we now turn to some 'ticking time bombs' that we will need to deal with sooner or later in pastoral care. The reality is that society has changed beyond recognition over the last few decades, and we are now encountering issues in church life we could never have imagined just a few years ago. These changes present a challenge for the church because it often exists in a religious bubble, sheltered from the worst excesses of our contemporary culture. However, if we are to reach out to society at large, we will need to confront a range of seemingly intractable topics, some of which we discuss below. How churches deal with them will determine whether they end up at the margins of society or at the heart of their community, offering support and love to broken people.

The imagery behind the title of this chapter compares these issues to bombs placed in a variety of places, ready to go off at any moment. We don't know where they are or when they will go off or what might trigger the explosion. We just know that at some point something will happen which will cause one or more of them to explode. The church can either pretend these bombs don't exist and go about its business as usual, or it can recognise the danger and prepare to meet the difficulty when it comes. Neither of these approaches will prevent the bombs going off, but the latter will help us to minimise the effects of the explosions. Churches which are serious about engaging with the local community will find themselves in difficult situations where they will be in conflict with societal norms. One wrong move and everything can blow up in your face.

What kind of issues are we talking about that could prove incendiary for the church? To begin with, there are those thorny issues such as same-sex marriage and the transgender movement, both of which feature regularly in the media and have become the touchstone of what is acceptable conduct by organisations. Then there is environmentalism and care for creation. Many Christians do not take environmental issues seriously, but they are important for society at large, especially for young people. Abortion continues to be significant, demonstrated in the fact that the number of abortions taking place annually in the UK has now exceeded 200,000. Political and social movements such as *Black Lives Matter* exert considerable influence, something akin to a cultural tidal wave. These issues are current and significant in society at large but, often, churches do not seem to regard them as important, until an incident or person demands urgent action.

We do not intend to unpack these issues to suggest what response the church should take towards them. Rather, our focus is on the wider context and its implications for pastoral care. Some might feel that such implications will be rare, but given the direction of travel of our culture, we may encounter them sooner than we think. They are complex issues, so we must take great care and give much thought in responding to them.

In pastoral terms, we need be in no doubt that there will be occasions when leaders will find themselves in a no-win situation. We live in a fallen world where, often, there are no right or wrong answers to complex problems. In the absence of clean-cut and complication-free pastoral responses, as churches we need to ensure that our actions do not make the situation worse, even though they may not solve the problem.

1. Same-sex marriage

We will begin with the very challenging question of same-sex marriage. This may sound fairly theoretical, but with the legalisation and wide acceptance of gay marriage, it is certainly not. Consider a scenario where a woman, whom we will call Louise, comes along to an Alpha course hosted by a local church. She has come because her work colleague, who is a member of the church, invited her. Louise thoroughly enjoyed the Alpha course and became intrigued and then absorbed with the person of Jesus. On the last night, Louise trusted Christ, much to the delight of the church outreach team. They were nervous, however, because Louise is married to another woman who is less than sympathetic towards Christianity. They also have two young children, and together they form a loving and close-knit family unit.

What kind of discipleship and pastoral care should a church give in a situation like this? There are no simple answers, and whatever decisions we take will have huge implications. Should the church encourage Louise to break up with her partner? If so, what effect would that have on the two young children? The question could also be asked as to what reputational damage the church would sustain in the eyes of the local community, especially as they would, in effect, be encouraging the break-up of a family unit.

On the other hand, should the church try to affirm and support the relationship, given that this couple is legally married? If this is what is decided, what damage would that do to the church, and could it continue to teach passages like Romans 1 without being compromised or hypocritical? Another option might be to encourage Louise to support her family and work at her marriage relationship, but abstain from physical intimacy. The question will arise as to how this would be monitored. And is it realistic, given that it requires the consent of Louise's wife, who is already antagonistic towards the church and who will probably consider physical intimacy central to her relationship with Louise? While all of this is being worked out, other questions press in—for example, should Louise be allowed to become an active member of the church community? Should she be encouraged to get baptised and take communion?

This situation is complex, and we should not pretend there are any neat answers. The questions raised demonstrate both the real challenges that we could face and how decisions reached can affect the church and the community. We have not attempted to suggest what the right course of action should be, but we must always remember that, alongside the thorny and delicate situation for the church, there is a new young Christian who faces massive personal challenges within the family home. It is true that the Bible does not support the idea of same-sex marriage, and Christians cannot condone obvious sin if they wish to remain biblically faithful. Nevertheless, the reality of this family unit is undeniable, and no pastorally sensitive person would want to cause emotional harm to young children. Examples like this highlight the importance of churches thinking through, in advance, the biblical principles relating to these issues, so they have the beginnings of an answer when confronted with such difficult situations.

Of course, there is always the temptation just to close the door on people with complicated lives so that the church does not have to deal with these issues. While this might seem like a reasonable response, it would have devastating results for the effectiveness of our evangelism. It is also not what Jesus would do. He offered hope to broken people and reached out to the outcast, so following him must involve doing the same, even if it creates challenges for the church.

Whatever pastoral decisions are finally made in a situation like this, we need to keep these realities in mind and the leadership needs to take the church with them as they work through the process. Keeping the church together when contentious issues arise is very difficult, but is a key task of leadership. Good leaders know that they will face situations like this one day, so they work hard over many years to build trusting relationships with their congregations. They show love and care consistently to all their members, and are very supportive of those in trouble. Members remember how the leaders cared for them in tough times and will be confident that they will handle the kinds of situation we are describing in this chapter with the same integrity and compassion—always having the glory of God and the welfare of his people at the forefront of their thinking.

2. Transgender confusion

The transgender challenge surfaced for one church when Tony came along to a church service. He had been on a business trip when he accepted an evangelistic book and DVD from a colleague, which led to his conversion. He then discovered that there was an evangelical church near where he lived, so he got in touch and began to attend, desiring to grow in his newfound faith. The challenge for the church was that Tony was going by the name of Margaret. He was a married man and had a child through that relationship, but he also suffered from the diagnosed medical condition of Gender Dysphoria, causing such embarrassment and humiliation that his wife left him. Feeling trapped in his body, he sought medical advice and had gradually transitioned to his new chosen gender, a process that included surgical intervention. Having become a

Christian, he now felt that he was getting his life sorted, but he was clear that he now identified as a woman and not a man. Tony was still in touch with his wife, who was prepared to take him back if he returned to his birth gender.

Our intention is not to suggest how churches should deal with this issue, but to make several comments from a pastoral perspective. One is that we should not rush either to make a judgment or to find an answer. Patience is important, both for those directly involved in pastoral care and for the church. We should also note that often pastoral care and discipleship work in tandem with each other. It is not realistic to think that we can solve a complex situation first and then go on to look at the issue of spiritual growth. Instead, discipleship should begin immediately; then we can tackle the problem over time and often a long time. In a situation like this, Tony will need to experience a measure of spiritual maturity before he can even address his gender dysphoria. In all of this, the job of the pastoral carer is not to be judgmental. Simply condemning Tony will only alienate him, especially when he is already emotionally and psychologically fragile. Instead, we need to think about what honours God and what will contribute to Tony's finding healing and wholeness in his life; we can be supportive as we encourage him in that direction. Again, the church members have a role to play if Tony is to receive the love and support necessary to make progress. How they relate to him will either contribute to his sense of rejection, or it will make him feel he has a family who will support him through this challenging period of his life and give him a sense of belonging.

3. Bandwagon issues

Another potentially difficult topic is the 'bandwagon' issues that periodically raise their heads. They become very newsworthy in society at large, and because we as Christians are part of the community, we cannot avoid them. Often, such issues raise genuine moral questions upon which Christians should have an opinion. Still, given the fallenness of our world, as Christians we need to be careful neither to swallow an entire agenda nor ignore its central component. A good example of this is how Christians relate to the *Black Lives Matter* movement.

On 25 May 2020, the world watched in horror as George Floyd, a 46-year-old black man from Minneapolis was asphyxiated as a police officer knelt on his neck. It was an appalling act which reminded us not just of the ugliness of racism, but also its prevalence in society. The *Black Lives Matter* movement was at the heart of the street protests that followed. Many Christians got involved and quickly identified themselves with the movement, though often without thinking about what it all meant or how it quickly embraced a range of other politically correct ideas. It is this element that makes it an important pastoral issue.

To be clear, racism is a sin, and all Christians should be opposed to it. Christians should speak out against oppression wherever they find it and stand up for the vulnerable, just as Jesus did. Churches need to preach about racism and ensure that their opposition to it is clearly articulated and understood. However, our motivation for opposing racism should be a deep conviction that we are all made in the image of God and therefore every human being has intrinsic value, irrespective of his or her ethnicity.

The problem with jumping on a bandwagon is that often social justice warriors and campaigners conflate different issues as if they were one. For example, some would say that a person who raises objections about homosexual behaviour is no different from someone who is racist, because in both cases they are prejudiced. Such campaigners rightly speak out against racism, but also believe that heteronormativity (the belief that heterosexuality is 'the norm' against which other relationships are compared) is also a form of prejudice and oppression. They would argue that anyone who believes homosexual practice to be morally wrong is equivalent to a racist. Equally, they would consider to be prejudiced anyone who has questions about a matter such as transgenderism and that they must be opposed with the same vigour as we oppose racism.

This is obviously a difficult issue, but a genuinely Christian response to racism, or any form of prejudice, should begin with a Christian worldview. We are not saying that Christians should not join a *Black Lives Matter* march or similar event. There will be times when it is appropriate for Christians to stand together with others on a whole range of ethical issues. We need to stand up for morality in the public square. However, it is important that Christians are discerning about how they relate to the wider culture. Scripture should shape their response, not the latest fad or political ideology.

4. The environment

Churches have often been silent on this subject, which is a mistake. We are stewards of God's creation and so creation care ought to be high on our agenda. It should matter to us that countries around the world are polluting the oceans and are also contributing to the destruction of the world's natural resources. We should care about poverty, exploitation, and the destruction of the world's forests. It should also matter to us that global warming is imperilling human and otherlife in a wide variety of ways. Our relationship with, and responsibility for the created world should also feature in our Bible teaching. Once again, however, as Christians we do not want to be caught up in any agenda that is driven by an anti-Christian worldview. For example, we cannot go along with campaigners who ascribe a sense of purpose and mind to the universe as if it were a living being as the *Gaia Hypothesis* claims. Equally, we should not go along with those who hold to a quasi-religious mystical attitude towards Mother Nature. While we may share similar concerns with such people, we base our reason for action on the teaching of Scripture. As we pastorally care for people, we encourage them to believe in the creation mandate to care for the created order, but not to follow anti-Christian agendas or belief systems.

5. Abortion

Statistically, around 200,000 unborn children are aborted each year in the UK, so this is a very significant moral issue. Again, Christians need to defend the defenceless and to value all life made in the image of God. Pastorally, however, this is a sensitive issue and there must be compassion for women who have felt that they had no choice but to end their pregnancy. The issue is also extremely politicised, as it involves questions about a woman's right to decide about her own body.

Stephen has written about abortion elsewhere[1], so our focus here is primarily on the pastoral dimension. The challenge that the church faces on a matter like this is that some key aspects get lost in the heat of the debate. When abortion is discussed in the public square, it focusses almost exclusively on a woman's right to do what she wants with her body. A Christian perspective recognises that the

---

1. Stephen McQuoid, *In His Image*, Wilberforce Publications, 2020, pp. 57–72.

unborn child also has a right to life. Often, the consequences of rape and incest are invoked as a justification for abortion. It is possible to have a legitimate moral discussion whether abortion might be justified in such cases, or to save the life of the mother when it is at serious risk if the pregnancy continues. But these arguments are not relevant to the great majority of abortions that have taken place in the UK since 1967.

It is important to recognise that we offer pastoral care against the backdrop of a broader culture which sees the woman's right as a fundamental human right. This is also an emotionally charged issue as the decision to have an abortion can have huge repercussions. Besides the personal and social pressures, there can be a significant amount of guilt and self-questioning, sometimes resulting in serious mental health problems. Pastoral care must therefore be done with great compassion and sympathy and a desire to look forward rather than judging the past. The difference this can make is enormous and can contribute to the woman's growing spiritually. Of course, if the mother-to-be is on her own and decides to have the child, the church must face the challenge of how best it can offer practical help in the years following the birth. This is no small matter, and it may be questioned whether churches always do as much as they should in this sort of circumstance.

6. It's all politics

We all have our political opinions, and many Christians are committed to their political party, voting with enthusiasm and conviction. However, there needs to be the recognition that God does not vote for any one party. This is not always at all obvious if you were to listen in to a conversation between Christians or look at their social media posts.

Christians need to be careful not to denounce people simply because they hold to a different political persuasion. Linked with this, Christians should also be careful not to make any assumptions that a given party line, policy, or economic system expresses the Christian perspective. That Christians can be found in every major political party is evidence of this. Since all political parties, politicians, and of course voters are fallen, the Christian response is to ask deeper questions about the principles that underpin any given political policy. Christians should be concerned about issues such as justice, integrity, hard work, and human wellbeing, not being neutral or apolitical but recognising that many people of all political persuasions share these concerns. Pastoral responsibility demands that we help the Christians whom we are pastoring to think through the ethical implications of public policies, but not to seek to influence how they might cast their vote.

Pastoral care may also involve a degree of political activism. After all, in caring for people we should also care for their environment. Everyone is part of a community and so the pastoral care must also keep the needs of the community in mind. Wider influences such as multiculturalism, capitalism, or consumerism affect the people we pastor. They may have experienced redundancy, harassment, anti-social behaviour, and even crime which will have impacted their personal circumstances and wellbeing. Good pastoral care will be concerned about this and want to make a difference.

Some would see socio-political concerns as being beyond the realm of pastoral care, but this is a mistaken view. If we are caring for the whole person, trying to make their lives better in a practical way ought to be part of the package of care. We once dealt with a situation where a family were being made homeless. Merely offering prayer in that situation would not have been enough. Rather, we got involved in the practicalities of the case, contacting government and local government departments and politicians, as well as asking Christians to offer practical support. We could term this holistic pastoral care, because it seeks to address not just the spiritual dimension, but the physical concerns and welfare of the family.

Desmond Tutu described himself as a pastor and not a politician, yet his concern for the people meant that he got involved in the political struggle for liberation in South Africa. He demonstrated that simply binding up wounds of hurt individuals is not enough. The pastoral carer will need to confront injustice when it is encountered and provide tangible evidence of the love of God.

7. Political correctness

Our final concern is the demands of political correctness. This is a fairly recent phenomenon that might at first appear to be a reasonable thing, but it has led to a range of damaging manifestations such as victim culture, the requirement of 'safe spaces' where people can be insulated from views which they or others consider they might find disturbing or disagreeable, and the suppression of free speech. It is this latter issue that is of particular concern. No Christian should be associated with offensive behaviour or speech. However, freedom of speech is a precious thing because, among other things, it allows us to preach the gospel and speak out for Christian values. From a pastoral angle, we need to encourage gracious and honest speech, as both have a place and are not mutually exclusive.

Lessons to be learned

What lessons can we learn about dealing with these and other potentially contentious issues? First, we need to understand that how a church responds to these complex situations will determine what kind of church it will become. Will the church close the door to people with complicated lives? Will its pursuit of purity and reputation exclude those who are messed up and struggling? If so, it will not be troubled by complexity, but neither will it be troubled by having a new generation of Christians to disciple. In a broken world such as ours, it is hard to see how a church can grow if it spares itself the complication of embracing broken people.

Second, maintaining biblical values in a fallen world is never easy, but it must remain our intention. Of course, as some of the examples above testify, there will be times when it will not be possible to ensure a biblically faithful lifestyle without significant collateral damage. In such cases, we must allow grace to overrule law, at least for a time, in order either to find a solution or to enable an individual to mature spiritually, to a point where they can make tough decisions for themselves. Such pragmatic decisions should not be a compromise and we should not perceive them as such. Holiness should always be our goal, and we should never allow standards to slip. We should apply Scripture wherever possible and continue to believe in, and preach it, even when human brokenness and complexity make solutions elusive.

A third lesson is that church leaders must communicate well with church members and work hard to maintain their trust. Pastoral matters are often sensitive, and confidentiality is important. It is not always appropriate for church leaders or those involved in pastoral care to talk openly about what they are doing. It is vital to gain the trust of the church so that there is no second-guessing, no gossip, and no questions about integrity. This will require church leaders to articulate their beliefs and standards, often through their preaching, while asking the church to trust that they will make wise and godly decisions in their pastoral care, decisions which it will on occasion be inappropriate to justify in detail to the church as a whole.

Fourth, it is important always to respond with love because life is complex and bruising. Doing pastoral care is all too often about caring for people who are broken and hurting. Over the years, we have met people who were hurt because of the way their church treated them and who, as a result, decided not to go back. Sometimes these situations are unavoidable and there is fault on the side of those who have taken offense, but where churches act with love, the wounds can be healed.

Finally, quality discipleship is key. Part of being a Christian is taking up the cross to follow Jesus. However, the crosses that God wishes us to carry are often heavy and splintered, requiring broad shoulders to bear them. Even while we give good pastoral care, we need to build people up spiritually so they have the fortitude to make the self-sacrifice that will lead to a life of holiness.

Having reflected on some of the challenges considered in this chapter, we need to remind ourselves that any one of them could be encountered in your church at any moment. Great wisdom is needed in dealing with them. It is also important that the church is always prepared and ready to respond whenever the need arises and this involves good planning, careful organisation, and constant vigilance.

For further study

1. Imagine you are a member of a group in church charged with the task of producing a paper on same-sex relationships. How would you go about this task and what would you include in the paper?
2. In difficult pastoral situations, how do we maintain the balance between biblical standards and caring for broken people?
3. Discuss the following case study, listing the range of pastoral questions that it raises. Then suggest ways in which each could be handled pastorally.

Case study: Lisa is a 17-year-old Christian whose family do not attend church and who claim no faith. She has a difficult relationship with her parents who are ambitious and driven, and they feel she is wasting her time at church. She has been accepted by a prestigious university to do medicine. Her boyfriend claims to be a Christian but does not attend church. She is involved in the praise band as well as being a leader in the youth fellowship. She is being mentored by an older lady in the church who is kind to her, but her mentor who is a forceful character is very critical of the elders and the church. One day Lisa tells her mentor that she is pregnant and that her boyfriend and her parents want her to have an abortion; she is beginning to think that is the right thing to do.

MAKING THE CHANGES

Focus on the process of change

CHAPTER 10

The Ground Rules

We are now at the point at which we can begin to reflect on what pastoral care looks like in practice. Pastoral care can sometimes occur from a chance encounter, but more often it requires thought, planning, and lots of prayer. We would not stand up to preach on Sunday without being adequately prepared and the same should be the case with pastoral care. There's an added complication in that we need to establish ground rules, so that we can work within a set of agreed parameters. This is because we need to make sure we are doing the right thing in the right way. Having good intentions is of itself not enough. We need to consider how we will deliver pastoral care and what rules need to be followed.

1. The glory of God is the bottom line

The first thing we need to ensure is that our ultimate motivation is the glory of God. Of course, that does not imply any reduction of care or focus on people. The object of our care is the people whom we pastor, and our concerns must always be for their welfare, but our primary motivation is still God's glory. If we did not have a love for God and a desire to serve him, our care would not be Christian. In that sense, a pastoral carer differs significantly from a social worker. The latter is concerned to help people to deal better with their circumstances, which, of course, is highly commendable. But the idea that God might become involved in an individual's life does not figure in secular caring, no matter how good it may be. Christian pastoral care is about encouraging people to know God in a deeper way and to commit to doing God's will in their lives, so that they can experience the blessing that that entails. The pastoral carer sees herself as partnering with God in bringing about change in the person's life.

Our hope in caring is that people's lives will be enriched through spiritual growth and holy living. The focus of our pastoral care, therefore, is not just that their lives will be emotionally healthy, but also that they are becoming more like Christ. When this happens, God is glorified. We care for people because we love God and want his will to be lived out in their lives.

Having clarity about our motives is very important because it is easy to do things—even the right things—for the wrong reasons. So rigorous self-examination is required. Pastoral care is a noble task, and our highest motivation is to ensure that God gets the glory. We need to ask ourselves why we're doing pastoral care in the first place, and what really motivates us to put ourselves out for others. Honesty in answering this question is essential.

2. Bad motives behind good actions

Some people get involved in pastoral care because they themselves feel the need for relationships. For them, pastoral care is a way of making friends and of dealing with loneliness in their own lives. They feel that, if only they can fill their lives with people, their own life will have meaning. This is not only a bad motive for being involved in pastoral care; it is also potentially dangerous. The problem is that the carer's need for friendship will become the driver in the relationship rather than focusing attention on trying to help the person being pastored. The carer will not primarily be thinking, 'What does this person need from me?', but 'What will I get out of this relationship?'

Closely linked is a desire to be needed. We can feel wanted and affirmed if there are people who depend on us. But this puts the focus on us rather than the glory of God or the person being cared for. If our motivation for caring is the desire to be needed, then we will encourage people to depend on us and their spiritual growth will be stunted as a result.

Ironically, another bad motive for getting involved in pastoral care is because we feel sorry for someone. Of course, compassion is important and pastoral carers should have genuine concern for the person whom they are helping. But merely feeling sorry is not enough. It is not sufficient if someone is facing a struggle in an area of their lives just to want to help them deal with that specific problem. The goal should be to help the person grow, so that they not only deal with the immediate issue but also develop the spiritual and emotional fortitude needed to deal with other trials that life may throw at them. This is important because it helps the carer to see the bigger picture. To use an analogy, if you are walking down the street and see someone begging, merely feeling sorry for them might compel you to buy them a sandwich. You might not feel quite so sorry for them after that. However, seeing the bigger picture might influence you to help the person find a job, which is a much more difficult thing to do, but it could result in the person no longer having to beg or go hungry. It takes genuine compassion to motivate us to make a difference in the person's life.

If our task is to ensure that God gets the glory, we need to ask what that will look like. What changes in a person's life will lead that person to honour God with their words, attitudes, and deeds? A clear picture of what this looks like will give us something to aim for in our pastoral care.

3. Respect for the individual

Another basic rule is that we must respect the individual. This is not always easy, especially if they have little respect for themselves. In some particularly difficult pastoral situations, we may be dealing with very needy people whose lifestyles and attitudes are, to say the very least, embarrassing. I once pastored someone like that. He was a man with considerable potential, but had never allowed that to develop. As a husband, he fell far short; as a father, he had little time for his children; as a businessman he was dishonest in his financial dealings. In addition, he had a drink problem, and these things combined to make him a generally unpleasant person. But he had become a Christian and therefore became my pastoral responsibility, which I found difficult because I was not drawn to him in any way. I had to see him as a new creature in Christ and learn to respect him as a human being if I was to see him grow as a person.

Respecting the individual has some practical implications. First, it means we need to be intentional about the aim of our pastoral care. We want the person to grow spiritually so that a genuine Christlikeness becomes part of their lives and they develop emotionally and thrive as individuals. In addition, we should want them to learn to make good decisions so that they can take control of their own lives and not be dependent on others. None of this will happen easily, but if we respect the individual enough to have high expectations of them, the outcome may well be a radically different kind of behaviour.

4. Keeping confidences

A third and fundamental ground rule is that of confidentiality. This is a crucial point to make because information is power, and we need to hold that power responsibly. When we get to know a person's deepest secrets and vulnerabilities, they have essentially entrusted us with some of the most sensitive aspects of their lives. If any of that were to leak out, the person we are caring for could be deeply hurt.

Confidentiality is a tricky thing. For example, we cannot just indiscriminately or absolutely promise to maintain confidentiality in every circumstance. In a worst-case scenario, the person might have committed some crime, or been a witness to a crime, or had a crime committed against them. Perhaps abuse has taken place and someone's life is in danger. In a situation like that, we cannot keep the information confidential, because the authorities need to be aware of it. Pastoral confidentiality is also complex when it comes to team leadership. Whether or not an actual crime has been committed, it may not be appropriate for the pastoral carer to keep the matter to themselves because, if a decision is needed by the leadership of the church, they can only reasonably do so based on a knowledge of what is going on. In such a case the person being pastored needs to be aware that information may be shared with at least some of the leaders of the church.

It is important to assure the person that you are trustworthy and will keep confidences, but this commitment has its limits, and you cannot guarantee it if what they disclose needs to be reported further. You could say that, if information does need to be passed on, you will let the person know what you are going to say and to whom. This will help to build trust. You should also assure them of your support through any consequences of this action.

Linked with this, we should stress that, when confidential information is disclosed, it must be given voluntarily. It is always dangerous to push for more information than people want to give. Sometimes this takes great patience. People who are dealing with very sensitive issues in their lives are often reticent to talk about them and so the pastoral carer needs to wait for the right time and gently encourage communication rather than to pressurise them to give information before they are ready. Unless those we're helping willingly open up, they will only tell us part of the story.

5. Maintaining boundaries

The maintenance of appropriate boundaries also requires thought. A boundary is a limitation that the pastoral carer establishes for their own protection and that of those being cared for. One boundary which they should impose is that of time. This would include the time that is allowed for pastoral care meetings, and the overall time the carer has to give to an individual. Without this, the demands of pastoring could dominate the carer's life. Some people lead very chaotic lives and therefore fail to adequately regulate their sleep patterns or their work and leisure time. They may want to meet with the pastoral carer at times which are inconvenient and unsuitable. They may also be needy psychologically, and express this by requiring other people to spend time with or on their behalf.

I remember being involved with a young Christian who had become quite nocturnal and was very undisciplined in managing his time. He arrived at my home at 11.00 pm one evening and stayed until after midnight. I did not mention how inconvenient this was for my wife and myself, but, when it happened a second time, I had to point out that, while I wanted to give him every assistance, we needed to establish when it would be appropriate to meet. It took some time to convince him that we needed new arrangements, but one good thing to come out of our discussion was that I was able to chat with him about the effect that his erratic behaviour had on other people.

6. Practical considerations

It is also important to begin any pastoral relationship with agreement on practicalities. Without these, the carer can become overwhelmed because the demands and expectations are too high, or they could find themselves in a compromising situation. This begins with reflecting on the time and place of any meetings. The pastoral carer must guard his or her own reputation and always be free of any suspicion, so the location and setting of any meeting requires careful consideration. Never meet in a location or setting that is compromising or which might allow for gossip or accusation. For example, if the carer is a married man who is meeting a woman, it would probably be fine to meet in the carer's own home if his spouse is also home at the time. Equally, the meeting could take place in a public venue like a coffee shop. However, it may not be appropriate to meet in the person's home, especially if the woman lives alone. Common sense should come into the decision. If an impromptu conversation is requested after Sunday worship (as often happens initially), it is better that that is conducted in public view, rather than withdrawing to another room alone with the person.

The same would apply for time limits. It is not unreasonable for a pastoral meeting to last for an hour, even if it is a relatively frequent meeting. However, longer meetings will become both problematic and counterproductive. The pastoral carer should also be aware of the possibility of sexual attraction or even co-dependency developing. Appropriate boundaries can protect against this eventuality. Tactile behaviour can also be dangerous and misleading, so the pastoral career needs to monitor and control this, especially, though not only, when dealing with persons of the opposite sex.

Meetings should only be arranged if there is a clear sense of responsibility and purpose attached to them. If the person being cared for regularly forgets to turn up or is late, then the underlying reasons need to be explored. Maybe the individual does not feel there is value in meeting or is not willing to commit to it. If no adequate explanation is forthcoming, it would not be unreasonable for the carer to discontinue meeting. There must also be clarity as to the purpose of meeting, for example, what are the matters to be discussed and what do we want to achieve.

It is important that the carer maintains control of the pastoral relationship. They should not let themselves be put in a situation where they are at the beck and call of the person being cared for. Such practicalities should be understood and agreed as part of the pastoral relationship. In this way, the care given will be purposeful and disciplined.

7. Pitfalls

Even with all these guidelines in place, there are still dangers we need to avoid.

First, we must not fall into the trap of believing we can solve everyone's problems. People are complicated and it doesn't take long working in pastoral care before we realise how little persuasive power we have in helping people to change. Of course, only God can heal a person or change their lives, and we must seek his will in every pastoral context. When we feel our own weakness, we remind ourselves that God chooses to use us; we are his hands and feet in ministering to others. But it is frustrating when we see people relapse and repeatedly stumble as Christians, despite our best endeavours to provide support.

It is also difficult to advise a person who is experiencing seemingly intractable problems. If for one moment we approach pastoral situations thinking that we have all the answers, then we set up ourselves and them for disappointment. There is no silver bullet and no perfect methodology.

Another danger is in directing people or making their decisions for them. There are various aspects to this. The best solutions are often those which are found by those we're helping. They are more likely to carry out a plan if it is their own idea. Also, being too directive creates a dependence which mitigates against spiritual and emotional growth. It also runs the risk of progress coming to a halt once the pastoral care ceases. Another important aspect is that, because we do not know everything about the person's circumstances, we might give the wrong advice.

A third danger is in socialising rather than giving counsel. This is a temptation we can easily fall into because intentional pastoral care is hard work, demanding focus and direction. It is much easier just to chat with people in a more relaxed way, wanting to strike up a rapport and develop a relationship with the other person. Of course, having a good relationship with them is important, but the pastoral carer is not just there to be a friend; their task is to help the person whom they are pastoring to find God's will for their life.

Finally, there is the danger of putting people in a box and being judgmental about them. When a person opens up in conversation, we get a chance to see what they are like, warts and all. Each of us has our failings and there are aspects of all our characters that are not very attractive. The pastoral carer must always be careful about not labelling the person and making assumptions about them. We may see the person as 'immature' or 'negative' or 'bitter', but they are still made in the image of God and valued by God. Pastoral carers need to see people in this way and believe in the possibility that God intends to do a work of grace in that person's life.

Pastoral carers should also focus on the real issues involved. It is easy to be side-tracked and miss what is actually going on in a person's life. People can often chat for a long time before they feel confident enough to raise the matter that is really on their mind. Good pastoral care involves entering every conversation with eyes wide open and being sensitive to every word spoken. Inevitably this will involve listening carefully and have the patience to keep listening so the person can genuinely open up. There is a spiritual component to this. Effective carers are not only listening to the person in front of them, but they must also be attentive to what God might be saying.

8. Trusting God

There is an important element of faith in pastoral care, and we need to rely on God in all that we do. We should consistently saturate pastoral ministry with prayer, but simply praying about a situation is not always sufficient. We believe that God can work miracles and there is nothing in his sovereignty that he cannot do. However, anyone who has had experience in pastoral work will tell you that people are not always willing to surrender to God's sovereignty in every situation. There are various reasons for this. First, it does not necessarily follow that, because someone is a Christian, they are walking closely with Jesus. Consequently, they may not have the spiritual fortitude to withstand the challenges which their pastoral situation requires. We can pray for them, but our prayers alone will not be enough to make a difference if they are not intentional about getting the spiritual basics right in their lives.

A second complexity we need to reckon with is regarding what God permits. While God is the great physician and can change any situation, there may be cases where, for reasons only God knows, he will allow people to suffer. This is equally true for people who love and serve him. Again, this can have major pastoral implications, especially when a committed Christian who has prayed about their situation and has found no relief, asks, 'why?' This is a question for which there is no simple answer. Ultimately, suffering is part of a fallen world and even fervent prayer does not change that. God might also allow the suffering because of the character building it provides. The pastoral carer must be sensitive to this reality, as well as to the hurts of the person being cared for. This should never take away from the need to constantly pray into a situation, but it should make the pastoral carer realise that just praying will not always bring about the result that was expected or sought.

9. Code of conduct

These ground rules are a necessary part of pastoral care. They give protection to both the carer and the person being cared for. If agreed and used properly, they will not be cumbersome. As a church establishes its pastoral care programme, it is a useful thing to have an agreed set of principles to which everyone involved in pastoral care signs up and follows.

There is great value in making these principles available to the wider church, so that everyone understands the basis on which pastoral care will be delivered.

For convenience, we have drawn up an example of a Code of Conduct, and print it below. Other examples can be found by seaching on the internet.

Code of conduct for pastoral carers:
An example

- Pastoral Carers will commit to respecting the rights and dignity of every person and to seeing them as a unique individual, equal in the sight of God, irrespective of and regardless of race, upbringing, religious belief, nationality, language, gender, marital status, sexual orientation, age, size, employment status, income, disability, or criminal record.

- Pastoral Carers will commit to being non-judgmental and to allow each person in their care the safety, freedom, and space to express themselves and to make their own decisions without coercion or manipulation.

- Pastoral Carers will not invade people's personal space and will always ask permission before physical contact. Physical contact must always be appropriate.

- Pastoral Carers will work to ensure that they do not misuse or abuse the trust that others place in them.

- Pastoral Carers will not threaten or subject any person to physical, psychological or verbal abuse or manipulate and spiritually harass them. They will not tolerate an environment where such behaviour takes place and will actively move to counter it. They will also commit to avoid insults, unwelcome sexual behaviour, inappropriate language, abusive humour, the display of offensive materials, and inappropriate gestures or signals.

- Pastoral Carers will not financially, sexually or emotionally exploit the people they are caring for.

- Pastoral Carers will maintain confidentiality, understanding that confidentiality does not necessarily mean secrecy.

- Pastoral Carers will be careful not to create an unhealthy culture of dependence for either themselves or others.

- Pastoral Carers will abide by all safeguarding regulations and the church's safeguarding policy, and take appropriate steps to seek medical, legal or other professional assistance where required.

- Pastoral Carers will seek to be honest and open, and to act with integrity.

- Pastoral Carers will commit to holding appropriate boundaries and will seek to relate appropriately without showing aggression.

- Pastoral Carers will seek to be good representatives of the church and to behave in accordance with prescribed church norms.

For further reflection

1. If a key goal of pastoral care is the glory of God, how should that inform our practice of pastoral care and our relationship with those we care for?
2. What difference will respecting a person have on the way we pastor them?

3. What challenges does the need for confidentiality pose, and how do we deal with those challenges?

4. Are there any other guidelines you think should be included in a pastoral care policy and, if so, what are they?

CHAPTER 11

The role of leadership

Having defined what a caring church looks like, we now need to think about the role of leadership in pastoral care. Unless leaders wholeheartedly embrace a policy of pastoral care for the church, it will never function effectively. Good will is not enough, there needs to be a commitment to develop pastoral initiatives. While much will depend on what church members themselves are willing to do, leaders need to be intentional about shaping and directing pastoral care. If they are not, it will not happen.

Of course, this presents a challenge regarding what leaders should do to transform their church into a caring community. We provide some answers to this question in the following pointers.

1. Leaders set the standard

We believe leaders set the standards and establish the culture, and it begins by modelling pastoral care in the leadership team. They can do this in several ways.

Pastoral care issues should be a regular part of the church teaching programme. This involves teaching pastoral theology, but it also means teaching basic Christian behaviour. For example, a new Christian who comes from a non-church background needs to learn the fundamental elements of what it means to live as a Christian. Examples of this might be learning how to read the Bible, how to behave at home or school, and learning how to behave when people disagree—that, as a Christian, it is not acceptable to lose one's temper, lie, or denigrate the other person.

It is not only new Christians who need to be taught how to behave in this context. As Peter says, Christians at every level need to be reminded again and again of basic Christian behaviour (2 Pet. 1: 12–15). I remember a brother who had a prominent position in a local church. He was a successful business executive and a good organiser. The problem was that he wanted to run the church in the same way that he ran his business. Everything needed to be done his way, so there was always hostility between himself and anyone who disagreed with him. He made life so difficult, and was so objectionable, that many good people, including two pastors, left the church. He was converted from a non-Christian background in his 40s, but no one had taken the time to explain to him that church life was not the same as business life. What he needed at the time was a Christian friend and mentor, but because he didn't have one, he assumed his business practices carried over into his Christian life. The church ended up in a much more difficult situation because of a lack of proper discipling at the early stage.

Leaders need to explain at the most basic level what kinds of attitudes and behaviours are required if all the members of the church are going to grow to maturity. The occasional sermon about behaviour will never be enough; a more systematic approach is required. This kind of training (and correcting of wrong behaviour) is vital if the church is ever going to establish a culture of mutual love and care.

Public preaching is one element, but so also is personal example. Leaders need to give priority to establishing quality relationships with each individual and family in the church. Each leader should seek the wellbeing of every person in the congregation. Ultimately, leadership is about maintaining good relationships with the people you lead. Great leaders will never be rude towards, or dismissive of people. They will have a genuine concern to see people flourish and reach their potential, and they will show a loyalty towards those they lead in good times and difficult times. In these ways, leaders establish trust and credibility. This is important because, when people feel confident about their leaders, they will be more ready to receive the pastoral care offered to them.

Leadership is not just about ensuring that the church functions efficiently; it is about equipping the saints for ministry. This too requires teaching, role-modelling, and encouragement. (Eph. 4: 12; Col. 1: 28).

Leaders also need to display unity as a team as they work together. Church members will always look for leaders who get on well with one another and support each other. They want to see a united team, graciously leading the church towards maturity. There is something very special about a group of leaders committed to Christ and one another.

But the church will not respect leaders who are seen to be arguing or undermining each other. It is particularly damaging when one leader maligns another behind his back. If leaders cannot resolve their disagreements, especially if they become public, church members will rightly see the huge discrepancy between their example and their teaching. If leaders are promoting a high level of pastoral care in the church and yet are failing to demonstrate it in the leadership group, the church will immediately recognise the hypocrisy. If they don't see care modelled in their leaders, they will never practise it in the church.

We must not assume that people automatically understand how Christians should relate to one another. Nor should we imagine that because the church has prepared a pastoral care policy that people will automatically buy into it.

2. Leaders assess the need

Building a caring community begins with assessing the needs in the church. This might seem a straightforward thing to do, but any proper assessment begins with asking the right questions. The first question we must ask is, do church members really care about each other? Many would assume that the answer is obvious and that it would be 'yes', but this is not necessarily the case. Sometimes Christians are not very caring, and some do not even think that it is their job to care. They go to church to enjoy worship and teaching, and to ensure that their family benefits from being part of a community, but they do not consider it is any part of their responsibility to care for other people or put themselves out for the benefit of others.

This lack of caring is not necessarily deliberate. Some churches are intimate communities where people know each other well and share their lives together. Others can be formal and distant: the church members may exchange polite greetings when they walk into the church building, but they don't go to the next level and get to know each other or get involved in each other's lives. In some churches there can be very little by way of conversation and interrelating. I have visited many churches (usually as a speaker) where very few people even say, hello. In such places, it would be possible to be a member, even for a relatively long time, and still not know anyone. It is the job of leadership to ask penetrating questions about what is really going on.

It is also the job of leadership to ask if the church structure lends itself to promoting a caring community. Structure is often an expression of what people think is important. For example, if a church focuses heavily on formal church services and expects members to attend, it may result in a lack of fellowship or sense of family. This could be solved by programming in opportunities for church members to come together in relationship-building activities. But such an outcome will only come about if leaders make it happen.

3. Leaders manage and review

Having set up pastoral care provision, leaders should take responsibility for managing and reviewing the ongoing process. Of course, managing something does not mean that leaders do it all. Other key people as well as members have a role to play. As we build a pastoral culture, our aim is to convince more and more church members to buy into the idea and commit themselves to caring for others. But, even so, the process must be supervised to ensure it stays on track.

How this is carried out in practice will vary from church to church, but good management of a project depends on such basic skills as observation, envisioning, motivating, and reviewing.

Regarding observation, church leaders must take note of two things: first, what pastoral needs exist in the church, and, second, how many people they can call upon to meet those pastoral needs. Some needs will be ever-present, such as those described in the chapter relating to the various stages of life and the challenges they present. Observant church leaders will know the age spectrum represented by their congregation and something of the personal circumstances of members. They will also have some awareness of those life-defining moments mentioned earlier in the book: who is getting married, who has significant and chronic health issues, who is approaching retirement, which families are experiencing heartache, and so on.

Good observation also notices people who will have something to offer in any pastoral care initiative. Actually, a range of skills will be useful. Clearly, people who are good listeners, empathetic, and who have naturally caring natures will be quickly recognised. However, given that good pastoral care requires organisation and consistency, church members who have good administrative skills can also play a vital role. They might not be on the 'front line' of the care being offered, but they can ensure that any pastoral care team or initiative functions efficiently.

Leaders also need to envision and motivate the congregation. Just because someone might be a naturally caring person, it does not follow that they will know how to deliver a pastoral care programme in a church context. If we rely only on their compassion, the pastoral care available in the church may be of outstanding quality, but it could also be patchy and erratic. It is a leader's job to paint the big picture, show what could be, and then motivate everyone to achieve the result. All of this means that the leaders of a church should ensure pastoral care receives the time and attention it deserves. We would suggest that every elders' or leadership meeting should give adequate time to pastoral care somewhere on the agenda. There is also real value in appointing an elder or leader to oversee the pastoral care of the church to ensure the vision is being delivered.

The leadership also needs to take responsibility for reviewing progress. A review process can make people nervous, as they fear being criticised for not doing something well enough. As a result, many churches fail in this critical element. But, if it is done in the right spirit in which everybody understands that the goal is the pursuit of excellence and not to find fault, the difficulties can be overcome. However, there does need to be recognition of human fallibility and willingness to learn and improve. This not only develops individuals; it also helps to grow the church.

Effective evaluation will depend on honesty and transparency, but it has to go further. It must also be positive, with leaders and members committed to finding good solutions, or at least the best way to progress. If we are afraid to fail or admit weakness, we will never get better at what we do. Exemplary leaders and committed ministry people can absorb disappointment, remain enthusiastic, and be willing to reinvent or reshape an approach to achieve maximum effectiveness. This will demand perseverance and willingness to keep thinking, but, if the alternative is a stalled or failing provision, effective review will be more than worth it.

A good evaluation process can pick up on important things. For example, it should identify if anyone is falling through the cracks and not receiving the pastoral care they need, or if those involved in pastoral care are struggling to meet their commitments. This is important for supporting people who have significant challenges in their lives. The evaluation might even conclude that some people in the church family have received a great deal of support and may no longer need it. Or perhaps an individual has been encouraged to make progress in his or her Christian life, but is making no attempt to put the necessary steps into practice. In cases like this, it might be reasonable for the carer to pull back a little. Whatever questions the evaluation raises, it should lead to a clearer understanding of how the church is functioning as a caring community.

4. Leaders create the culture

Leaders need to create the culture of a caring community. You can have all the programmes, the best technology, and endless announcements, but unless the church embraces a culture of caring, it will never be achieved. People often define culture as 'how we do things around here'. The expression reflects what is actually going on, and if the church is genuinely caring, as we indicated in chapter four, an obvious spirit of compassion and concern will permeate every aspect of its life. In one sense, it is something intangible yet real.When it is absent, there is a pervading sense of deadness which the visitor can immediately detect.

Creating that caring culture comes back to the leaders. If they teach that everyone is important—that being a Christian is not just about doctrinal correctness, but rather how we live together; if they emphasise the importance of brotherly love and insist that God's love needs to be mediated through each of us to others, then this will shape the church culture. Likewise, if the leaders model Christian love by taking an interest in people and showing that they care, their example will permeate the church and impact all its members. A positive, God-honouring, Christ-exalting, mutually loving culture doesn't just happen.It has to be worked at. It does not appear automatically.

There is no simple formula that leaders can use to produce this desired atmosphere. No leadership or management textbook can provide a tool or sequence of tasks that, when completed, will produce the radical change implied in the words, 'truly caring church'. It will only be achieved by the determined effort of leaders and members of the congregation to follow Christ and live as authentic Christians, caring for and loving each other every day as Christ cared for and loved us. There is no shortcut to this.

5. Leaders care through preaching

Finally, we must expand a little on pastoral care through the preaching programme. One of the most important functions of leadership is to make sure that the teaching and preaching programme is well thought-out and purposeful. Churches that don't pay enough attention to this will find their members lacking in spiritual maturity. Good teaching also provides a strong foundation for building a caring church. The preaching needs to include good content and be delivered by preachers with personal credibility.

As to content, preaching needs to be both theological and biblical. Theologically, many themes inform and shape the worldview of the hearers. We shall need to speak of the love of God, his grace and patience, but we shall also need to speak of his holiness, majesty, and sovereignty. We shall need to teach the value of each human being as made in the image of God, along with what it means to be a child of God. The practical outworking of these great themes will also figure in our programmes—themes such as developing a Christian lifestyle, demonstrating forgiveness and forbearance among Christians, and having compassion for lost people. If this theology saturates the minds of church members, it will be genuinely transformative.

The church preaching programme should also be biblical in the sense that we preach through the whole Bible. This will add to the theological knowledge of the congregation and bring other benefits besides. Think of the impact of teaching through the gospels and being challenged by the example of Jesus as he lovingly cared for people, including the outcast and the marginalised. Or consider some of the marvellous stories of the Old Testament in which people such as King David, Jonathan, Hosea, and Jeremiah showed great sacrificial love for others. And what about the challenges laid down by the Apostle Paul in iconic passages like 1 Corinthians 13 where he eloquently defines true Christian love, not to mention John's writings which are full of the concept of love. Consistently teaching biblical truth will mould a church and shape it for pastoral caring.

Pastoral preaching will combine diligent study with a real engagement with the congregation. Those who preach take an interest in the lives of the people they are trying to reach. They are willing to 'take up the towel' and serve through Christian love as well as teaching from the Bible. They are relational, and their concern and care for people comes out in their tone, eye contact, and empathy. They are known not just for their pulpit presentation, but for their desire to genuinely impact and support their congregation.

Preaching like this is ultimately the responsibility of leadership. Church leaders must decide who is qualified to handle and preach the word of God. This decision will determine whether the teaching programme in the church will just be an output of information or a transformative experience based on quality relationships and effective communication of great biblical truths.

Physician, heal thyself

We cannot overstate the importance of the role of the elder/pastor in the circumstances we have already described. Leaders are crucial to the success (or otherwise) of everything that goes on in church, because growth or decline so depends on the vision and leadership given by them. In most churches, the members have put their leaders in positions of authority, recognising their commitment and abilities, their extensive service to the church, and their years of study and patient teaching. Members recognise that they are the best people to lead the church, holding them in high esteem and sometimes mistakenly seeing them as living on a higher spiritual plain than 'the rest of us'.

Showing such respect is commendable, but it raises the question, 'who pastors the pastor?' In this section we will use the word 'pastor' to speak of full-time workers and those in the most senior positions of influence in the church or organisation (often termed 'elders'), though the questions raised apply to some extent to leaders at all levels.

Congregations can make it more difficult for the pastor when they hold him in too high esteem. Members often see their pastor as different. He is the one who knows the Bible, can answer difficult theological questions, and exhorts the congregation to follow Christ more fully. You can tell from his prayers and preaching that he is a spiritual person who has got it all together! (Historically, churches led by elders have regarded them as special in the same way.)

Many of us find it difficult to imagine that our church leader could struggle with the same issues that we face. But the reality is that those involved in full-time ministry, or who are leaders in churches, face exactly the same challenges. They have the same temptations and struggles. They battle to overcome sin in their lives; they struggle with resentment and jealousy, lustful thoughts, and undisciplined habits; they worry about finances, health, and family relation-ships as we all do. In short, they face the same temptations as everyone else. The only difference is that they are often much better at hiding it.

The pastor knows his people have high expectations of him, that he is supposed to be spiritual in all circumstances and must always be positive, encouraging, and godly. But he knows what he is really like and he often feels guilty about it. Too often, he goes about the business of the church on automatic pilot, going through the motions, but his heart is far from God. Somewhere along the way, he has lost his first love. He knows he is not the man he used to be and while he presents a spiritual front, inwardly he is a spiritual wreck.

Nobody knows what is going on in his family—that he fights with his wife night after night, or that his children are beginning to hate the gospel because he only has time for the church. Nobody knows what a burden preparing sermons every week has become, or what an effort it is to drag himself to his study. Putting on this show of spirituality has all but sucked the life out of him and his solution has been to numb himself with hours of late-night television, including programmes he would never have watched a few years ago.

This is the problem: that nobody knows what is going on behind the façade and nobody knows because nobody asks. A number of years ago I had got into the way of chatting with one of our young people over coffee after the Sunday service. We got on well together and spoke about all kinds of things, but on one occasion I asked, 'how are you doing spiritually?' He expressed astonishment at this question and commented that nobody had ever asked this question before. We talked for a while and I suggested that every time we met in church I would ask him the same question. Out of the blue he said to me, 'well if you are going to ask me, should I not ask you the same question?'

Actually, no one has ever asked me that question either. It's just not done in our polite, sophisticated society. Imagine a teenager asking an elder how he was doing spiritually. But my friend had made a valid point, so we had a little pact between us for several years that when we met on a Sunday, we would ask each other about our spiritual wellbeing.

It has only struck me now, when writing this chapter, that I had stumbled upon the solution to the problem highlighted in this section. The pastor is responsible for training the members to care for each other, but is, himself, in the greatest need of the very ministry for which he trains others. When Paul says that we are to teach and admonish one another (Colossians 3: 16), the pastor is not excluded. If we are to keep ourselves in the love of Christ, all of us, including the pastor, need the input of others. It is therefore most important for the church to ensure that means are available for the pastor to hear the voice of God. Paul Tripp says, 'Teaching enables you to see life God's way. Admonishing is helping you to see yourself God's way. It is standing you before the perfect mirror of God's Word so that you are confronted with the reality of who you really are.'[1] Tripp continues, 'Pastor, you need to be surrounded by well-trained teachers and faithful, loving admonishers.'

Church members must be willing to challenge the pastor about his spiritual life, not in a critical or judgemental way, but with love and concern—and the pastor must be willing to hear the word from God through his parishioners. But someone might say, 'the Bible says we are to respect our leaders (1 Thess. 5: 12; Heb. 13: 7), so surely it would not be right to rebuke or admonish him?' It is precisely because we hold our leaders in such high regard that we must challenge them. If the church is to grow, it needs its leaders to do their very best in leadership, and the membership must encourage the pastor to provide that leadership, even if it means raising tough issues.

It also follows that where the church is led still by a body of elders of equal standing with each other, one of their responsibilities is to challenge each other in the way implied by the preceding paragraphs. And as a body and individually they need also to seek the same spiritual openness with the congregation for which they are responsible.

---

1. Paul David Tripp, *Dangerous Calling*. IVP: Kindle Edition, p. 91, loc 1277.

What we are saying is that we are all in this together and that includes the church leaders. They must be prepared to remove the mask of pretend spirituality and acknowledge their vulnerability. Their job is to give advice to others, but their ministry may depend on accepting the gentle, caring rebukes of those who love them and understand they are still on their own sanctification journey.

The heading for this section is 'Physician, heal thyself' is taken from the words of Jesus in Luke 4: 23. Applied to pastors or elders, it would read 'Pastor/ elder, mind thyself,' which means not only lovingly teaching and admonishing the people in our care, but humbly allowing those we serve, to teach and admonish us.

For further reflection

1. It is said that the need for (and demand by church members for) pastoral care is almost limitless. What criteria should leaders and pastoral carers set as a way of deciding what priorities should govern their pastoral care?

2. How do you assess if someone is providing quality pastoral care?

3. What are the signs that someone is responding well to pastoral care?

4. Do you agree there is a difference between a preacher who is merely an expositor and a pastorally aware preacher? If so, how are the two different? And why should all preachers aspire to the second?

5. Suggest ways members of the congregation can provide pastoral care to their leaders and hold them to account.

CHAPTER 12

Church discipline and pastoral care

1. Distinctions

Pastoral care cannot deal with every problem or issue that occurs in a church. While good pastoral care can encourage people and help them draw closer to God and grow in their faith, there will still be times when even the best pastoral care reaches its limits. Human beings are free agents, and if they are determined to disobey God or live in a way that displeases him, pastoral care will not prevent this. There comes a point when church leaders, if they are being consistent with biblical expectations, may decide they need to act more robustly and apply church discipline.

The move towards church discipline is not a simple one. The very idea is countercultural, and it can leave a church open to criticism for intolerance. When the church's reputation or spiritual health is at stake because of the behaviour of some of its members, there is sometimes a need to act (Gal. 6: 1; Titus 1: 13). The New Testament is not slow in urging church leaders to do what is required to maintain the purity and health of the body of Christ.

Church discipline is something that I have written about before.[1] In my research for that book, two things gave me pause for thought. First, I spoke to a number of people who had been subject to church discipline and in most cases they were no longer involving themselves in a church. I realised that this was evidence of failure, especially as the purpose of church discipline is to challenge and help the individual to come back into full fellowship within the family. Second, having investigated several situations, I was surprised by how

---

1. Stephen McQuoid, *Discipline with Care*, Day One Publications, 2008.

quickly church leaders rushed into draconian disciplinary measures, when a gentler approach might have resulted in a better outcome.

Clearly, the interface between pastoral care and church discipline is very important, and we need to begin by thinking about some of the challenges that make this difficult for the church.

We first need to remind ourselves of the fallenness of our world. The Bible spares no blushes as it describes human society as utterly fallen and depraved (Rom. 1: 18–32). Of course, that does not excuse Christians who behave badly, but when the pervasive influence of a fallen culture is all around, we need to be realistic about the effects that it can have in the lives of Christians. Added to that are the twin evils of western individualism and the lack of objective moral standards in society. The latter means that, when we deal with Christians either pastorally or in the context of discipline, we need to recognise that the moral framework of our broader culture will make it difficult for them either to recognise what sin is or how serious it is. There will be many occasions when we simply have to recognise that many people will not see a particular action as wrong. But if the Bible is clear on the issue, we must submit to it. Even then, the individualism of our culture will leave a person asking what business it is of the church if they chose of their own volition to act in a certain way. The prevailing view of the culture around us greatly complicates many of these issues, so we must carefully explain that the church is not a democracy, and we are called to obey God rather than man. These situations will be among the most difficult that the church and its leaders are likely to encounter.

Given the challenges, we need to think hard about what our pastoral care and discipleship looks like. We should be slow to move towards church discipline and do it prayerfully. An interesting analogy which the Bible itself uses is that of an athlete who lives a very disciplined lifestyle in order to excel (Phil. 3: 14). In much the same way, we should see pastoral care and church discipline, not as a controlling mechanism to keep people in their place, but as a way of encouraging Christians towards excellence in their personal lives.

Another useful biblical analogy is that of the shepherd. A shepherd dedicates himself to caring for and protecting the flock, as well as leading it to nutritious feeding places. In the New Testament, Jesus is the great shepherd of the sheep (Heb. 13: 20). He then appoints church leaders to be shepherds of God's flock

(1 Pet .5: 2). Far from being a negative picture, it is positive and affirming. Jesus said that he lays down his life for the sheep (Jn. 10: 11) and this should be the attitude of those under him. This picture of a shepherd should inform how we do pastoral care, and if church discipline should prove necessary, it should also influence how we carry it out.

Before anyone protests that they are not a church leader, we must remember that no one involved in pastoral care is exempt from this responsibility. The job of encouraging each other and caring for one another is not just for church leaders, it is for all of us. Indeed, helping each other grow and experience the touch of God in our lives is a responsibility we all carry. We are all part of God's priesthood and therefore all have a duty to hold others spiritually accountable (1 Pet. 2: 9). It is not the leaders who exercise discipline; it is the whole church which must endorse and apply the leaders' conclusion on the matter (1 Cor. 5: 11).

When the rubber hits the road

We must now explore how pastoral care and church discipline fit together. What does the relationship between the two look like, and at what point and for what reasons might a church need to move from one to the other?

First, some things need to be said about pastoral care. Prayerful observation and early intervention are important. I have a Christian friend who is an alcoholic and, in the past, she has suffered much because of it. She realises the extent of her problem and is very self-disciplined. In twenty-five years of being a Christian, she has never touched a drop of alcohol, but she has other struggles which she is less able to handle. In some ways this is surprising, as she has proved to be disciplined and committed in her Christian life. Good pastoral care is about getting to know people and being able to identify what challenges they face. Equally, when problems do arise, we need to deal with them quickly. Better to 'nip it in the bud' than allow something to grow into a major challenge for the individual concerned.

Take Michael as an example. He is a successful business executive and committed Christian. Rumours began to spread that his business was in trouble and that some of his dealings were less than ethical. A couple of his church leaders were in the business community and were aware of the rumours, but did nothing until news broke that he had been arrested. At that point, they thought about church discipline. But it hadn't occurred to them that they had already missed the boat on pastoral care. We are not suggesting that better pastoral care would in itself have prevented disaster, but if applied much earlier it might have resulted in a different outcome.

2. The role of community life

Linked with the idea of the priesthood of all believers is the role which community life plays both in pastoral care and church discipline. We have already noted that the New Testament teaches that all of us as Christians are responsible for each other. We all have a role to play in encouraging each other to excel in our spiritual lives. The church is also a body that functions in unison in order to serve God (1 Cor. 12: 12–27). Communities, however, do not just happen automatically: they only come together through the process of shared experience and commitment. In essence, this is one of the defining marks of a church. It is not just a group of random believers, but people committed to sharing life together.

Even though church members share a common commitment to Jesus Christ and a desire to serve him, that does not mean that people in the same church will necessarily know each other well. I have visited many churches where the members are comparative strangers. Where there is no genuine sense of community in a church, we reduce the possibility of members helping each other to live successful Christian lives. People are not robots; relationships require time and effort to develop, and we can put no timescale on this process. However, when we put in the effort, the benefits to the community are significant. Some of these benefits are listed below.

First, genuine fellowship creates a sense of accountability. In the story of Cain and Abel, Cain kills his brother out of jealousy and when God asks, 'Where is your brother?', Cain replies, 'I don't know. Am I my brother's keeper?' Such distance had crept between them that Cain felt no sense of responsibility towards his brother. This kind of attitude exists within churches and can become the norm. In genuine community, members feel a responsibility towards each other, and this means sharing and speaking into each other's lives.

Love is also a feature of community. A fellow Christian challenged a friend of mine about his attitude to others. Interestingly, my friend did not get angry when rebuked, because he realised that the other Christian genuinely cared about him and the correction was done in a sensitive and loving way. He thanked the other Christian for his concern. An atmosphere of love and trust will ensure that Christians will be able to speak into each other's lives without judgment and in a spirit of friendship.

Third, real community promotes empathy. Even where love exists, there can be impatience which can inadvertently cause friction. A gentler approach will be taken if the person doing the correcting tries to understand the weakness and struggles of the Christian who has fallen. Moreover, if a forgiving spirit is part of the package, then the relationship can be preserved.

These attitudes need to be expressed in the church at all times. Churches that work at their relationships and create this kind of loving and compassionate community life will be better placed to maintain unity even in the context of church discipline.

3. What sins should be disciplined?

Good pastoral care will save the church a lot of grief and hurt. Ignoring it will lead to a build-up of problems, some of which may never be solved. That said, even with the very best of pastoral care and genuine spiritual growth taking place in the church, there will be occasions when this is not enough. We live in a fallen world and even committed Christians struggle to be utterly consistent in that kind of environment. Also, we are in a spiritual battle with the devil doing his very best to bring us down (Eph. 6). Given this, no one can assume they will never fall (Gal. 6: 1). Christians make mistakes and sin, and sometimes they develop patterns of sin that scar their lives and the lives of others. When this happens, there comes a time when the church must take assertive action through church discipline. The question is, what kind of situations require church discipline? The New Testament names a few such scenarios which we now explore.

Conflict between church members

The first problem is conflict between church members (Mt. 18: 15–17; 1 Cor. 6: 5–6). Of course, Christians can disagree over a whole range of issues and yet remain friends. But, sometimes an argument can be so heated that it can sever their previously cordial relationship. If the breakdown is long-lived and draws others in, the potential for division is very real: hence the need for decisive action. Jesus mentioned this in the context of an actual offence that one member commits against another (as in the Matthew passage referenced above). Again, the severity is such that there needs to be a process to deal with it.

The process outlined by Jesus was practical and uncomplicated. Stage one is for the person who has been hurt or offended to speak honestly, one to one, with the person who has caused the offence. Often this has the desired effect and the two people involved can talk it through and may even develop a stronger relationship. Sometimes this doesn't work, perhaps because the person refuses to recognise fault or is not sorry. If that happens, the offended party takes a couple of witnesses, to add moral pressure and enable constructive discussion to take place. If this does not work, the last stage is to involve the church or at least the church leadership, so that the issue can be finally dealt with.

Inappropriate social behaviour

A second issue that necessitates discipline is where Christians are involved in behaviour that people in the broader culture regard as inappropriate. If Christians do not conform to basic standards of conduct in society, they risk being a poor example to their non-Christian peers. In 2 Thessalonians 3: 6–14 for instance, Paul condemns Christians for being lazy and 'sponging' off others. This really gives Christianity a bad name.

Unspiritual behaviour

Similarly, Christians can get bogged down with unspiritual and frankly stupid behaviour, like the people Paul referred to in Titus 3: 8–11 who engaged in foolish and fruitless arguments. This was unhelpful within the church context, so Paul called for action.

Undermining leadership

Another obvious danger to the church is if members try to oppose or undermine the leadership. Hymenaeus and Alexander opposed Paul's ministry (1 Tim. 1: 20), so he took the radical step of handing them over to Satan so that they would learn not to blaspheme. Then in 2 Timothy 4: 14, 15, Paul mentions Alexander once more, stating that he opposed the apostle's message and did a great deal of harm. The apostle John indicates he would take the strongest action against Diotrephes (3 Jn. 10).

Gross moral sins

Gross moral lapses come into this category, as was the case in Corinth. In 1 Corinthians 5: 1–13 and 2 Corinthians 12: 21, Paul lists some sins which Christians should stay away from. They include such evils as incest, greed, idolatry, drunkenness, and robbery. If a member is guilty of such sins and refuses to repent, the leaders would need to take action.

Heresy

One last area is that of heresy, which the word itself suggests is a cause of division (*hereticos*—divisive person). When a Christian begins to believe something false, that is one thing; when they spread that belief around the church, it is quite another. Of course, Christians disagree about many matters, but the problem that the New Testament warns about are false beliefs that relate to the fundamental teachings of the Christian faith. These might include false teaching that relates to the resurrection (1 Cor. 15: 12, 2 Tim. 2: 18), or the gospel (Gal. 1: 8), or salvation (Col. 2: 8). Several New Testament books including, Hebrews, Peter and John's epistles, and Jude, warn against false teachers and state that if the church is not vigilant, they will creep into the church and cause massive damage. If leaders take no action, such false teaching spreads like a virus through the congregation with devastating results.

4. Beyond church discipline

The matters listed above may require church discipline. We have already questioned how we move from pastoral care to church discipline and stated that if good pastoral care is in place, the effects of these issues can be minimised.

So pastoral care is the best form of prevention. But what is the relationship between the two? When do you decide that pastoral care is not enough and move towards discipline? To answer this, we need to reflect more deeply by using some keywords, all of which have a bearing.

One such word is **grace**. Churches should never rush towards church discipline. While pastoral care should be given quickly and lavishly, church discipline should be a last resort when all else has failed. Leaders who are eager to 'punish' are not good shepherds; they are a danger to the flock and to the church itself. Grace should characterise all we do, and anyone who might ultimately need discipline should equally realise that we love them and that the church has shown them great grace.

Then there is the all-important word, **humility**. This has to do particularly with the attitude of church leaders, as they make the progression towards church discipline. When we help other Christians in their struggles, we are not claiming to be better than them, nor are we pretending that we don't have our own struggles. We are all sinners who do our best to follow Jesus, and we all fall short in many respects. But when the sin is of such a serious nature, leaders need to act decisively and any action should be taken with humility and tears. There is nothing more damaging or hurtful than a church leader carrying out church discipline in a smug or self-righteous manner.

The next keyword is **proportionality**. By this I mean that not only should we be slow to apply church discipline, but when we do so, we must not use a sledgehammer to crack a peanut. A surgeon would not create a large, open wound when keyhole surgery would be just as effective. This concept is entirely biblical because the New Testament provides a range of disciplinary procedures, beginning with very simple steps before getting to the more serious measures. For example, in Galatians 6: 1 Paul commands the believers to speak out when they see a fellow Christian sinning so that they can be restored. Likewise, in 1 Thessalonians 5: 14 he tells church members to warn the idle, encourage the timid, and help the weak. Jesus also spoke of Christians having a conversation with those they had been offended by (Mt. 18: 15).

Taking the issue to the next level would involve speaking to someone with two or three witnesses present (Mt. 18: 16, 17) and if this fails, it may be necessary to involve the wider church. The worst-case scenario is when leaders advise the church to withdraw from fellowship with the individual (1 Cor. 5: 11). At each step, we need to be very careful not to move too quickly to the next level and always pray that the ongoing pastoral care will bear fruit.

The last word we need to mention is **forgiveness,** and here again, the whole church has a role to play. If we as Christians cannot forgive each other, we should not be entrusted either with pastoral care or church discipline. Remember, Jesus forgave each of us so much, so we have not fully appreciated the forgiveness of Christ if we are not prepared to forgive others.

All of the key words we have just mentioned are very important, but we also need to recognise that we live in a fallen and broken world where life is not always as we would like it to be. Even when we deal with difficult situations with the right attitude, things can still go wrong. There are often unexpected developments which require leaders to act quickly to keep in advance of the situation and prevent further deterioration. Damage limitation is a negative concept, but it is very important because people can get hurt, the church's reputation can be tarnished, and the church itself can be divided because of the way things are handled. Church leaders need to recognise that perceptions matter and be very careful to communicate well with each other and with the church. It is extremely difficult to control perceptions, but honesty and transparency are the minimum requirements in seeking to mitigate further damage.

The end game

In all of this, we need to keep the end game in mind. The purpose of both pastoral care and church discipline is to encourage Christians to keep walking with Jesus and in full fellowship with their brothers and sisters. The scenario I mentioned at the start of this chapter, where people were subject to church discipline and then did not return to church, can only be seen as failure. It is not necessarily the church's fault, because the person themself could have become so spiritually cold that they really do not want to follow Christ. However, often the church has contributed to the problem by being too quick to move towards discipline, or by lacking pastoral care, or having wrong attitudes in either case.

For further study

1. Someone once said, 'Moving from pastoral care to church discipline is a difficult road for a church to travel along, and there are many casualties by the wayside'. What do you think they meant by this?

2. What are the main reasons why a church should begin to exercise church discipline?

3. Does church discipline bring pastoral care to an end? If not, how should we relate pastorally with someone who is being disciplined and what should be our guiding principles?

4. The crucial factor in the restoration of a fallen Christian is pastoral care. What issues do we need to consider as we support a person back into active life in the church family?

CHAPTER 13

The spiritual dimension 1— how God changes my life

We have emphasised in earlier chapters that the goal of pastoral care is to help people become fully mature in Christ. This involves a series of interactions between two people where one seeks to help the other to grow in faith. The helper, however, is not a dispassionate observer in this process, for he or she is also being transformed and from time to time requires help from someone else in his or her own journey to maturity. Change is taking place in both lives.

In this chapter and the next, we shall explore how this change takes place. We begin by looking at how God changes us. This will help us to have a deeper understanding of the change process which will not only deepen our own spiritual lives but will throw light on what is going on in the lives of those we are caring for. Not only that, when we see how difficult it is for us to make changes, we will be much more sympathetic and patient with those who are experiencing times of deep trouble and darkness.

When we observe God working in our lives, we will be in a much better position to help others in their time of need. In this chapter, we explore how God changes the life of an individual (this process is called sanctification). In chapter 14, we will look at how he uses the individual to change others (the process of pastoral care). A study of the doctrine of sanctification will require a much more theological approach than in our earlier material, but we strongly encourage you to work through the chapter because an understanding of this teaching will give you the tools to make significant advances in the life of faith.

1. Sanctification and pastoral care

Some basic principles are common to both processes.

Paul says regarding sanctification in 1 Thessalonians 4: 3, 'it is God's will that you should be sanctified', and talking about pastoral care, his instruction is 'bear one another's burdens' (Gal. 6: 2 RSV). There should be no doubt what God wants for our lives and for those we seek to help. God loves us as we are, but he does not want us to stay as we are. He has begun a work in us, and he intends to complete it (Phil. 1: 6). So, whether our concerns are for our own sanctification, or we are encouraging others to pursue it, we can have total confidence that all the resources of God are available to us. He has given us everything we need for life and godliness (2 Pet. 1: 3).

With this background, we must now explore what the Bible teaches about sanctification, not just theologically, but how it affects us practically. As we look back over our lives, many of us know there were times when we made significant spiritual progress, and other times when we felt we were failing badly. Why were we able to make progress at some times and not at others?

The answer is, it's all about the heart. Do you remember when you first fell in love? It was so exhilarating, and you couldn't wait to be in the other person's company. For many people, when we first became Christians, we felt like that about Jesus. We were amazed that the Son of God left heaven, came to earth, and died on a cross to save us from our sins. Our first encounter with Jesus created within us the desire to know everything we could about him. We knew the Bible was all about Jesus, so we couldn't get enough of it, reaching for it first thing in the morning and last thing at night.

It was our supreme delight simply to wait in his presence. Prayer and Bible study were not chores for us. They were the means of bringing us closer to the one we loved. Because of our love for him, we wanted to do what pleased him. We turned away from sin. We sought to magnify his name by speaking of him constantly to other people. There was no third party in this relationship.

Reflecting on those occasions when we made little or no spiritual progress, it is immediately obvious that the problem lay in the condition of our heart. Like the church in Ephesus, we had left our first love (Rev. 2: 4); like Demas, we had turned away because we loved this present world (2 Tim. 4: 10).

This is why the writer of Proverbs says, 'Above all else, guard your heart, for everything you do flows from it'.(Prov. 4: 23), and Jesus says 'For it is from within, out of a person's heart, that evil thoughts come—sexual immorality, theft, murder . . .' (Mk. 7: 21).

The fundamental lesson is that, if we are to make progress towards maturity and holiness, we need to get the heart right, and to do that:

(a) there are things we need to know (and believe) and,

(b) there are things we need to do.

2. Things we need to know (and believe)

Meaning of sanctification

Sanctification is a theological term used to describe the believer's standing before God and their growing in holiness. It is both an act and a process. The act is where God changes our status, setting us apart and making us holy in his sight. The word literally means to be separate or set apart for God. Every believer is 'sanctified in Christ Jesus' (1 Cor. 1: 2) and is called a 'saint', which basically means a 'sanctified person'.

The process is that progressive work in which the redeemed sinner (now a saint) is transformed to be more like Jesus in his or her life. It describes the moral requirement to resist sin and pursue holiness.

Sanctification begins

We begin with the initial act of sanctification which is called 'positional sanctification'.

At the moment of conversion, we were united with Christ and, because of our association with him, were sanctified—set apart by God as holy in his sight (Acts 20: 32; 1 Cor. 1: 2; 6: 11). Paul described the Corinthian Christians as 'saints' or sanctified ones. They fell short in so many ways, yet they are described as sanctified because of their new relationship with God. Positional sanctification has to do with our standing before God and not our spiritual state.

In Romans 6, Paul describes this change using the imagery of slavery. Before we were Christians, we were the slaves of sin, which meant we obeyed sin because sin was our master. But Jesus paid the ransom price for us on the cross as a result of which, another owner, God himself, bought us. This change of ownership means that there has been a decisive break with sin and our obligations are to our new master. Sin no longer has authority or jurisdiction over us. We are no longer under its dominion (Rom. 6: 14). It is most important that we grasp the significance of this truth.

Sanctification continues

Another change also takes place at the moment of conversion which the Bible describes as regeneration. This is when God gives us a new nature (Eph. 4: 24; 2 Cor. 5: 17). So, God not only changes our status, he changes our nature by giving us the Holy Spirit who takes up residence in our hearts, to guard and develop the new life within us.

Regeneration begins the second phase of our sanctification—sometimes called 'progressive sanctification'. We are no longer the servants of sin and Satan; we now belong to God. But our old master will not give up without a struggle, and progressive sanctification is a description of how we overcome our old nature and become more and more like Jesus. Sin has been deposed but not eradicated in our lives, resulting in a condition of spiritual warfare which Galatians 5: 16–23 vividly describes as the flesh warring against the Spirit. The flesh always works to pull us down, whereas the Spirit always wants to lift us up. Our task is to submit to the Spirit and crucify the flesh. Romans 7: 13–25 describes the intense, personal nature of this struggle.

This battle will continue throughout our lives, so we will never be able to say this side of heaven that we have achieved complete holiness. But neither should we ever say, 'I will never be able to overcome this sin, it will always be too strong for me.' That's what the devil wants us to believe and is totally contrary to what God wants for us. There may well be times of defeat, but there will also be times of glorious victory. The graph of our spiritual progress will not be a straight line, it will be jagged, but steadily pointing upwards.

Sanctification completed

Now we have arrived at phase three of our sanctification which will not be completed until we see Jesus and we shall be saved from the presence of sin. In that day, our struggles with sin will be over, and we will rest in perfect holiness in the presence of Christ. Jesus will transform our bodies (Rom. 8: 23; Phil. 3: 20), and we shall be completely conformed to his image, with nothing to mar our fellowship. We shall be like him, for we shall see him as he is (1 Jn. 3: 2).

The three phases of sanctification are illustrated in the following diagram:

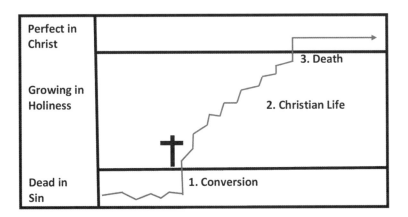

In summary, this is what we need to know:

> *God's plan for us is that we be holy, and he has given us everything*
> *we need to make it happen.*
> *God has bought us out of the slavery of sin, so we are no longer*
> *under its dominion.*
> *God is our new master, who calls us to obedience.*
> *God has given us the Holy Spirit as the source of power to*
> *overcome sin.*
> *We are engaged in a lifelong struggle with sin, but 'the one who*
> *is in you is greater than the one who is in the world'* (1 Jn. 4: 4).

Let me urge you not to skip over these statements but pray over them and ask yourself if you really believe what the Bible says about you. Take time to reflect on each idea and listen to what God is saying to you.

When I think of the importance of sanctification, I always remember the words of the great Scottish preacher, Robert Murray McCheyne: 'My people's greatest need is my personal holiness.' McCheyne was a powerful evangelist whose spirituality governed the whole of his life and ministry.

3. What we need to do

We not only need to know and believe certain things; we need to do certain things. The discussion for the rest of this chapter will focus mostly on 'sanctification continues'.

How do we become more holy?

All of us are aware of this struggle with sin and conscious of how often we fail, yet deep within us there is a desire for better things. We want to love Jesus and live the way he wants us to live. Our new nature craves that more than anything else. We know we need to be holy, but how do we actually achieve it?

The first thing we should notice is that growing in holiness is our responsibility. We need to be intentional about it. In positional sanctification, God did a work within us to which we contributed nothing. In progressive sanctification, we decide how we are going to live, so it is our responsibility to guard our hearts and be ruthless with sin. We must not think that change will come through some mystical experience; rather we need to learn to obey God in everything. God will not force holiness upon us against our wills.

Read the following verses carefully to see what God expects of us.

2 Peter 1: 5	Make every effort to add to your faith goodness; and to goodness, knowledge
Romans 6: 12	Do not let sin reign in your mortal body
Ephesians 4: 22–24	. . . put off your old self . . . and put on the new self . . .
Colossians 3: 5	Put to death whatever belongs to your earthly nature: sexual immorality, impurity . . .
Matthew 5: 29	If your right eye causes you to stumble, gouge it out and throw it away . . .
James 4: 7	Resist the devil . . .
2 Corinthians 7: 1	let us purify ourselves from everything that contaminates body and spirit, perfecting holiness out of reverence for God.

The thrust of these verses is unmistakable. If we are to become like Jesus, we have to work at it, but it is not something we do in our own strength; it is something we do by the power of God in us. In one sense, sanctification is active as described above, but in another sense, it is passive. We lay ourselves open toward God and allow him to do his work in us. Paul says, 'work out your salvation with fear and trembling, for it is God who works in you to will and to act in order to fulfil his good purpose.' (Phil. 2: 12, 13).

It is very encouraging to know that the Triune God is passionately interested in our holiness. God the Father sanctifies us completely (1 Thess. 5: 23); God the Son gave himself for the Church that he might sanctify and cleanse it (Eph. 5: 25, 26); God the Holy Spirit is transforming us into the image of Christ (2 Cor. 3: 17, 18).

God sanctifies us by an inward change which affects our intellect, emotions, and will. He has given us a new mind to know him (Rom.12: 2; 1 Cor. 2: 6–12), a new heart to love him (1 Jn. 4: 10) and a new will to obey him (2 Thess. 3: 4; Phil. 2: 13, 14). We are truly new creatures in Christ Jesus (2 Cor. 5: 17).

Sanctification not only makes demands on us spiritually; there is a very real physical dimension. Paul tells us that our bodies belong to God—therefore, we are to glorify God with them (1 Cor. 6: 19–20). We are not to let sin reign in our bodies, nor are we to present our bodies as instruments of unrighteousness to the service of sin (Rom. 6: 12, 13). We must give every member of our body to the service of God. As the children's chorus says, 'Watch your eyes, your ears, your lips, your hands, your feet; what do you see, what you hear, what you say, what you do and where you go'. It's an old chorus and it sounds simple and childish, but if we fail to heed it, it will have serious repercussions for our spiritual development. We all know there are things we do and places we go that stimulate the flesh, bring doubts or evil thoughts to our minds, and weaken our resolve to follow Christ, so we must reject them completely.

This active dimension of sanctification involves co-operation between God and the believer, as seen in Romans 8: 13 and Philippians 2: 13. This does not mean that the work is partly ours and partly God's: it is God's work. Growing in holiness only happens because God makes it happen. But he has chosen to make this growth possible through human beings as rational creatures, prayerfully and intelligently submitting to his commands.

4. The process of sanctification

The Bible describes several actions we need to take if we are serious about growing to maturity. We will look at three.

Mortifying the flesh, renewing the mind

The word 'mortify' is not a word we use very often, but it describes a powerful and logical concept. When we do use the word, we mean something quite different from its biblical sense. For example, we say 'I was mortified' when something highly embarrassing happened. But in the biblical sense, 'mortify' means to kill or subdue something. The word 'mortuary' belongs to the same word group. The idea of mortification is found in two passages in the New Testament: first in Romans 8: 13, where Paul says we shall live if we, through the Spirit, 'mortify the deeds of the body' (KJV).[1] The second occurrence is in Colossians 3: 5: 'Put to death, therefore, whatever in you is earthly: fornication, impurity, passion, evil desire, and greed . . .' (NRSV)

These passages stand in marked contrast with how we view sin in our lives. We rationalise it, accommodate it, and often give in to it. The Bible says there is only one thing we should do to it; we are to kill it stone dead. These verses make the same point:

> (1 Pet. 2: 11)   abstain from sinful desires, which war
> against your soul.
>
> (1 Cor. 6: 18)   Flee from sexual immorality.
>
> (Rom. 13: 14)   . . . do not think about how to gratify the
> desires of the sinful nature.

These, and many other verses, leave us in no doubt as to what the Bible demands of us. We are to stop sinning and do all we can to be holy. This will involve taking whatever action is necessary to remove ourselves from temptation and asking the Holy Spirit to give us the strength to see it through.

---

1. You can hear an excellent sermon on this verse by Martin Lloyd Jones at https:// www.youtube.com/watch?v=a0pGve9pVVo

This process is demanding because it is not always easy to say 'no' to self and 'yes' to Christ. The problem is that we love our sin; therefore, we need to love Jesus more. It is a matter of the heart.

Sanctification is an inner work with outward consequences. Mortification focuses on outward actions, which we will only achieve by the renewing of the mind and reviving of the heart. Turning away from sin requires us to set our minds on things above (Col. 3: 2) and focussing on Jesus. The mind (the Bible sometimes refers to it as the heart) is the powerhouse of our life; whatever is going on there, determines our attitudes and behaviour.

If we are to experience mortification and renewal, we must develop a biblical mindset—meaning that we will need to learn to think biblically. This means we must give ourselves to a regular and concentrated study of Scripture. There can be no progress in holiness apart from daily interaction with God through his word.

We would encourage you to look up all the Bible references mentioned in this section, meditate on them, and memorise them. The most important thing is to immerse ourselves in the word and let it saturate our being. We need to appropriate these truths in our thinking, so that we can leave behind our old thought patterns and replace them with new, spiritual thinking. There is no shortcut to this, nor is there any substitute.

Willpower alone cannot accomplish this inner transformation. We need to be reprogrammed through the Word of God by the power of the Holy Spirit (Phil. 4: 8). Satan seeks to keep the believer's mind unrenewed by constantly plying us with negative, sinful thoughts. Unless we replace the old ways of thinking with a new Spirit-inspired mindset, we will almost certainly fall back into old sinful habits, unbiblical beliefs, and harmful behaviour patterns.

Putting on and putting off

Closely related to the above point is the picture of 'putting off' and 'putting on' clothes. Paul exhorts us to 'put off' our former nature and 'put on our new nature' (Eph. 4: 22–24; Col. 3: 8–10). When we decide to finish with a habit, we create a vacuum, which if not filled with something better, will cause us to return to the old routines. So, we need to learn to replace sinful habits with biblical ones, which we can do through disciplined living in the power of the Holy Spirit, remembering that the ruling power of sin has been broken.

A couple of months ago, my wife and I agreed that we needed to get rid of some clothes to make room for some new things we had bought. Among the clothes destined for the bin was a fifteen-year-old jacket of mine. The problem was that I liked that jacket. I felt comfortable in it and still thought I looked smart in it. I struggled to put it away and I confess that, when my wife was not looking, I sneaked the jacket back into the wardrobe.

As I write, I realise that this is an excellent illustration of how we feel about sin. We know there are habits we need to put away, but, somehow, we have grown accustomed to them and, if truth be told, we quite like them. We can't bring ourselves to finish with them, and while we may make some progress in putting on the newer spiritual habits, every so often we just slip back into that old jacket. If we are going to embrace the new life of the Spirit, we must make a clean and decisive break with our old life.

The practice of the spiritual disciplines

God commands mortification and renewal—putting off and putting on—and he provides the means to achieve that through the spiritual disciplines. We reach maturity and holiness through discipline (1 Tim. 4: 7). Top-class athletes make their sport look easy, but it has taken years of rigorous discipline, long hours given to practice, and constant pushing of their bodies through every kind of pain barrier. They put themselves through these rigours because they want to be the best and they know only the highly motivated will achieve such levels of excellence. Paul uses the sporting metaphor for the spiritual life in 1 Corinthians 9: 24–27, which reads, 'I train like a champion athlete. I subdue my body and get it under my control . . .' (TPT). Paul goes on to say that if athletes submit themselves to such rigours for earthly recognition, how much more should we discipline ourselves for the Kingdom of God.

Christians through the ages have identified a range of spiritual disciplines to help us achieve spiritual victory. [2] They are rightly called 'disciplines' because

---

2. The following books have been much used by God in helping Christians understand the disciplines:Donald Whitney, *Spiritual disciplines for the Christian life,* NAV Press & Tyndale House, 1991 & 2014. & Dallas Willard, *The Spirit of the*

they are hard, and we would normally choose to do something else. They are designed to break existing behaviour and thought patterns so that new godly lifestyles can replace them.

There is no one definitive group of disciplines, but we have found Foster's arrangement helpful. This is shown in the table below:

Inward Disciplines	Outward Disciplines	Corporate Disciplines
Prayer	Simplicity	Confession
Fasting	Solitude	Worship
Study	Submission	Guidance
Meditation	Service	Celebration

Spiritual disciplines are not a guarantee of spiritual growth; rather, they put us in the place for God to work out his purposes in our lives. 'God has given us the disciplines of the spiritual life as a means of receiving his grace. The disciplines allow us to place ourselves before God so that He can transform us.'[3]

There are so many sins to be conquered and disciplines to be mastered that we might feel overwhelmed by it all. Our advice would be to deal with one habit or one discipline at a time. There is no way we can do everything at once. A good place to start would be to master the discipline of Bible study first, because knowing what the Bible says will be required for virtually every other area of life. It begins with really wanting to do it and, if you have no desire for this, you need ask God to change your heart. Choose what book of the Bible you want to study, then set aside a place and a time, free from distractions. There will be many occasions when you will not feel like doing it or are tired but being disciplined means you will do it anyway. I can tell you that when we drag ourselves kicking and screaming to the place of prayer, these are the times when God draws especially near to us.

Similarly, if you have some sin or habit preventing your progress, focus on overcoming it. Study what the Bible says about it and what help it offers

Disciplines: Understanding How God Changes Lives, HarperSanFrancisco, 1988.

3. Richard Foster, *Celebration of discipline: The path to spiritual growth*, Hodder and Stoughton, 2008, p. 6.

for dealing with it. Ask yourself questions about this sin, for example, when and in what ways does it most impact on your life, how does it affect you and the people around you, why does it have such a grip on you? These kinds of questions will help you, not only to understand the problem, but to devise a strategy for dealing with it. We might need to curtail or even eliminate certain activities, for example, choosing to spend time with different friends, putting filtering software on our laptop, or setting up an accountability arrangement with someone we trust.

All this takes time and perseverance but, as we deal with one aspect then another, we discover that the new habit is becoming second nature to us and the old has gone. It takes an initial commitment, but one which needs to be renewed every day, for this is a fight which will never let up.

This can be illustrated in the context of dieting. We know that we will lose weight if we eat fewer calories each day than we need and, if we do this over a period of weeks, we will see ourselves becoming the slim, trim person that we want to be. We know there will be some foods we must not eat, so we don't buy them in. We know that other foods will help us to lose weight, so we make sure they feature highly in our diet. It's the same in the spiritual life. If, each day, we do those activities that lead to holiness and refuse the things that lead to sin, we will establish habits that will build our faith and enable us to live a life of victory.

If we don't start the diet, we shall never lose weight. Similarly, if we never start those daily habits with God, we shall never build our faith. If we completely blow our diet one day, we can get back on track the next day, and so it is with the disciplines. We can fail badly today, but God will welcome us back when we confess and repent, and we can return to the spiritual routines tomorrow. It's one thing to want to lose weight or progress towards maturity; it's another thing to actually start and keep going. Start today . . . and every day.

5. Bringing all this together

In the first part of this chapter, we identified several things we needed to know and believe.

Here, now, is a summary of what we need to do:

Be intentional about turning from known sins.
Learn to see sin the way God sees it.
Identify specific behaviours that drag you down and devise
strategies to help you overcome.
Walk in the Spirit and be obedient to his promptings.
Get to know Jesus—crucified and glorified.

The bottom line in this pursuit of holiness is that we must integrate into our thinking all the things that God has provided for us; and then we must obey the instructions that God has given to us in his word. What we believe about God and ourselves determines how we live and behave.

The idea of holiness is often ridiculed in today's society. Many see it as puritanical and embarrassing, often characterised by negatives—prohibiting people from doing things or going places that they enjoy. The caricature is one of stern, intolerant, critical people who take a position of superiority over others. It is very unattractive, showing so little of the grace of Christ to whom we must look to see what perfect holiness is. His outward actions and attitudes sprang from an inner relationship with his Father. He was separate from the world in heart and mind, and yet visibly associated with sinners, whom he loved to the extent of giving his life for them. He rejected the world's values, having no concern for fame or power.

Holiness is the end result of giving ourselves, as Jesus did, to the service of God—laying aside our ambition, helping the vulnerable around us, and standing against personal sin and social evil. This kind of holiness is not wimpish, weak, or cowardly; it is strong, noble, and resolute, and is the only kind of holiness that will make a difference in this world and be pleasing to God.

6. The final word

We recognise this has been a long and sometimes difficult chapter. We have devoted much time and space to it for two reasons. First, because it allows each of us to reflect on our own progress to maturity; this is most important because if we are not growing in faith, how will we be able to help others to do so?

But, second, when we understand how difficult it has been for us to increase in holiness, we will be a little more understanding of the challenges facing those we are caring for. We will also be a little more patient when they do not progress as quickly as we would like.

For further reflection

1. Define in your own words what sanctification is and how we can achieve it.
2. How do we renew our minds (Rom. 12: 2), and why is this important if we want to be holy?
3. Part of sanctification involves 'taking off' our old nature while 'putting on' a new nature (Eph. 4: 22–24). Give some actual examples of what is involved in this process.
4. How do we establish new spiritual habits and remove old ones?
5. In your own words, describe the activity required of Christians from these verses (Col. 3: 5, 8; Mt. 5: 29; 2 Cor. 7: 1).

CHAPTER 14

The spiritual dimension 2—
How God uses me to change others

In the last chapter, we looked at how God changes us to be more like his Son. Since the Bible gives the same instructions to all Christians regarding spiritual growth, it is reasonable to assume that God's work in others will be similar to his work in us. So, in helping others towards maturity, we are in a position to offer insights from our own experience, although these will only be tentative because we must not assume their circumstances are exactly the same as ours. One further source of help in caring is the recollection that many people drew alongside us in moments of difficulty, so now it is our turn to do the same for others.

In addition, many more resources are available to us as we enter this helping process. Over the last few decades, there has been a revival of interest in biblical counselling, fostered by such writers as Adams[1] and MacArthur[2], and more recently by Kellemen[3] and Tripp[4]. These writers have helped to establish such organisations as the *Biblical Counselling Movement*[5] which exert considerable influence, particularly in North America.

Two basic principles of the biblical counselling movement are that the resources available to us in Christ and his Word are sufficient to deal with all

---

1. Jay E. Adams, *Competent to Counsel: Introduction to Nouthetic Counseling,* Zondervan, 1970 & 1986.

2. J.F. MacArthur & W.A. Mack, *Introduction to Biblical Counseling: A Basic Guide to the Principles and Practice of Counseling*, Word Publishing, 1994.

3. Robert Kellemen, *Gospel Conversations: How to care like Christ (Equipping biblical counselors),* Zondervan, 2015.

4. Paul David Tripp, *Instruments in the Redeemer's Hands: People in Need of Change helping People in Need of Change,* P&R Publishing, 2002

5. https://www.thegospelcoalition.org/reviews/biblical-counseling-movement/

the issues of life and the instructions given in the Bible are addressed to the whole people of God and not just a few leaders. We very much welcome these emphases, but the counselling and church contexts in North America are much more structured than in the UK, and American churches make much greater use of formal counselling processes. We agree that pastoral care is a job for the whole church, but we also recognise that some difficult cases are better handled by skilled professionals.

That said, we have found the writings of the counselling movement very helpful in understanding how God uses pastoral caring to influence others. As the title of Paul Tripp's book suggests, every church member is an instrument in God's hand to make a difference in the lives of those around us. Tripp calls this 'personal ministry' and Kellemen describes it as 'one another counselling', but both are based on the conviction that God works out his purposes through caring relationships for the benefit of both participants. Much of the material in this chapter picks up on some of the key themes of Tripp and Kelleman.

1. 'One-another caring'

Kellemen insists that biblical counselling must not be given over to professional experts, but should be part of the life of every local church. He shows that every believer has some level of competence to care for someone else. He bases much of his teaching on Romans 15: 14, where he identifies four qualities of the pastoral carer:

- Character: 'full of goodness'
- Conviction: 'complete in knowledge'
- Competence: 'competent to instruct'
- Community: 'brothers/one another/'

He makes much of the contribution of the Christian community, emphasising that every church must train people to care for others. The role of the pastor is not only to do pastoral care, but to equip the congregation to do it. A therapist can have an input into somebody's life for an hour a week, but a church can provide care by a range of people, in different ways and over many months and even years. This explains the benefits of providing pastoral care through the natural networks and ministries of the church.

Tripp makes the same point when he says, 'God uses ordinary people to do extraordinary things in the lives of others.'[6]

The apostle Paul provides further details of his approach to pastoral care in 1 Thessalonians 5: 14, where he uses five distinct words to describe his care for these young believers: (urging, warning, encouraging, helping and being patient): 'And we urge you, brothers and sisters, warn those who are idle and disruptive, encourage the disheartened, help the weak, be patient with everyone.' So pastoral care is about urging, warning, encouraging, helping and being patient with everyone.

Kellemen sees the first two words in the above list as important: 'urge'—from the Greek 'parakaleo'—carries the meaning of comforting someone and walking with them in times of trouble. The same word group speaks of the Holy Spirit as our 'paraclete' or 'advocate', signifying one who comes alongside us to help. Getting close to someone in times of trouble is called 'parakaletic' counselling.

The second word from the list above is 'noutheteo', translated 'warn', which was developed by Jay Adams into the system known as 'nouthetic counselling'. That system claims the answers to all life's problems are found in Scripture, so Adams is very sceptical of contemporary psychology. Nouthetic counselling takes sin seriously and seeks to effect change by encouraging greater conformity to the principles of Scripture. This explains the emphasis on admonishing and instructing towards a different way of life. We would see value in both the parakaletic and nouthetic approaches, without confining ourselves to any one system, so carers will sometimes use one approach, then the other, but always based on loving concern for the individual so he or she can benefit from the blessings God has for them.

2. Ambassador

Paul Tripp helpfully compares the pastoral carer to an ambassador. The job of an ambassador is to speak on behalf of the person or country that he represents. He does not offer his own thoughts or opinions, but says what he believes his master would say were he present. This is our task as pastoral carers. Every time we care for others, we must remember we are on duty for

---

6. Paul David Tripp, *Instruments in the Redeemer's Hands*, Kindle edition, p. 18, location 401.

Christ as his ambassadors. Conversations are not just chance encounters, but are opportunities to further the Kingdom of God.

In every conversation with friends or people whom we meet, we should be open to the possibility that God might use this encounter to communicate his message for us through our interlocutor, or that he might want us to speak into the life of that person. We have all experienced chance encounters which ended up in deep conversations where the other person has thanked us for being with them at a critical point in their lives. Most of these encounters were unplanned, at least by us, but not by God. But maybe we need to be more intentional in asking ourselves, 'What does Jesus want me to say to this person, and how should I say it so they can hear the words of Jesus behind this human voice?' Tripp says when we learn to think like this, we can become God's instrument of change in another person's life.

Being an ambassador

The question is 'how do we do this?' Tripp says, 'It is almost embarrassingly simple. Love people. Know them. Speak truth into their lives. Help them do what God has called them to do.'[7]

When we tease out these four elements, the instructions are clear:

1. We must offer **love and hope.** We show that we care and that there is a way ahead.
2. We must **know and understand.** This requires careful listening, to find out why the person is so upset.
3. We must **speak and encourage.** This involves sensing God's truth for our interlocutor and helping him or her to see God's purpose for them for the future.
4. We must **plan and act.** This involves preparing an action plan for lasting change.

Whenever we engage in helping another person, focussing on these four elements will help us keep on task as ambassadors for Christ. Although there is some logic to the order, we should not regard this process as consecutive,

---

7. Paul David Tripp, *Instruments in the Redeemer's Hands*, Kindle edition, p. 275, location 4354.

but rather, we hold all four elements in our minds, emphasising each one at various points, as the discussion dictates.

Let's imagine that a friend (whom we'll call Ruth) has come to you for help with a problem, perhaps an illness or losing her job or some family problem. It could be any of a hundred things. The situation is affecting her emotionally and spiritually, because she thinks she has let everyone down and doesn't know what to do to make it right. Even worse, she is questioning her faith in God and wonders if she believes any more.

The question we want to explore now is, 'How do these four elements guide us in providing the encouragement that Ruth needs in order to get to a better place?'

Element 1: offer love and hope

Proverbs 27: 6 says, 'Wounds from a friend can be trusted.' We are most receptive to advice from trusted friends, because we know from our past relationships that they are with us and for us. They can speak to us frankly about our faults, and though we may feel offended at the time, we know they are trying to help because they are concerned for us. Pastoral care is best done when that kind of relationship already exists.

We should point it out that there is no standard procedure or model appropriate for every situation. Caring for other people is not a tick box exercise or a pre-scripted programme. It requires wisdom, sensitivity and much dependence on God.

The apostle Paul is a great pastoral care role model. With the Ephesian church, he admonished them: 'for three years, I never stopped warning each of you night and day, with tears' (Acts 20: 31). To the Corinthians, he says his heart was 'opened wide' to them (2 Cor. 6: 11), and to the Thessalonians he says he had been like a loving mother and a strong supportive father (1 Thess. 2: 7, 11). Paul was totally committed to his people, and we need to say to Ruth that we are committed to her.

Basic to good pastoral care is the building up of warm, trusting relationships over many years. When we have a history of integrity and reliability with our people, they know they can trust us and will be much more prepared to turn to us in times of trouble. They need to know that we will care and not stand in judgment on them.

Show love

When Ruth comes to us, the first requirement is to listen carefully and sensitively to her story. We need to give her time to explain her situation and express her feelings. We remember the word 'parakaleo' and show a willingness to enter Ruth's world—to walk with her for whatever time it takes. Ruth needs to know that we have heard her struggle and that we are there for her. We're not going to just offer a few platitudes and then walk away.

Our task is to stand with Ruth at this low point in her life. We may agree that her situation is very difficult and acknowledge that there is a temptation to give up on faith, but we disagree with her conclusions. We cannot accept that God no longer loves her, or that she has no future. Kellemen says we want to establish the point that 'God is good, even when life is bad.'

We can gently say to her that she may turn away from God, but God has not turned his back on her. Instead, he is inviting her back to himself. We will seek to convey that there is light at the end of the tunnel and, even in a terrible situation, it is possible to hope.

Instil hope

People who have had life-shattering experiences, like divorce or the death of a loved one, need hope and to come to believe that God is on their side. We can remind them of a verse in Isaiah 63: 9 that 'in all our distress, he, too, is distressed'. It's not a good idea at this point to preach a sermon, but when the time is right, we will want to remind Ruth that God loves her and has a purpose in and beyond her present difficulties, even if she cannot immediately see or understand what that purpose is. Our task is to help her to see Jesus, who is our hope (1 Tim. 1: 1), and to understand that, in him, change is possible.

As ambassadors for Christ, we are messengers of hope, but it must be a biblical hope, not a false hope. Many people think their problems will disappear if only they could change their circumstances. They might think, 'if I could just get married' or, 'if I could get a better job' or 'if only God would heal me of this sickness', then everything would be fine. We must never encourage them in that error by promising their desires will be met.

False hope is based on human ideas of what is pleasurable and desirable, and the problem with this kind of thinking is that we base it on the physical and the temporal rather than on the spiritual and the eternal. Genuine hope is a biblically based expectation of good, based on the promises of God (Rom. 4: 18; 2 Pet. 1: 4). It is the acceptance that God's plans for our lives will bring true and ultimate happiness. We need to help Ruth to look away from the problems and look up to see God's solutions. Kellemen's point here is that, 'It's normal to hurt, but it's possible to hope.'

In the approach laid out above, we have assumed that Ruth is a Christian. If someone asks for our help who is not a Christian, of course we offer our services, but at some point, we must go back to basics and explain the gospel. We must constantly keep in mind that, while we may work with hurting friends, in trying to find practical solutions to their problems, our main aim is not just to get them to feel better, but to experience change at the deepest level. For non-Christians, this begins with a saving commitment to Christ.

Element 2: know and understand

This is the next stage in describing the process, but in practice, just by listening to Ruth's story, it has already begun. These steps are not sequential, but concurrent, with one or more taking priority as required. With Ruth, we have been listening carefully and offering hope at the same time. Getting to know someone is not as easy as we might think. The reality is that we don't know people as well as we think we do. We have many casual, superficial conversations which allow us to hide who we are. If someone asks us how we are doing, the standard reply is 'I'm fine, thank you.' We have almost designed these kinds of conversations to maintain a distance between us. How often the person asking doesn't really want to know, and the person answering doesn't really want to tell.

If we're going to know and understand someone, we will need to get beyond the casual. It will take our best listening ability to understand what is going on. We will also need to ask the right questions in the right way, gently and lovingly to ask such questions as 'what exactly is the problem?'; 'how did the situation arise and was there anybody else involved?'; 'why do you think this has happened to you?'; 'can you describe any reason for it?' Always ask open-ended questions (what? how? why?) which cannot be answered with a simple 'yes' or 'no'.

This element functions alongside the love and empathy which undergirds the relationship. We love the person sufficiently to give the time to listen to their story. We also love them sufficiently to ask some deep, penetrating questions, but we must remember it is not an interrogation—it is a conversation.

Having listened carefully, we must not rush to make assumptions. How often in conversation do we think, 'I am not sure if I trust this person' or 'This person is so self-centred and manipulative' before we have allowed them to finish what they have to say? We must guard assiduously against jumping to conclusions. We don't have all the information about the person, nor will we ever fully understand why they are in this predicament. In the well-known Bible story, when Eli saw Hannah's lips moving but heard no sound, he assumed she was drunk and condemned her without so much as smelling her breath (1 Sam. 1: 12–14).

What about the hard cases?

Ruth's request for help is fairly typical of the kind of situations where pastoral carers at level 1 and 2 (as described in chapter one) can make a difference. External circumstances had caused her life to collapse, and she sought help from someone with whom she had a long-standing relationship. But sometimes we are confronted with much harder cases. The remainder of this chapter offers advice on one such case. The application of elements three and four will illustrate the kind of work that still needs to be undertaken with Ruth, but at a much deeper level.

In cases like the one outlined below, we recommend that, if anyone feels in any way out of their depth, the case should be referred to someone with more experience. This is not an admission of defeat; it is an acceptance of reality, and does not imply failure.

Advice for elders

Let's imagine the case of a man we will call John, a long-standing member of the church, who has approached you as his pastoral elder because he has got himself into a terrible mess. He admits he has been unfaithful to his wife and spends a lot of time watching pornography on the internet. Over several years, he has become addicted to gambling, which has resulted in the accumulation of significant debt. He does not try to excuse himself, freely admitting his life is a total sham and his behaviour has brought great distress on himself and his family.

As with Ruth, we will begin by extending love and hope, then seek to know and understand. So we let John know that we see him as a brother, a friend, and a fellow Christian. No matter what the outcome may be, we want the best for him and, as far as we are able, we will stand with him at this difficult time, even though we cannot condone his actions. We will be very careful not to be critical or judgmental while we listen to his story. We must resist the temptation to think something like, 'How could he have got himself into this mess?' A more relevant question to ask might be, 'How could he have got into this mess and no one in the church has noticed?'

Kelleman's advice, as noted above, when dealing with people whose circumstances have brought them to their knees, is help them get to the point at which they recognise that, 'God is good even when life is bad.' But, where an individual's sinful lifestyle has contributed largely to his or her downfall, our task is to journey with the person to reach the point of conviction that 'God is gracious even when I am sinful.'

We must allow John to state both the facts and the feelings of his wrongdoing, and then explore together with him what the Bible has to say about the issues. Our goal is to help him come to realise how God feels about his actions and how he can come back to God to find peace. This will be a very painful conversation, requiring great wisdom and sensitivity. We must ask the deep penetrating questions if we are to really know and understand what is going on in John's life. This process may well be embarrassing for both of us, but the aim is to bring John to where he accepts that he needs to have an encounter with God in order to bring about a permanent change from the inside.

These discussions will take place over many meetings and will generate a great deal of information which we must sort out in our minds to understand what is going on. This will require much prayer and study as we seek to find what the Bible says about John's circumstances. We want our conclusions to be biblical, so that John can hear what God is saying to him. In all of these discussions, of course, we must not forget the issue of confidentiality. We may not always be in a position to share the details with our fellow leaders, but if we do, they must also be aware of the importance of confidentiality. If we do not share details with them, for whatever reason, we at least need to highlight that there is an issue and ask for their prayer support.

Element 3: speak and encourage

Most of us probably feel relatively comfortable in helping people in the ongoing business of life. However, the problem comes when we get involved in difficult, one-on-one situations, particularly those requiring tough conversations. Most of us baulk at having to rebuke or criticise a friend. It doesn't feel right, and we are afraid that it might destroy our relationship, so we stay silent.

But saying nothing is not in our friend's best interests, and it is not what God wants. If God has brought John to ask for our help, it is because he intends to use this relationship to further his purposes. This is how God brings about personal transformation. We remember that we are ambassadors for Christ, so our task is to bring John face-to-face with God's word but not in a harsh or humiliating way; it will be persuasive, thoughtful, and kind. We are to 'speak the truth in love' (Eph. 4: 15). Often it is best to have two people in leadership involved in such a challenge as they can keep each other accountable and also because, if the challenge leads to any complaint, there are witnesses to what was said.

Tripp says, 'The question to ask yourself is, "What does this person need to see (about himself, God, others, life, truth, change) that he does not see, and how can I help him see it?" Our goal is that through the things we say (message), the way we say them (methods), and the attitudes we express (character), God will change the heart of this person. God is connecting us with people so that he might complete his work in their lives.'[8]

Having listened very carefully and considered what John has disclosed about himself and his circumstances, in a spirit of prayerful submission, we are now ready to speak with John. It is better to express our thoughts as questions by saying something like, 'This is what I think is happening in your life just now, here are some issues I see at the heart of the problem and here are some suggestions for what I think you need to do to turn your life around. Do you think I have got this right?' We mustn't tell him that this is God's word for him. He has to arrive at that conclusion for himself and acknowledge the part he has played in creating the situation in which he now finds himself.

If John agrees our understanding is correct and expresses his willingness to put his wrong behaviour behind him in the spirit of repentance, then he is ready to move on to the next stage. Evidence of a genuine desire to move on with God will be seen if he does not try to rationalise his behaviour, blame someone else for his problems, or point to some mitigating factor to explain his actions. He is acknowledging that the problem is his, and he is looking to God to guide him through it.

At this point, we might think we have finished our task, but we must be careful not to leave too early. One further element remains.

Element 4: plan and act

God has challenged John to make some changes to his life. He has learned about things he needs to 'put off' and things he needs to 'put on': he wants to commit to a different lifestyle. He knows that change is not some automatic, mystical experience; it will demand hard work, but he is ready for that to achieve his goal. He also recognises that he cannot do this in his own strength, but he believes God will give him the power to make the changes.

So, how does this work out in practice? Over many years, John has developed a range of habits which will need to be broken and replaced with new ones. He will need to develop alternative ways of thinking, different strategies for dealing with temptation, and new routines to help him grow in grace. He

---

8. Paul David Tripp, *Instruments in the Redeemer's Hands*, Kindle edition 2002, p. 213, loc. 3429.

will need to spend more time in Christian activities and with Christian people, while also severely restricting the time he spends on the internet. All of this will be necessary, because he knows the temptation will be intense and he means business about not going back to his former way of life.

Our task here is twofold: we help John identify what he needs to change, and then we help him prepare a strategy to implement that change. It is tempting to think that, because John is now ready with God's help to change his life, we can just leave him to get on with it. He may know what he needs to do, but it is unlikely that he knows how to do it. So, we will want to assure him that we will continue to give him every support until the old habits have gone and new habits are the norm. We will commit to walking with him until he can stand on his own.

Habits are learned ways of living, established by doing them repeatedly until they become so ingrained as to be second nature. This kind of life change will require an action plan through which John will commit to undertake certain actions to deal with the specific changes that he wants to implement in his life. It will also involve a level of accountability so that he can report on progress made. John needs to agree that he will take responsibility for and be accountable for the three issues requiring immediate attention: his marriage, his debt, and his pornography addiction.

Each of these issues presents its own difficulties and the process will be much easier if John has help from a variety of people; his wife and family, his pastoral carer (who may also involve the church elders), and perhaps a small group of male friends who will study and pray with him or include him in more healthy pursuits. He needs a group of people around him who will spend time with him, particularly when temptation runs high.

But John must also agree that he will be honest with his wife and be willing to account for his movements, 24/7. Similarly, he will report to his group of friends weekly regarding progress, or lack of progress he has made in finishing with gambling and pornography. There must be honesty and transparency in 'putting off' his past life, and we must hold him to account for 'putting on' the alternative lifestyle in the power of the Spirit. Accountability means that we are not leaving John to 'get on with it'. We know he can't do it by himself, so we are walking with him for a while. But we are making demands on him not to lie to us and say he has changed if he has not. Our intentions are not to catch him out doing wrong, but to give him every help to do what is right.

We do not pretend that this chapter has been easy. Working through the details has been demanding, but if we remember the 'embarrassingly simple' quotation at the beginning of this chapter, with God's help, we can make a difference. '*Love people. Know them. Speak truth into their lives. Help them do what God has called them to do.*'

We finish this chapter by quoting Tripp's summary of an ambassadorial lifestyle:

Core truths of an ambassadorial lifestyle[9]

Truth #1. We need God and his truth to live as he meant us to live.

Truth #2. God has called each of us to be his instruments of change in the lives of others.

Truth #3. Our behaviour is rooted in the thoughts and motives of our hearts.

Truth #4. Christ has called us to be his ambassadors, following his message, methods, and character.

Truth #5. Being an instrument of change involves incarnating the love of Christ by sharing in people's struggles.

Truth #6. Being an instrument of change means seeking to know people by guarding against false assumptions, asking good questions, and interpreting information in a distinctly biblical way.

Truth # 7. Being an instrument of change means speaking the truth in love.

Truth # 8. Being an instrument of change means helping people do what God calls them to do by

---

9. Paul David Tripp, *Instruments in the Redeemer's Hands*, Kindle edition, p. 272, loc. 4309.

clarifying responsibility, offering loving accountability, and reminding them of their identity
in Christ.

For further reflection

1. In what sense are pastoral carers acting like ambassadors (2 Cor. 5: 20)
   and why is this element so important for their ministry?
2. Read the following verses and discuss how they apply in a pastoral
   context: Prov. 27: 6 & 9; Acts 20: 31; 1 Thess. 2: 7 & 11. To what
   extent do these verses describe the pastoral care that takes place in
   your church?
3. How can a church get beyond superficial relationships, so that real
   caring and spiritual support can take place?
4. Read through the 'Core truths of an ambassadorial lifestyle'. Which
   three do you most need to give attention to in your life and why?

CHAPTER 15

Pastoral care: the web and social media

Perhaps the most significant and life-impacting change in recent years has been the development of technology, especially in the area of communications. Today, it is virtually impossible to find a house that does not have a TV, Wifi, and a whole range of other electronic devices. Likewise, it is almost inconceivable that someone would not have a mobile phone. These things are now necessities, not luxuries.

The question could be asked, what is the relevance of a chapter on social media to a book about pastoral care. Given the significant influence social media can have in the lives of Christians, those charged with offering pastoral care ought to have a concern about this and want to highlight its potential dangers. Many Christians spend more time online and watching TV than they do in church or reading their Bibles. The influence this can have on their lives should not be underestimated.

The use of social media has become virtually universal. An increasing number of people have a Facebook page, use their Twitter feed, and regularly post images on Instagram or a similar platform. These are popular media and great tools for communication. We use them to keep in touch, to build and consolidate friendships, and also to learn. Few people who make use of social media are unaware of this, but there are dangers we need to watch out for.

When we look at the book of James, it is interesting to see how he deals with the way we communicate with each other. He is aware of the blessing speech can be but, given our fallenness, there is always the temptation to use our tongues for wrong purposes such as lying, gossiping, or slander. As James says, the tongue is set on fire by hell itself (Jas. 3: 6). We could say much the same about social media which can bring many benefits, but which can also cause much harm.

Pastoral carers should also be aware of what people are posting, not in any monitoring way, but simply because a person's social media postings can be an indicator of how they are doing spiritually. The information in the remainder of this chapter is intended to help carers understand the influence and workings of social media, and be able to help anyone caught up in it.

1.   The benefits of social media

We will start by looking at the blessing social media can be for pastoral care. Used properly, it can be a real asset to any church. The essence of platforms such as Facebook is that they tell a story about people. That story is not always accurate because people only tell us what they want us to know. People will post happy photos and comments, because they want to portray only the positive things about their lives. But this may be a cover for lives that are deeply troubled. That caveat aside, it is nevertheless a good way of keeping in touch with people and being aware of important events in their lives. Much the same is true of platforms such as Instagram and Twitter. A general awareness of what people are posting online can give us an understanding of what is going on in their lives.

These platforms are not only useful for getting to know people and their circumstances; they also provide a facility for communication. Texts and Messenger fulfil the same function and are a great asset in pastoral work. If someone hints or overtly states through a social media posting that they are struggling or have had some disappointment, it is good practice to get in touch with them. What you say does not need necessarily to be visible to the general public, though it is appropriate for a message of encouragement to be open to view in some contexts. More often, a message sent by Messenger or a text to the person will be better. The point is that once you pick up on something, it is good to be able to respond quickly. I have often spoken to Christians who have expressed great appreciation for all the encouraging messages they have received and all the promises of prayer. In some cases, that encouragement made a significant difference and enabled them to go on.

2. Ground rules to prevent harm

Having noted the positives of social media, we must also recognise its potential for harm. Just as we can be guilty of sinning with our tongues, so we can use social media in a destructive way.

While this technology did not exist in Jesus' day, other spiritual dangers did, and Jesus warned his followers there were wolves that would scatter the sheep (Jn. 10: 12). Paul also warned the Ephesian elders to 'be alert' because of the 'fierce wolves' who would not spare the flock (Acts 20: 29–31). For many people in churches today, the internet and social media can be like a fierce wolf that could cause significant spiritual harm.

The challenge for pastoral care is that technology presents us with lots of different 'wolves', each of which is easily accessible to church members and can be accessed in the privacy of their homes, offices, social settings, and hotel rooms. Danger is just a click away. The Covid pandemic exacerbated the problem as many Christians found themselves isolated in their homes because of lockdowns and devoid of meaningful church fellowship.

Given this, it would seem clear that we should consider media habits to be a discipleship issue. Since it can be toxic as well as helpful, we need to teach Christians how to be discerning, how to develop good habits, and be disciplined about their media use. This, of course, will involve more than just including it in Sunday sermons. Conversations about social media and the internet should be a regular feature of pastoral care, both one-to-one and in small group and discipleship group settings. It is also helpful to offer practical advice on the use of social media. One way of doing this is to establish a simple list of 'don'ts' that we need to watch out for, such as the following.

Don't complain

The first thing to watch out for is people who are always complaining—for example, on their Facebook site. Of course, we have all struggled at times and it is appropriate to share that struggle with interested 'friends'. However, there is a big difference between sharing a struggle and continually populating social media with complaints and moans. A negative frame of mind is not healthy, and neither is it good for the people who read constant negative comments. When a Christian constantly expresses hurts, grievances, and disappointments, we must ask if that is a reflection of their relationship with God and their inability to deal with life's struggles.

Equally, it is not healthy to convey constant positivity and optimism, especially if it does not reflect reality. Yes, it is good to be thankful and to rejoice in the good that God has provided, but we should also guard against a boastful attitude. I have noticed some social media sites where users are always posting pictures and making comments about holidays, luxury weekend breaks, new clothes, the latest gadgets, or expensive jewellery that they have purchased. They present a picture of how wonderful and successful their family members are and how much other people admire them. Three issues here are worth considering. First, it can be a form of pride. Second, it may be an overworked attempt to convey a false impression that life is all sorted, covering up deep-felt feelings of insecurity and inadequacy. Third, it can have a negative impact on others who can't afford such luxuries, or on hurting people from broken families. Rejoice in God's goodness, but don't boast about it.

Don't criticise people

A critical attitude is also something we need to avoid. Sometimes, we should use our social media platform to speak out about issues that matter. I have spoken out against such things as racism, abortion, greed, the persecution of Christians, human trafficking, and a range of other issues. This is entirely appropriate. What is not acceptable is criticism of specific people, in intemperate or abusive language. The problem with social media is that we can be so 'brave' saying things from the safety of our laptops that we would never say if we were speaking directly to the people we are maligning. Even hard words should be 'gracious, seasoned with salt' (Col. 4: 6).

I have cringed as I have read posts written by Christians who have de-nounced politicians and leaders referring to them as 'idiots' and 'liars', not only questioning their every move and motive, but also suggesting that they have never done anything virtuous or good. Of course, there are many politicians whom I strongly disagree with, but that does not make them bad, nor does it make me correct or accurate in my analysis of them. This can sometimes be the gossip and slander that the Bible warns us against. Equally, I am troubled when Christians criticise fellow believers and churches. Such maligning is unhealthy, especially in such a public forum.

Don't engage in meaningless theological speculation

It is inadvisable for Christians to engage in online theological debate in an aggressive and un-Christlike spirit. There is, of course, a place for discussion in which the participants are seeking deeper understanding of the matter. Years ago, at Bible college, I took part in a debate with a fellow student on the question of baptism. I held believer's baptism, and he was committed to infant baptism. We both argued our views strongly, but with respect. He was a good friend and someone whose spiritual life I greatly admired. The strength of our relationship was evident, and it was both sincere and good-natured. That was a good context for Christian discussion, not least because all the witnesses were also Christians.

Social media can, however, be a bad place for theological debate, because anyone can observe, and the discussion can get out of hand. I have witnessed several such debates which quickly descended into *ad hominem* (against the person) attacks. One of these was on the authority of Scripture, which is an important, but complex, subject that needs to be treated with care. A friend of mine inadvertently began the debate by quoting one of his favourite writers who was a controversial evangelical scholar. It wasn't long before someone chastised him online with the assertion that this writer was a 'heretic' whose books no true Christian should read. This led to a serious, ill-tempered argument on the reliability of Scripture with new people joining in. Many of the points being made in the debate were inaccurate and even untrue, and it was clear that some participants only had a very superficial understanding of the subject matter. This, however, did not stop them expressing their opinions forcefully and often showing no grace or tolerance for the opinions of others. The fact that this debate could be witnessed by many, including non-Christians, negated whatever good the participants hoped to achieve. It was embarrassing and unedifying.

Keep private things private

A similar problem is when people use social media to speak negatively about others. I have witnessed the unpleasant reality of people who talk about their family members, fellow church members, or workmates in a critical manner. This is unfair as the person being talked about cannot defend themselves. It is all about perspective. The person who is being critical about someone else or about hurts they have sustained may not be accurately describing the situation. What they are claiming may not be true, but even if it is, social media is not the place to raise it. Again, I have witnessed everything from one Christian condemning the alcohol consumption of a friend to someone who stated online that her father had abused her. Neither comment was appropriate, and the audience had no way of verifying the truthfulness of either statement.

Don't drop hints

Of course, all the above can be done using vague language and terminology. Christians do not usually want to be accused of gossip or criticism, so they use language that is suggestive rather than overt. They do not name the other people, churches, or situations, but they write so as to leave no doubt as to whom they are referring, using their version of events. Maligning others by inferring wrongdoing does not make such interventions right, nor excuse tittle-tattling about it.

Don't virtue signal

This is another nasty habit where people make themselves appear 'virtuous' by condemning things that they believe to be wrong. It is a kind of 'one-upmanship' common among celebrities and people in the media, but is not pleasant or appropriate coming from Christians. In essence, it reveals a moral pride.

Of course, we are right to condemn things that we know to be wrong like injustice, racism, or human trafficking. However, our motive can be to make ourselves seem morally virtuous, which is a very different thing. For example, during the Covid-19 lockdown, some people criticised others for not keeping to all the guidelines, while stating as loudly as their digital medium permitted, that they had been 'model citizens'. In a similar vein, I have witnessed people saying that they would not go to a high-profile Christian event because the organisers were not sufficiently discerning about the speakers or worship leaders invited. Such false piety in a public setting does the Christian faith no credit.

Don't fight every battle

A final challenge worth reflecting on is that of people who respond to everything that they don't like on social media. Responding is a huge temptation, especially if you are someone who reacts strongly to injustices, hypocrisy, stupid comments, poor arguments, and unpleasantness. There are times when we should all feel compelled to respond if people make offensive remarks. I have often observed arguments brewing online, and I have tried to pour oil over troubled waters to prevent the online debate from going too far. Wisdom dictates that we should not only choose our battles, but we should also be careful about how we fight them. All too often well-meaning Christians react in such a way that fuels the argument rather than resolving it. We should always consider the nature of the audience for any social media posting. We can express some opinions in a small close-knit group, which might create havoc if taken to a larger audience. It is part of our Christian responsibility to be peacemakers as well as defenders of the truth.

Of course, it is one thing to note these misuses of social media; it is quite another to deal with them. That does not mean we should do nothing. If church leaders and pastoral carers do not get involved in situations like this, they will continue unchecked. Once someone gets used to using social media inappropriately, they will continue to do so and often push the boundaries even further. When pastoral carers note regular misuse of social media, they should act out of a sense of love and encourage those involved to be wise in how they contribute.

3. Dark side of the web

As already stated, the misuse of social media is not the only issue about which those involved in pastoral care need to be concerned. Other dangers lurk beneath, the most obvious of which is pornography. We have already mentioned this in a previous chapter as one of the addictions raising pastoral concern. However, it deserves mention here because of the sheer accessibility of pornographic material on the internet. It is said that pornography was the first product to make money on the internet and this is where most people engage with it.

Not only is pornographic material very easy to access: it also spawns some deeply unpleasant issues such as sexting and online grooming. The lack of regulation of the internet means that the depth of online depravity is limitless and much of it is available for free. We should not be so naive as to assume that Christians don't dredge through the worst of this material and become addicted to it. If a church is to take the matter seriously, then this must become a pastoral priority.

Because of the enormous stigma attached to pornography, it is important to talk about its dangers openly and preach on the subject. Peer groups also have a vital pastoral role to play. I have participated in several men's events where there was serious teaching and discussion on the dangers of pornography and many churches set up accountability groups which are in themselves a safeguard. When pastoring men of all ages, we should bring this subject up regularly and create a safe space for honest discussion. There are also practical things that we can do to help. It should be mentioned that pornography can also be a challenge for women.

First, there needs to be a reminder in our teaching and pastoral counselling that women are made in the image of God and should be respected. Whatever women a man may look at as he views pornography, we need to remind him that she is someone's daughter, or sister, and possibly even someone's mother. She is a human being, loved by God and created in his image. Pornography is inherently demeaning and must be rejected. There also needs to be a reminder that we are called to be holy and to act radically against lustful thought (Mt. 18: 9). Where pornography is being used, there is also masturbation, which can also be habit forming. The accompanying fantasies also objectify people which is spiritually and emotionally harmful.

Second, pastoral care involves praying with those who struggle and encouraging them to pray for power to resist. It is also a good thing to encourage them to pray for women caught up in and exploited by the porn industry. A friend of ours who is a pastor has suggested that among the young people in his congregation, there are very few who don't watch pornography in some form or other. The prevalence of this issue is exemplified by the popularity of TV shows such as *Naked Attraction*, which demonstrates the seriousness of the issue.

A third thing is to encourage healthy habits and practices in life. Many small steps can be taken which will work cumulatively to provide safeguards. For example, married men can be encouraged to share their computer password with their wives and talk openly with them about holiness challenges. There are computer software programmes that build in accountability structures. It is equally helpful to be aware of danger zones, like channel hopping when on your own, or computer browsing when no one else is around. Also, the regular reading of scripture and Christians books that build up faith are important habits to foster.

A second significant addiction worth returning to is that of gambling. In much the same way as Christians can get caught up in pornography, they can also form gambling habits. Once more, the internet provides easy access. Here is where the danger lies. Most Christians would not frequent a bookmaker or ever visit a casino. However, in a world where most vices can be found online, they don't need to. No one needs to know, not even members of the family. Gambling may not be as widespread as pornography, but it is just as addictive and destructive.

As we've already said, good pastoral care will take various forms. There needs to be clear teaching on the subject. It is not something that a Christian can justify doing, but in the complexity of life, we often blur the distinction between gambling and entertainment. Many Christians do not see taking part in the lottery or bingo as gambling. Neither would they be concerned about things like slot machines, seeing them as entertainment rather than gambling. The problem here is that something which may appear benign can lead to something more serious, dangerous, and addictive. The analogy of a slippery slope is appropriate here.

We should also encourage practical, realistic, and open pastoral conversations on these issues. When we care for people, we get to know them and that is the appropriate context for speaking into someone's life. A general rule of thumb is that, where we see behaviour that might become destructive, we should lovingly speak up—not to criticise, but gently to caution and encourage a healthy lifestyle of holiness that avoids any appearance of wrong. Of course, this is much more difficult when these things are being done in the privacy of home and with the anonymity that the internet provides. This is where quality relationships pay dividends because it allows for openness and a better awareness and knowledge of those who struggle.

For further reflection

Project 1: Draw up a code of conduct for church members on the use of social media.

Project 2: How would you respond to someone who might argue that pornography is nothing more than harmless entertainment?

Project 3: Here is a short list of do's and don'ts of internet use:

Do: Be careful what you say.

Use what you say to bless others.

Avoid wasting time.

Be a bold witness for God.

Pause before you publish.

Keep Jesus at the centre.

Remember your internet use reveals who you are.

Be careful of cyber friendships.

Ignore constant negativity.

Don't: Text and tweet while having dinner or conversation.

Text it if you can't say it in person.

If you wouldn't say it, don't text it.

Don't blindly trust all 'Christian' sources.

Don't give in to 'Christian' peer pressure.

Do you agree with these lists? Are there any other aspects you think should be added?

CHAPTER 16

Caring for carers

In recent years, the media have profiled a good many cases in which very prominent people—politicians, journalists, CEOs, celebrities—were accused of abusing their colleagues or staff. The abuse was mostly verbal, where the person in power used the tactic of shouting, being rude, or publicly humiliating those under them. The defence offered was always that the 'boss' was so focused on the task that that he or she needed to use a confrontational approach to get the job done correctly. Such aggressive tactics have no place in church leadership.

Coincidently, I was aware of a couple of Christian workers who had to take extended sick leave because of burnout. For me, this pointed to the opposite extreme where congregations were completely unaware of the pressures which these workers faced. The church has a duty to support everyone involved in any kind of ministry, and while our focus here is on pastoral carers, we believe the principles described apply across all the activities of the church.

In previous chapters, we have described what pastoral care is and the range of needs pastoral carers often encounter in the church. We now want to discuss the church's obligations and commitments towards those who engage in a caring ministry.

We have defined the purpose of pastoral care in the words of Colossians 1: 28, 'that we may present everyone mature in Christ.' We will have a better idea of our task if we reflect on how Paul understands this expression. The complete verse reads: 'He is the one we proclaim, admonishing and teaching everyone with all wisdom, so that we may present everyone fully mature in Christ.'

1. The task

The verse begins, 'He is the one we proclaim'. The reference is, of course, to Christ who, as verse 27 says, lives in the heart of every believer. Paul does not preach himself or his opinions on politics or theology. He preached Jesus as the Creator and Reconciler of all things (1: 16, 20). This is where pastoral care must begin. We must direct people to Jesus, to whose likeness we will, one day, be conformed and who alone has the power to transform us in this life.

We point people to Christ by admonishing and teaching. Admonishing means warning or gently reproving and, in Paul's case, tears often accompanied it. Teaching means to impart instruction or explain doctrine. Both verbs are in the present tense (1: 28), meaning they are done continuously and often. Paul adds that we must do this with love and wisdom, always in the individual's best interests and for the glory of God.

Further, Paul says in this verse that his instruction is for 'everyone'. He is not speaking to a few people, but to every Christian. The word 'present' is sometimes used in the technical sense of a priest placing an offering on the altar. Paul's aim, as he labours for his people, is not to offer dead sacrifices, but living saints, fully grown in Christ.

Verse 29, and the first few verses of Colossians 2, highlight that Paul gives every ounce of energy to this task. He uses a range of words to describe intense struggle and labour that leads to exhaustion. For Paul, this task of caring for new Christians is not optional but an all-consuming passion. But he is also careful to point out that the source of his energy comes from God, who provides the power to change the lives of the Colossian Christians (1: 29).

Using 'ordinary people'

I suspect most of us would say in response to Paul's example, 'I could never care for others in the way that Paul did.' Paul was an experienced pastor when writing these words, but his ministry was with fear and trembling (1 Cor. 2: 3). All of us have to start at the beginning. We can be confident that the God who called and equipped Paul for service will prepare us for whatever ministry he has for us. We can see parallels to this in the world of sport. Suppose we want to be a great tennis player. We don't become the world's number one on our first day. We will need to train and practise for years, and the chances are that we will never be number one, but that should not stop us from getting started.

Another factor in getting started in pastoral care is that our involvement will be within our own circle of influence, that is, our friends and people we meet on a regular basis. We have already established relationships with those around us, some very close to us and some a little further away, but at least we have some measure of contact.

Several years ago, my wife and I were friendly with a lady and her husband in the church. She was very outgoing and committed to the service of Christ. There was an older couple in the church who were struggling to deal with the changes taking place and were negative about almost everything. My friend found it very difficult to cope with this and would go on and on about the older couple. On one occasion, following a rather lengthy tirade, I suggested to her that she needed to repent of her attitude. It was a kind of throwaway remark, and we all laughed. However, it must have got through to my friend because in the following weeks she reached out to the older couple, eventually establishing a very warm relationship with them and being of considerable help to them in their later years.

I would never have dreamt of speaking like this to someone whom I didn't know well, but I could make the remark without offending because of our long-standing relationship. Pastoral care sometimes begins in small ways, but can often have profound effects. If our relationships are healthy, it is possible to raise matters which might otherwise be difficult. For the record, I would need to say that my friend occasionally called me to repentance, if she felt I had not done things quite right. All of this in no way impaired the relationship.

In rounding off this section, we should take a moment to look at the fourth chapter of Colossians. From verse seven to the end of that chapter, Paul expresses deep gratitude to a whole range of people who laboured with him—ordinary people, but who each contributed in their own way. Paul expresses his debt of gratitude to so many people who made his ministry possible. He did not see himself as a 'lone ranger', or in any way superior to those with whom he laboured; he knew that pastoral care is best delivered by people working together.

I am always been affected by the last two verses of chapter four. They are a kind of postscript—almost an afterthought. Here's what Paul says: ' Tell Archippus, see to it that you complete the work that you have received in the Lord.' Whenever I read these verses, I think this is a word from God for me. Could it be for you too? If so, do not let any obstacle get in the way of doing what God wants you to do.

2. The support

The examples of Jesus and Paul highlight the importance of looking after the people whom we lead. There are many situations where the pressures of caring for others can be quite overwhelming. This section offers some advice on how we can support others in difficult times. Here are some points to consider.

Make sure everyone understands the job

Confidence and satisfaction, even in difficult times, are easier to maintain if, right at the beginning, members of the team have a clear understanding of what is entailed. A solid base will be stablished if everyone understands:

- *The purpose of the pastoral care team and the vision that the leadership has for pastoral care.*
- *The leadership's policy for pastoral care and strategy for its implementation.*
- *The standards expected, the qualities required in carers.*
- *That the leadership highly values the team and will provide support whenever it is required.*

Make sure everyone is appreciated

One of the great motivators in any kind of service is to know that we are appreciated. Caring for others can be demanding and draining. Pastoral carers can go through periods of discouragement and frustration. It is important to affirm them during these times, and throughout their period of service, so that they know their contribution is valued. Carers, like everyone else involved in Christian ministry, need to have the assurance that they have the leadership's full confidence and approval. It is essential that carers realise their gifts have been recognised and that the leadership believes each carer can make a difference in the life of the church.

We have spoken in earlier chapters about the need to challenge those responsible when things are going wrong. This is often neglected because it is so difficult to confront a colleague. It is not difficult to express appreciation when someone does well, yet this, too, is often neglected. Failure in both cases is to the detriment of the individual and the church. In the first case, the person will continue with the bad habit and, in the second, they can become discouraged, perhaps thinking that no one cares how they perform.

The moral is that if someone does a good job, then tell them you have appreciated their contribution. It is not too difficult to say, "I want you to know how impressed I was by the way you handled that very difficult situation" or "You need to know that your attitude is a source of great encouragement to this team". The team leader is not excluded from these expressions of thanks. Team leaders also get discouraged at times, and don't always know how they are being perceived by the team. They get feedback mostly when they get it wrong, but, when they get it right, make sure someone says, "Thank you for your leadership of this team. We appreciate your support and guidance, and recognise how much time and energy you give to help this team do all that we do. We couldn't do it without you."

Of course, the caveat is, don't say it if you don't mean it or it isn't true. But if you do mean it and it is true, don't forget to say it.

Make sure everyone is appropriately prepared

Mature carers don't just appear out of nowhere. They grow and develop over the years. For most individuals, it starts by having an interest in and an enthusiasm for helping friends and those around them. They have the right character and aptitude for the task, so in many ways they just grow into the job. It's a kind of learning by doing. But, if we want to make the best provision for our churches and help the carers to survive the storms that they will encounter, we must be more intentional about training. This can be done at a variety of levels.

Individual training

When someone expresses an interest in pastoral care, one way of helping that person to develop is to link him or her with a more experienced carer. It can be done very informally at the beginning but may become more structured as the relationship develops. This process is now called mentoring and is used extensively in secular contexts. The Bible also provides many examples of experienced workers who invested in preparing the next generation for service: Elijah and Elisha, and Paul and Timothy, come to mind.

Mentoring goes back a long way. According to Homer, when the Greek warrior Odysseus went off to fight in the Trojan War, he left his young son Telemachus, in the care of a trusted guardian named Mentor. The siege of Troy lasted ten years and when Odysseus returned home, he found the boy Telemachus had grown into a man—thanks to Mentor's influence.

The word 'mentor' thus means someone who functions as a kind of father figure (in the best sense of the term), a man or woman who fundamentally affects and influences the development of another, usually younger, person.

In our book, *Learning to Lead*, we highlight four elements essential to the mentoring process:[1]

- it is a relationship between two people
- it includes a planned process
- it brings about accelerated growth in the mentee
- it includes transferring experience as well as knowledge from one generation to another.

We know it is not always easy to find mentors, but where appropriate people are available, we would urge church leaders to make maximum use of their expertise, knowing that their input can make a huge difference for the mentee, not only in the early stages, but later when carers may be getting to breaking point. Good mentoring can be a lifelong investment.

---

1. Clarkson and McQuoid, *Learning to Lead: Next Generation*, OPAL, 2013, pp. 149–179.

Lifelong leadership Development

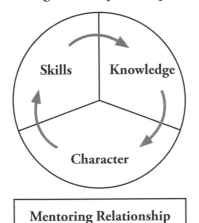

Group training

In addition to personal mentoring, we believe it is essential to provide basic training in pastoral care which will be required for members of the pastoral care team. This training should also be open on a voluntary basis to every church member, so that everyone understands what pastoral care is about.

We should also encourage ministry leaders, e.g., of youth groups or music ministry etc., to attend these sessions and see their activities as opportunities to care for their own teams. Such training will establish the principle that pastoral care is not the exclusive responsibility of leadership or pastoral team members.

These introductory training sessions will enable members of the church to:

- See pastoral care as an integral part of the mission of the church.
- Have an increased awareness of the needs of the congregation.
- Develop skills of caring for our brothers and sisters.
- Recognise the need to create strong teams where the members are unconditionally committed to one another. In this context, we can develop gifts, provide care, and give support.

The point of these sessions will be to emphasise the 'one another' teaching of the Bible.

Ongoing training

When the basics have been completed, the church should offer training in more specialised areas of pastoral caring. They could consider such subject areas as:

- Understanding the needs of people across the stages of life.
- Understanding the biblical foundations for pastoral care.
- Awareness of safety legislation and the safeguarding policy of the church.
- Understanding how to use the Bible and pray in pastoral contexts.
- Developing pastoral skills, such as listening, asking pertinent questions, being accepting and non-judgmental, and maintaining confidentiality.
- Learning how to do some practical activities, such as hospital visitation or providing support in times of bereavement.

The diagram below shows how one church structured its training programme :

PASTORAL CARE DEVELOPMENT PROGRAMME

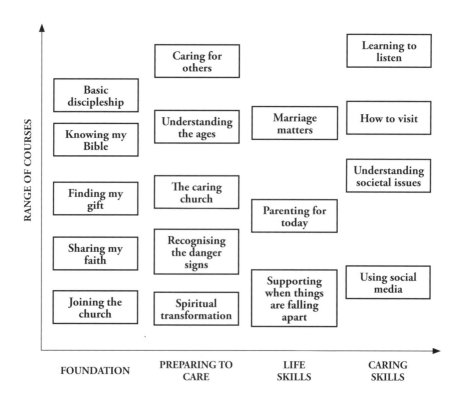

The foundation courses could be offered annually, with others available on rotation over several years. Pastoral team members should do all the basic courses and should be encouraged to attend as many others as they can manage. Some churches prefer to provide the training in six-week blocks; others spread it over the year. The method will depend on personal preference and availability of personnel. This kind of training requires careful planning, so that people can give themselves a programme to learn new skills or keep up-to-date with new knowledge. Most of the sessions should be open to members of the congregation to join with the team. This will keep everyone informed of what is going on and may stimulate interest in potential future members for the pastoral care team.

Deliver imaginatively

Preparing and delivering a training schedule like this might appear daunting at first sight, especially for people whose lives are already busy and pressurised. However, working as a team over a period of time can greatly reduce the workload. The task is to deliver the training interactively, with creativity and enthusiasm, so that the church benefits from the learning opportunities.

We strongly believe that training should be much more than lecturing: it must contain vital practical elements. We should encourage new team members to partner with more experienced carers and accompany them in their pastoral activities wherever possible. Thus, hospital visitation, for example, can best be learned by being with a skilled practitioner. This allows the opportunity to discuss how to approach the visit, and a debrief will help elaborate on lessons learned. It also gives the trainee credibility in the eyes of the congregation.

We would emphasise that this training model offered for pastoral care can be adapted for any church activity. Our firm conviction is that before anyone takes on any ministry in the church, they should have the church leaders' backing and be given training appropriate to the activity. Throwing someone in at the deep end with no preparation might create problems for the church at a later stage, and may perhaps cause immense damage to the individual.

Take stock occasionally

We would encourage periodic review of pastoral care in the church. In terms of the team, this should be relatively informal, with the aim of discussing how we could improve in particular areas. It should not be unduly critical or with the intention of finding fault or attaching blame. After all, the team members are volunteers who want to do their best. So the discussion should focus on questions like "How we could do this better?", "Do we need additional resources?", or "Could we function better as a team?"

We would also encourage team members to reflect privately on their own performance. This should not be seen as deep introspection which highlights our failures, but rather just taking time, say, once a year, to think about what we are doing and what God is saying to us.

Some people find a questionnaire like the one copied below, helpful to focus their thoughts.

Questionnaire for personal reflection

> *Do I still see myself as being called by God to this task? Am I still as passionate about it as I was at the beginning?*
>
> *Am I still seeking to give God the central place in my relationships? Do I still believe that God can change the lives of messed-up people?*
>
> *Do I try to help people to move forward towards Christlikeness and not just stop at reducing anxiety?*
>
> *Am I still convinced of the dignity of each individual and relate to them in a non-judgmental way?*
>
> *Do I maintain confidentiality?*
>
> *Do I respect everyone's privacy?*
>
> *Do I deal gently and lovingly with people?*
>
> *Am I patient?*
>
> *Have I made progress in such skills as listening, accepting people, using the Bible, and praying to bring people closer to God?*
>
> *Are there particular areas in which I need to improve?*
>
> *Are there any specific issues that I should raise with my mentor?*

3. The pressures

We have stressed how important it is for churches to have procedures and support in place for those involved in pastoral care, particularly in the early stages. But even with the best programmes in place, there will be occasions when carers feel under pressure, and the church needs to be ready to provide support when these arise. We have three such possibilities in mind.

Disappointment

There will be occasions in the work when disappointment sets in. It is easy to imagine that working with people will always be successful and that we will be able, relatively quickly, to bring change into people's lives. This is not usually the case. It is possible to work with an individual for months and see very little progress. This can be very dispiriting. How do we handle the disappointment of seeing someone for whom we had high hopes turn away? The reality is that there will be disappointments and there will be occasions when we feel that what we do is futile.

We live in a fast-moving world—fast cars, fast foods, instant coffee. Amazon's significant selling point is that they can deliver whatever we want, often on the same day but certainly by the next. But God is not in a hurry and, while he could do everything in an instant, he chooses to work in peoples' lives over time.

The Japanese theologian, Kosuke Koyama, wrote a book entitled, *Three Miles an Hour God*.[2]. He discusses the speed at which things move and observes that humans are often frantically rushing to fill every moment with activity, but God is not governed by our speed requirements. Koyama observed that humans walk at around three miles an hour and suggests that our loving God chooses to walk with us at our speed. Love has its own inner speed—a spiritual speed which cannot be measured in miles per hour. God is prepared to walk at our pace and does so because of his patient love.

While we may wish to see change taking place in our friends' lives very quickly, we need to remember that the journey from darkness to light, from confusion to understanding, takes time and companionship. Therefore, we

---

2. Kosuke Koyama, *Three Mile an Hour God: Biblical Reflections*, SCM Press, 1979, pp. 6–7.

need to learn to walk slowly with them, so that each person can hear what God is saying about the way ahead.

Other circumstances also bring great disappointment. For example, we can become involved in a friend's life who, for a variety of reasons, has concluded that Christianity is not for him or her. There are doubts about the truths proclaimed in the Bible or the cost is too great. Jesus encountered exactly this situation. A young man with great potential asked Jesus about inheriting eternal life. Interestingly, Mark says that Jesus looked at him and loved him and, because he loved him and wanted his best interest, Jesus laid out the demands of discipleship, only to see him turn away because he was unwilling to give everything to the service of Christ (Mk. 10: 17–22).

In these circumstances, the pastoral carer can only commit the friend to God and point out that, unless he or she is willing to obey the word of God, sadly we cannot help further. This does not mean that we abandon this friend. We continue with the relationship as far as possible, but we cannot change the advice.

Carers may well feel that the problem lies with them—that they are not good enough at caring, and perhaps the time has come for them to resign from the pastoral care team. These are genuine emotions and church leaders need to be aware of how disappointments and setbacks can affect those on the front line.

Criticism

Criticism can be devastating in Christian service. No matter how well we perform our duties, there will always be critics. Leaders need to prepare their people to deal with criticism and support them when it arrives. The question is how we deal with it, and our response will be an indicator of how mature we are. Criticism directed at us can spring from perceived inadequacies, actual shortcomings, or unmet expectations. Its source can be pettiness, jealousy, or personal animosity.

When criticism is directed at us personally, we must first determine if there is any truth in it. Did we make a mistake, act unfairly, or not meet our promises? If so, we must acknowledge it and apologise. We put our ego aside and make no attempt to pass the blame to someone else or make excuses. We got it wrong and now we want to find God-honouring solutions to put it right. When personal criticism is approached in this way, we will emerge stronger, and our relationships will be on a better footing.

Our response will, of course, to some extent, be dependent on the nature and source of the criticism. If it comes from someone who strongly supports the ministry, we need to listen and take heed. This person will have our best interests at heart and want to see us succeed. If it comes from someone who is hostile or resentful, we need to determine the root of the problem, try to resolve it, and seek reconciliation. As Jesus said, if we can do that, 'You have gained your brother' (Mt. 18: 15).

We must never turn criticism into a personal canpaign in which we see winning as the only acceptable solution. Neither should we allow revenge to motivate us or seek to strike back at someone we now regard as an opponent. We must know when it is better to lose a battle in order to win a war. Criticism can be a growth opportunity, depending on how we respond to it.

Sometimes criticism is directed at the pastoral team or at the way in which the ministry is conducted. Again, it is important to know where the criticism is coming from. If the criticism comes from the key influencers in the congregation, we will be more than ready to listen to their constructive suggestions, knowing that they also are looking for better outcomes.

If it comes from the regular complainers, the leaders need to tackle the situation quickly by identifying the basis of the complaint. If there is substance to it, the leaders should address the issue and put it right, but if there is no evidence to substantiate the complaint, they should insist that the criticisms cease. The leaders should take the initial heat for the team until they can adequately investigate the problem. This gives an opportunity to meet with the team to discuss the problems objectively and create solutions together.

Mistakes

Leaders need to care for the carers when they make some drastic mistake. Many carers worry about getting things seriously wrong. "What will happen if I screw things up?", we ask ourselves. The question is not *if* we screw things up but *when* we screw things up. Mistakes and mishaps are inevitable; after all, we are human and fallible. We (Stephen and David) have made many of the mistakes which we have urged you as readers, not to make. We both cringe with embarrassment as we look back over so many things we have said or done and, even yet, blush when we ask, "did I really say or do that?"

Other leaders will have had similar experiences, so they are able to point out to despairing pastoral carers that mistakes can be very significant learning experiences. One counsellor has said, 'I believe I learned more through my mistakes and failures than through the successes.'[3] Getting things wrong impresses upon us the need to make sure that the same mistakes don't happen again and forces us to consider how we would do things better in future. This is why it is essential for leaders to discuss the details with the carers, identify where mistakes were made, and what lessons can be learned. We must not ignore the incident and go on as if nothing had happened, for this will only increase the carer's isolation and deprive them of the benefits of talking through the events with a trusted and caring leader. It is also important to deal not just with the facts, but with the emotions.

Bill Jordan in his book *Helping in Social Work*[4] wrote

> from the start, I recognised that social work, even with the best of intentions, could as readily be unhelpful as helpful. It was clear to me that every attempt to influence a person in trouble entailed a risk of making things worse for him, and that social workers often did this. Far more painful for me was the gradual recognition that often it was when I minded most about my clients, tried hardest, or liked them best that I did the most harm. The risks of damage were highest where the investment was greatest.

We can say the same for pastoral carers.

Every parent knows that risk is implicit in every change situation. At some point, they need to allow their children to make their own decisions, otherwise they will never grow up. Likewise, every stage in pastoral care involves risk. The carer takes a risk getting involved in someone's life in the first place. Then they

---

3. Quoted in: Steven Pattison, *A Critique of Pastoral Care,* SCM Press, 2000, chapter 7.

4. Bill Jordan, *Helping in Social Work*, Routledge & Kegan Paul, 1979.

take risks by journeying alongside those they care for, not telling those they are caring for what to do but encouraging them to make their own decisions wisely. Finally, there is the risk of stepping back a little so that the person being cared for does not become dependent. Each of these steps is risky, but without taking risks, growth and development are not possible.

Pastors are human and imperfect, as are the people they deal with. Like them, we fail because we are weak, confused, and inconsistent. Weakness and flaws are part of the very stuff of our nature.

Failure in pastoral care is inevitable. We should neither seek it out nor try to avoid it, but, when it happens, recognise it, face up to it, and learn from it. Learning from our mistakes demands an enormous amount of courage and is one of the most challenging tasks that pastoral carers need to undertake. It brings us to recognise that we are not as competent as we thought we were, and that we need God's grace to help us every step of the way. Hence the need for reflection and learning in what we do.

Everyone involved in ministry will at some point face discouragement. This may be because it is not proving successful, but it could also be that the carer involved is going through their own personal struggles. The trigger for this could be a family matter, a health matter, a spiritual matter, or they may simply be jaded and in need of a break. Whatever the reason, as we care for carers, we need to be there for them when they experience these low points.

People cope with discouragement, and even encouragement, in different ways. Some carers will be very open about the fact that they are discouraged and will share their personal struggles. Others will keep it to themselves and just keep going regardless, but those who know them will recognise their actual condition. It is important to be alert and sensitive to the needs of carers and be able to draw alongside them when they are down.

The response to discouragement can vary, but the task of leadership is to be available to people. Given that team members have devoted themselves to caring for others, the least they can expect is that church leaders will be at their side to offer support when it is really needed. Beyond this, the carer needs encouragement and assurance that God values them and can work through them. If their discouragement is persistent, they may need a break from responsibility so that they can recharge their spiritual and emotional batteries. This break should not be for long though, because getting back to a useful ministry is also a good counterbalance to discouragement.

Conclusion

We have considered some support structures that should be in place for caring for the carers. If church leaders want their carers to thrive and be effective for the long haul, they need to look after them. Investing in this area of church life is very important because, if a church has motivated and able carers, this will pay a huge dividend for the future.

Of course, the kind of support we have been advocating also applies for everyone involved in church ministry.

For further reflection

1. What are some stresses carers experience?
2. From the list of short courses shown in the diagram on page 224 above, which do you think would be the most helpful and why?
3. What are some of the signs of burn-out and what steps should be taken to prevent it and recover from it?
4. Some believe that disappointment and a fear of failure are two of the biggest challenges that carers face. Do you agree with this and, if so, why do you think this is?

APPENDIX 1

Some Practical Guidance

Pastoral care is an intensely practical activity. It is about doing things that help people grow in their faith and working through issues in their lives. The very best pastoral carers are those who are willing servants, prepared to give of themselves for the benefit of others. However, it requires more than just a willingness; personal qualities and specific skills are also needed. Good carers will develop listening skills which will enable them to get to know the people they are helping. They need both tact and patience as well as the ability to relate well to others. It will also be important to learn to pray with people, and read and share Scripture with them.

Pastoral care is also a very diverse ministry. Consequently, carers will need to develop a basic competence in dealing with a range of challenging situations. This will include knowing how to relate to people struggling with end of life or mental health issues, depression, or dementia. Carers will need sensitivity in coming alongside couples struggling with infertility, miscarriage, disability, or perhaps the stress and challenges of adoption. This is just a small sample of the kind of situations which will require great empathy and support.

As well as these qualities, practical skills will be required for specific situations some of which are described below.

1. Doing a pastoral visit

Pastoral care is all about relationship. It is not really possible to provide pastoral help unless there is some sort of rapport, which can only be developed by being with people. Pastoral visitation at its best should be done regularly, first, because this is how relationships are built and, secondly, if people are only ever visited when there is a crisis or they have done something wrong, then visits are automatically associated with trouble and that produces a sense of foreboding. While pastoral visitation is a time-consuming activity, it is more than worth the effort. Even the very busy apostle Paul gave himself to this task (Acts 20: 20).

Pastoral visits usually take place in a person's home. That can be a good thing because you get a better perspective of the person when you are in their home environment. However, this is not always suitable, especially if they live with other people who are unchurched. There are lots of alternatives, such as coffee shops, which are great places for a pastoral meeting. They provide a relaxing and informal atmosphere, creating a natural gathering place. The carer can also invite people to their own home, and the hospitality they provide is an important component in the pastoral care. Indeed, hospitality is one of the most useful gifts a pastoral carer can develop.

Whatever the location, the importance of this simple activity cannot be overestimated. People generally remember visits they have received and appreciate the fact that someone took an interest in their life. What is important is that visits do not become random; rather, they should always have a purpose. We must not confuse pastoral visits with socialising. Whether the visit is requested by the person or decided on by the carer, there must always be a rationale for the visit which will determine how it is conducted.

Before looking at the rationale, a word should be said about when people request a visit. This is a very common thing. Indeed, experienced carers will receive many requests for a visit and may struggle to meet the demand. Consequently, a little wisdom is necessary as pastoral care can easily become a bottomless pit. Some needs are chronic but not urgent, while others are acute, and action needs to be taken immediately. The carer needs to judge every situation individually. For example, I once got a phone call from a friend whose wife had died suddenly. Clearly, he was feeling anxious and emotional, so I cancelled the plans I had for that afternoon and immediately went to see him.

On another occasion, I had a phone call late at night from a young woman who said she was distressed and wanted me to come and pray with her. I knew her situation well and, while she had genuine matters to be helped with, loneliness was the main one and, in her loneliness, she 'invented' issues which were not real but rather a way of getting people to spend time with her. She still needed care and spiritual guidance, but this was far from an emergency and did not necessitate a 'drop everything' response. Instead, I arranged to see her in a coffee shop about a week after the phone call and she was happy with that arrangement. Discipline as well as wisdom is important in pastoral visitation.

When a visit takes place, the pastoral carer should know why it is happening and what they want to achieve. The visit might be as light-touch as a catch-up, or it could be weightier—for example, bringing support when someone is going through a difficult time or speaking into a particular situation in their lives. Often, I will think of questions I want to ask beforehand or things I was to say and will write them down, so I don't forget. In addition, I will often tell the person why I want to come and see them which helps them prepare. Even if it is just a catch-up, I will tell them that, so they arrive at the visit ready to talk and share.

The tone of the visit will depend on the circumstances. To reference the earlier examples, visiting someone who has just lost his wife will be very different to a catch-up visit. But there are basics that become virtually universal. For example, keep the visit relaxed, and don't forget to smile. Listen more than you speak and don't dominate the conversation or steamroller the person. After all, the visit is about them, not you. When asking questions, listen to the answer, not just to respond but to understand. Use Scripture where appropriate: this doesn't mean you necessarily carry a Bible with you, but quoting Scripture in conversation, or applying it, can be powerful. Don't rush the conversation or keep looking at your watch or mobile phone, especially if the issue is a serious one. It is also a good habit to offer and use prayer. Visits build relationships if done well. Try to ensure the visit leaves the person looking forward to the next time.

2. Doing a hospital visit

Much of what was said about general pastoral visitation could be applied to visiting someone in hospital. However, we need to be aware that hospital visitation is a particular matter that requires careful thought. Consideration needs to be given to the tone of any conversation, which should be purposeful and prayerful.

To begin with, we need to ask about an appropriate time to visit. If someone has just had surgery, it is usually better to wait a couple of days, both to allow immediate family to see them and to allow the person some recovery time. On the other hand, if someone has gone into hospital for tests and may only be in for a short time, delaying may not be helpful, particularly if the person has little family support. Sensitivity to the particular situation is important. It is also useful, if the hospital allows it, to go outside of normal visiting hours where a proper and private conversation can take place.

The situation confronting the pastoral carer will vary greatly. A person who has come through an operation successfully with no complications will be in a different frame of mind from someone awaiting news of tests. Likewise, a young person having their tonsils taken out will be feeling differently from someone having chemotherapy treatment that does not appear to be helping much. Again, sensitivity is the key.

Basic rules also apply in hospital visitation. Don't stay too long. This is particularly important in busy hospitals where lots of activity and interruptions are almost inevitable. Comfort, cheer, empathy, and encouragement are always welcome. Confidentiality is vital and you should be careful not to push for more information than the patient is willing to give. If the patient does open up and share about their prognosis, and consequent emotions, be sure to offer prayer. This is the case whether or not the person is a Christian. In my experience, many people who would not claim to be Christians still appreciate being prayed for. However, if the person you are visiting isn't a Christian, just make sure you ask if it is alright to pray for them, and never be pushy about it.

It is also important to offer support for the family. Concern for a loved one in hospital, and the hospitalised person's concern for their family, are often two-way. Again, Scripture and prayer can be very helpful. It's advisable always to have a Bible passage in mind before you visit someone in hospital, because you don't want to be fumbling around thinking about what verses to read. It is also essential to encourage the person to trust God during this particularly difficult situation.

3. Taking a funeral

A funeral is a profound experience for any bereaved family and the way in which it is conducted can have a significant impact on loved ones and anyone else who attends. It is imperative to think carefully about what will happen and what will be said. There are two aspects to a funeral: the graveside or crematorium, and the church service. Both have important functions.

From a pastoral perspective, the context of the bereavement is of great significance. If the person who has died was a Christian, the funeral can actually be a time of celebration and gratitude, filled with hope and expectation of a better world. On the other hand, if the person had no faith, it is important—though much more difficult—to bring comfort to the family.

In general, we recommend that the burial takes place first and then the service at the church afterwards. The committing of the body to the ground is a highly emotional time and if that is done first then the bereaved family can go to the main service with less pressure and trepidation. Depending on the circumstances of the death, and other factors, we sometimes recommend that the graveside event is attended by family and close friends only. For example, I once took the funeral of a small child and because the family were so overwhelmed, it was agreed that a family-only burial would be more appropriate so that they could grieve in private.

What happens at the graveside can set the tone for the whole funeral. Given that this takes place in the open air, it is a very weather-dependant event. In winter, it can be very cold and the atmosphere of a graveyard can contribute psychologically to this, so the service by the graveside should be short. A hymn, prayer, and a few short comments are sufficient. It should also be said that the singing of a hymn is not essential, and it is probably better to sing only if there are enough church people there to make it sound credible. It is certainly not necessary to sing every verse of a longer hymn and an appropriate choice of hymn might be one which celebrates the life-giving power of the gospel.

What is said at the graveside is very important for whoever is there. This is a poignant moment, and the speaker should say something that will be of real support to friends and family who will be experiencing acute grief. If the deceased person was a Christian, it is a great opportunity to celebrate the hope of eternity. Christianity has something very special to offer people who are broken-hearted through bereavement. The death and resurrection of Jesus offer hope: the resurrection of the body and eternal life in heaven. Declaring these truths clearly and boldly will present a challenge any non-Christians who are there, but it will also give comfort and reassurance to Christians who are going through the pain of loss. Of course, if the person who has died is not a Christian, it is more difficult to stress the hope of resurrection and eternal life. In such a situation, sensitivity is paramount, and the message should be one of God's comfort for people who have a broken heart.

The service at the church also has an important pastoral component. Once again, the truths that were emphasised at the graveside can be repeated and expanded upon. It is also important to remind those present, especially the immediate family, that God understands and is aware of all our suffering—that he wishes to draw near to support and heal. And it is a time to celebrate the life of the person who has died—a life full of relationships, memories, shared experiences, fun times, hard times, laughter, and tears. Everyone leaves an indelible mark on the lives of others. It is because of this that we each value the lives of the people we love. The funeral service is a time to reflect on all of this, to be reminded of the stories of a person's life, and to celebrate the memories that the mourners will have of the person who has died. Such reflection will not only bring comfort, but it will allow family and friends to experience a degree of closure—an important pastoral consideration.

4. Marriage guidance and preparation

Few events in life are more significant for people that getting married. The marriage relationship will either provide the joy and stability in a person's life, or, if it goes wrong, will bring sadness and disappointment. Marriage is a big commitment, and therefore preparing someone for that event is an important pastoral duty.

Pastoral guidance in regard to finding a life partner should begin early. There are two aspects to this: teaching someone what to look for in a partner, and training them to be the kind of a partner they should be for someone else. With regard the first, the pastoral carer should be encouraging young people to look for and wait for a person of character. In our superficial culture, looks and popularity are huge draws. It is more important, however, to find someone with shared values and the same spiritual interests. Likewise, young people, for example, who are dating need to be encouraged to demonstrate faithfulness, restraint, and selflessness in their relationships.

Relationship guidance then morphs into marriage preparation, once a couple have committed themselves to each other. The importance of this cannot be overstated. The saying goes, 'Love is blind, and marriage is an eye opener', but there is real truth in it. In the romance of an early relationship, eccentricities seem less annoying, problems smaller, and of course there is still a freshness to the relationship. Once married and the normality of married life settles in, it is then that matters of contention can emerge. These issues need not prove very difficult to deal with, but the job of marriage preparation is to enable a couple to enter marriage with their eyes open and equipped to talk about contentious questions as they arise, and how to deal with them.

There are several matters that are worth investigating pastorally as part of marriage preparation. The first of these should be the importance of communication. It is probably this more than any other matter which causes relationship stress. The couple need to be made aware of the importance of communication, as well as to receive advice on how to improve in this area. Ambitions and aspirations also need to be addressed, so that they each understand where they want their lives to lead. This should include the ambition to have a family as well as discussion on how to take responsibility for children, should they be blessed with them. It is also important to look at conflict resolution in marriage as couples need to learn to work through their difficulties. Adequate time should also be given to reflecting on spiritual commitments, disciplines and practices within marriage. It should never be assumed that a couple will behave in their marriage in a spiritual way just because they are Christians. All couples need to determine to honour Christ in their marriages and this should be central to marriage guidance.

5. Conducting a wedding

Many people enjoy weddings because, quite apart from the romance, they are significant social events. However, they can also be times of stress and nervousness, not least because of the significance of what takes place. Weddings involve not just the couple themselves, but their families and friends, and Christian weddings are of course conducted 'in the presence of God', who is asked to give his blessing to the union.

Most of the time when a Christian gets married, he or she will marry another Christian. However, this is not inevitable. If a Christian marries a non-Christian, it adds to the pastoral sensitivity of the occasion. Some churches are not prepared to accept or officiate in such circumstances. If a church does allow for this, it is important that there is good preparation for the event by talking to the couple about the importance of faith and explaining to the unbelieving partner not only why Christians see faith as important, but also why Christians believe that marriage is most successful when God is involved in the relationship.

It is much more straightforward to marry two people who are Christians, but there are still important things to be done and emphasized. It goes without saying that all the legal requirements and processes need to be tended to, so that the couple are properly married in the eyes of the law. However, the wedding itself takes on a great significance from a Christian and a pastoral point of view. Wedding vows are not just ritualistic sayings that the couple utter as they tie the knot. They are solemn promises that are made in God's presence, with witnesses present to hold the couple accountable for what they have promised to do. It is important that the couple are involved in deciding the vows. While there are certain required legal undertakings in the vows, there is room for creativity and personal expressiveness. I often encourage couples to write their own vows, so that they express what they really feel and mean, in their own words.

Weddings are also worshipful events where God should be glorified. It is a particular kind of worship because, after all, the wedding is about the couple themselves. Since marriage is given by God for human flourishing, God's role in the relationship, as well as in the ceremony, should be recognised, with thanks offered to him. The marriage ceremony is also an important time to emphasize the importance of marriage and all it signifies. For this reason, short sermons and the reading of Scripture are important. The sermons need to be short, so that they don't detract from the specialness of the occasion . However, what is said is very important. It is generally helpful to speak directly to the couple. They can be reminded of important matters, such as bringing God into their relationship, praying together, demonstrating Christian love and self-sacrifice in their own relationship, and creating a home life that welcomes others and honours God.

A final matter that is important to remember is that of prayer. The Christian life is challenging and one area where we need help to live it out is in the marriage relationship. The soaring divorce rate, even among Christians, is testament to the struggles that people can have in marriage. Praying for the couple is not a mere formality or something that fills the programme: it is a key pastoral event in which those present can lift the couple up before God, supporting them in prayer, and calling upon God to strengthen and help the couple in their marriage commitment.

Facilitating in all of these life-events will become routine for those involved in pastoral care. They are the 'bread and butter' of the job. It is for this reason that we need to do them well and give thought to our words and actions. Over time, we can become accomplished in fulfilling these duties, but we should always guard against complacency. People will remember and value the input we have had in their lives through these key stages. With careful consideration and prayer, we can enhance peoples' experiences and be a blessing to them through the routine of these pastoral encounters with them.

Legalities

Introduction

This book has focused on the spiritual and practical dimensions of pastoral care, with the aim of helping people to do it better. But churches are not free agents to do whatever they please in the pursuit of this aim. Churches are required to comply with a range of legislation—for example, pertaining to the safety and wellbeing of everyone who uses our buildings or the safeguarding of children or vulnerable adults. Complying with government legislation can sometimes be demanding, but it can also help us to do pastoral care better.

We do not propose to detail the requirements of the various laws which apply to churches in this appendix. To do so would require legal expertise beyond our abilities and would be inadvisable because legislation constantly changes and takes different forms in different countries. We will simply highlight a number of areas that leaders should be aware of, and encourage them to check out the requirements in their own context.

Every church is strongly advised to comply fully with the law, with transparency and integrity. Government legislation is important because it will mean the church will be a safer place, and difficulties arising from serious incidents should be minimised. It is better to have policies in place in advance rather than become consumed with damage limitation after an event. Furthermore, the very act of producing policies or protocols is very helpful in thinking through the issues.

The purpose of this appendix is to point us to those areas where churches need to have protocols in place to meet the increasing demands of the law. Many churches find it helpful to have written policies on a whole range of issues so that the church's position is clearly established. These policies will cover the legal requirements, outline good practice for undertaking the business of the church, and indicate how each policy will be supervised. This will help explain to non-members what the church is about and also remind members how the church expects them to behave. Policies remind us of areas of potential danger and help to keep us accountable. And as Christians, if it is reasonably within our power, we should not wish simply to fulfil minimum legal requirements, but to go beyond them when appropriate as a matter of Christian testimony and of doing good to and for those with whom we deal.

1. Policy areas to consider

We recommend that churches give serious consideration to at least the following:

1. Constitution or Trust Deed—should include definitions on key matters to which the church is committed, e.g., in what constitutes Christian marriage.
2. Health and Safety—including fire safety and food hygiene, maintenance of gas and electricity appliances, building and public liability insurance.
3. Finance—compliance with the requirements of the charity regulator and relevant professional bodies on maintaining and reporting of accurate accounts.
4. Safeguarding Policy—this is discussed more fully below.
5. Data Protection Policy (GDPR)—including on the range of data held and for how long, use of photography, email, and internet. Compliance with copyright and licencing requirements (Churches Copyright Licencing International (CCLI)).
6. Employment—including on appointment procedures, conditions of service, complaints and disciplinary procedures and employer's liabilities.
7. Volunteers—including on selection procedures, code of conduct, support and training, instructions about working alone.

Some of the above policies have no bearing on pastoral care and others impinge only slightly, but we have included them here for the sake of completeness.

However, there are a number of policy matters relating directly to pastoral care which we discuss more fully below.

2. Policies specifically relating to pastoral care

Four areas are particularly important.

1. Safeguarding

We begin with safeguarding which is arguably the most important policy any church will produce. Every church should have a safeguarding policy as well as a safeguarding coordinator whose job it is to ensure that the requirements of the policy are adhered to. It is also important that everyone involved in pastoral care is familiar with this policy and appropriately trained in safeguarding issues, and how they apply in the context of pastoral care. In the United Kingdom, the relevant charity regulator expects charities to have a policy which covers a variety of possible harms to its staff, volunteers, beneficiaries, and trustees. This is particularly important if they are dealing with children or vulnerable adults. Carers should also be subject to any necessary disclosure checks. How these disclosures are operated varies from country to country within the UK.

Any safeguarding policy will take particular interest in children as they are a particularly vulnerable group. Typically, the policy should highlight areas such as neglect, and physical, sexual and emotional abuse. The policy should outline how church members should respond if abuse is discovered and the actions that should be taken. It should also outline the safeguarding coordinator's role and how police and social services are notified. In the UK, organisations such as *thirtyone:eight* and Christian Safeguarding Services or local Children's Services can offer invaluable help and advice and should be consulted as necessary.

The safeguarding policy should include information as to how the church will handle issues relating to vulnerable adults and cases of domestic abuse.

These safeguarding issues have been discussed in chapter 8 and fuller details of the legal requirements can be found at:

https://thirtyoneeight.org/

https://thecss.co.uk/

https://learning.nspcc.org.uk/safeguarding-child-protection/
writing-a-safeguarding-policy-statement

https://www.ageuk.org.uk/about-us/people/safeguarding/

https://www.bond.org.uk/resources/safeguarding-policy-
templates

2. *General Data Protection Regulation (GDPR)*

Data protection requirements are about how we hold and use data and information about people. There are rules about how this information is obtained, held, and protected, as well as what churches can and can't do with that information. Churches will have contact details and addresses of their members on file. If they run an activity such as a toddler group or a youth club, they will also have contact details of those people and their parents. All of this is legitimate and necessary, but there are also laws that protect these data so that they are not misused or inappropriately used. Many church leaders and especially those involved in pastoral care may have recorded some sensitive material which was volunteered during, for example, a counselling or pastoral session. This material is personal data for the purposes of data privacy legislation and needs to be treated with discretion and care, and, as required, to meet the standards of data privacy legislation and the requirements of the Information Commissioner's Office. Policy details will need to be in place outlining the extent to which confidential material can be shared among the leadership and pastoral teams.

It is important that church leaders are aware of these laws and comply with them. Someone will need to be appointed to look after GDPR and to be accountable for it. There are regulations surrounding the length of time data can be kept and for more sensitive information there is also the matter of confidentiality. While these matters appear to be mundane, they are important, and attention should be given to them.

3. *Reporting and confidentiality*

One of the most important questions you will need to answer is in regard to the kind of reporting is necessary in any given situation. For example, in the course of your pastoral work, you may discover that an adult may have behaved inappropriately towards a minor. In what circumstances, are you obliged to contact the social services department and the police? And to report the matter to your charity regulator? What internal procedures within the church should you follow in such a case? How this is handled is important because the church or individual pastoral carer could be in potentially significant trouble if they get it wrong.

Confidentiality is an important issue, but there are times where keeping confidences is illegal, for example, knowledge that a crime may have been committed. In such situations, leaders have a duty of disclosure to police or other authorities.

4. *Trustees*

Trusteeship is an important role as trustees are accountable in law for all that a charity does. They need to ensure that it fulfils its charitable objects. They are also charged with the responsibility of risk management, including financial, reputational, operational, etc. risks. Given this, it is easy to see how, if something goes badly wrong in a pastoral situation, the trustees who stand behind any activity are in fact liable for that matter. In such a situation, they cannot merely state that it was the fault of the pastoral carer because it is their job to ensure that the pastoral carers operate within the law and the legislative framework. Among other things, this means that pastoral carers must keep the trustees informed in good time about pastoral matters which may engage the trustees' interests, even if the threat is only reputational to the charity and to themselves as trustees. In pastoral matters, trustees normally work through the elders or leadership team, though this does not dilute the trustees' responsibility. This is another reason why pastoral carers should not make inappropriate promises of confidentiality to those who are being cared for and should avoid creating unrealistic expectations in this regard.

Guidance on the duties of trustees can be found at:

> https://www.gov.uk/government/publications/the-essential-trustee-what-you-need-to-know-cc3

> https://www.oscr.org.uk/guidance-and-forms/guidance-and-good-practice-for-charity-trustees/charity-trustee-duties/

https://churchgrowth.org.uk/wp-content/uploads/2020/01/
Good-Practice-for-Charity-Trustees-January-2020.pdf

https://www.stewardship.org.uk/blogs/charity-commission-
updated-guidance-managing-faith-charities-trustees

Insurance

In a perfect world, nothing would go wrong, but we do not live in a perfect world. It is therefore necessary that we take whatever precautions are necessary. Taking out an insurance policy is one such necessity. Given the litigious nature of our society, it seems sensible that a church (including trustees) be properly insured, especially as aspects of its work—like pastoral care—have potential risks attached to them. The existence of insurance does not however protect pastoral leaders and trustees from the charge that they have been negligent in carrying out their duties. They must always be able to show that they have given due consideration to any matter before them and be able to demonstrate that they have acted reasonably and lawfully in all the circumstances.

APPENDIX 3

Resources

Over the years and in the context of writing this book, we have found a number of resources to be very helpful. These are listed in the categories below:

Books

We have benefitted greatly from Gary Collins's book and would recommend it as a comprehensive reference book for the many aspects of pastoral care:

> Gary R. Collins, *Christian Counselling: A Comprehensive Guide (Revised and Updated)*. Thomas Nelson, Third Edition, 2007.

The following have been written in recent years and are useful as a more general introduction:

> Lynne Baab, *Nurturing Hope*. Fortress Press, 2009.
>
> Alison Moore, *The Puzzle of Pastoral Care*. Kevin Mayhew, 2018.
>
> Penny Nairne, *When I needed a Neighbour: Enabling Pastoral Care in the Local Church*. Marshall Pickering, 1998.
>
> Trevor Partridge, *Paraclesis: Journeying Together*. CWR, 2018.
>
> Hongsuk Um (Ed), *Learn: Pastoral Care*. Saint Andrew Press, 2018.
>
> Edward T. Welch, *Side by Side: Walking with others in wisdom and love*. Crossway, 2015.

Those who are looking for more in-depth material will find some of the following helpful:

> J.F. MacArthur & W.A. Mack, *Introduction to Biblical Counselling*. Word Publishing, 1994.

Robert Kellemen, *Gospel Conversations: How to Care Like Christ.*
   Zondervan, 2015.

Robert Kellemen, *Gospel-Centered Counselling: How Christ changes
   lives.* Zondervan, 2014.

Paul David Tripp, *Instruments in the Redeemer's Hands.* P&R
   Publishing, 2002.

We are mindful of the wealth of pastoral writing from earlier years and many
of the following still provide valuable historical and pastoral insights:

Jay E. Adams, *Competent to Counsel.* Zondervan, 1986.

Richard Baxter, *The Reformed Pastor.* Banner of Truth, 2020.

William A. Clebsch & Charles R. Jaekle, *Pastoral Care in Historical
   Perspective.* Prentice-Hall, 1994.

T. D. Edwards & W. R Kimball, *Common Care Counseling Handbook.*
   Christian Equippers International, 1992.

R. E. O. White, *A Guide to Pastoral Care.* HarperCollins, 1976.

Some of these are now out of print, but can be obtained second hand.

Video Resources

For those who prefer a video introduction to pastoral care, we recommend the
following two conference videos, one from Scotland and the other from Canada:

Introduction to Pastoral Care: three excellent talks by Ken Jeffrey, 2017
   https://www.churchofscotland.org.uk/resources/learn/events/content/
   pastoral-care-conference-2017

Several very helpful talks from different speakers at the Canadian Biblical
Counselling Coalition
   https://biblicalcounselingcanada.ca/2019conference/

Web Resources

UK Context
Biblical Counselling UK provides resources and training opportunities from a UK perspective.

> https://www.biblicalcounselling.org.uk/resources/

Pastoral Care UK: Association of Christian Counsellors—a useful site offering a range of resources.

> https://www.acc-uk.org/pastoral-care

CWR International: material based on the work of Selwyn Hughes.

> https://www.waverleyabbeyresources.org/courses/paraclesis/

US Context
RPM Ministries: contains lots of pastoral resources (many are free) from Bob Kellemen.

> https://rpmministries.org/2019/03/11-resources-for-one-
> another-ministry/
> https://rpmministries.org/2020/10/12-biblical-counseling-distinctives/

Insight for Living: good range of resources.

> https://insightforliving.org.uk/

Online Courses
The following are a series of classroom lectures:

Biblical counselling and discipleship: lectures by John Street.

> https://www.youtube.com/playlist?list=PL4sbg6ng23C6kxXcn035
> efwnLf2lB4rSb

There are some thirty lecture videos with notes included. Good stuff, but not for the faint hearted.

Master's Seminary: series of lectures by Dr Stuart Scott and staff from The Master's seminary. The link below is for lecture one.

> https://www.youtube.com/watch?v=NYx6B1gNj4Y